Ukraine

The Social Sectors during Transition

The World Bank
Washington, D.C.

Copyright © 1993
The International Bank for Reconstruction
and Development/THE WORLD BANK
1818 H Street, N.W.
Washington, D.C. 20433, U.S.A.

World Bank Country Studies are among the many reports originally prepared for internal use as part of the continuing analysis by the Bank of the economic and related conditions of its developing member countries and of its dialogues with the governments. Some of the reports are published in this series with the least possible delay for the use of governments and the academic, business and financial, and development communities. The typescript of this paper therefore has not been prepared in accordance with the procedures appropriate to formal printed texts, and the World Bank accepts no responsibility for errors.

The World Bank does not guarantee the accuracy of the data included in this publication and accepts no responsibility whatsoever for any consequence of their use. Any maps that accompany the text have been prepared solely for the convenience of readers; the designations and presentation of material in them do not imply the expression of any opinion whatsoever on the part of the World Bank, its affiliates, or its Board or member countries concerning the legal status of any country, territory, city, or area or of the authorities thereof or concerning the delimitation of its boundaries or its national affiliation.

The material in this publication is copyrighted. Requests for permission to reproduce portions of it should be sent to the Office of the Publisher at the address shown in the copyright notice above. The World Bank encourages dissemination of its work and will normally give permission promptly and, when the reproduction is for noncommercial purposes, without asking a fee. Permission to copy portions for classroom use is granted through the Copyright Clearance Center, 27 Congress Street, Salem, Massachusetts 01970, U.S.A.

The complete backlist of publications from the World Bank is shown in the annual *Index of Publications,* which contains an alphabetical title list (with full ordering information) and indexes of subjects, authors, and countries and regions. The latest edition is available free of charge from the Distribution Unit, Office of the Publisher, The World Bank, 1818 H Street, N.W., Washington, D.C. 20433, U.S.A., or from Publications, The World Bank, 66, avenue d'Iéna, 75116 Paris, France.

ISSN: 0253-2123

Library of Congress Cataloging-in-Publication Data

International Bank for Reconstruction and Development.
    Ukraine : the social sectors during transition.
       p.   cm. — (A World Bank country study, ISSN 0253-2123)
    Includes bibliographical references.
    ISBN 0-8213-2584-1
    1. Ukraine—Economic conditions—1991–   2. Ukraine—Social
conditions—1945–   3. Social security—Ukraine.   I. Title.
II. Series.
HC340.19.I68   1993
338.947'71—dc20   93-21580
                                            CIP

CONTENTS

TABLES

FIGURES

BOXES

THE INDIVIDUAL AND THE STATE

Today Ukraine is facing a complicated period of its history. The institutions of the newly independent state are being created, the political system is being composed, and the main principles of domestic and foreign policy are being developed. There are many opinions about what is the best development strategy for Ukraine but there is one dominant idea common to them all: we must create a society that ensures a reliable social partnership between the state, the market, and the individual.

The path to achieving this type of society requires creating the conditions necessary for the realization of the creative potential embodied in each person, to release and promote the entrepreneurial spirit. A well-balanced economy, effective employment, up-to-date education, reliable medical care, and social protection for the most vulnerable groups of the population form the prerequisites for this society.

That is why we truly appreciate the initiative of the World Bank, whose experts managed to perform an extremely complicated task and conduct a thorough analysis of the social sector in our country. This report highlights the whole range of problems related to this vitally important sector and above all defines tendencies of its development and reform trends.

On evaluating the state of humanitarian development, it must be noted that Ukraine has a well-defined system of education and medical care, a wide range of social welfare and protection, and a relatively low level of unemployment. It ranks in the group of developed countries, being the 45th in the GNP per capita in the world. However, these impressive social indicators come at great cost, almost 45 percent of GNP is spent on social programs.

It is obvious that the state is unable to maintain such expenses, especially considering the current economic situation. So the great value and importance of the recommendations given in this report stem from recommendations on how to make the social sector institutions more efficient under conditions of reduced budget allocations.

The main conclusions of the World Bank coincide in principle with the state policy of Ukraine. Their value is increased by learning from the experience of other countries in transition. Steps to be taken include the adjustment and improvement of the labor market, introduction of the system of targeted benefits and financial aid, restructuring of the system of education, and training of specialists. Many of these recommendations have already been implemented, others will form the context for the human development strategy of the Government of Ukraine.

The publication of this report is the product of our mutual collaboration. But it is just the beginning and I would like to express my strong belief that in future our joint projects will become an important factor in the social and economic development of Ukraine and will promote my country's integration into the world community.

M. Zhulinsky
Deputy Prime Minister for Social Rehabilitation
The Cabinet of Ministers of Ukraine
Kiev, June 18, 1993

ACKNOWLEDGMENTS

This report was prepared by William McGreevey, Principal Population Specialist, Population, Health, and Nutrition Department, Human Resources Development and Operations Policy Vice Presidency. It is based on World Bank missions that visited Ukraine in 1992 and 1993. Contributors to the report include Mr McGreevey, Mission Leader, Michal Rutkowski, Deputy Mission Leader; Charles Griffin, sector analysis and performance; Arvil Van Adams, training and active labor market policies; Ms Teri Bergman, unemployment and cash benefits administration; Ms Jeanine Braithwaite, cash benefits under the Former Soviet Union; Ms Barbara Dabrowska, statistical data; Myroslaw Kohut, population and health; Ms Marisol Ravicz, sector finance; and Irving Sirken, education and training. Cooperation of officials of the Government of Ukraine is gratefully acknowledged, especially senior officials and staff of the Deputy Premiere for Social Rehabilitation and the Ministries of Education, Finance, Health, Labor, Social Welfare, and Statistics, and with the Funds for Chernobyl, Pensions, Social Insurance, and Employment.

Mission members visited government offices and facilities in Kiev, Kharkiv, Donetsk, and Yenakiyevo (Donbass region). Members had visited Chernihiv, Lviv, Yavoriv, Vinnytsia, and other cities during previous missions. The International Renaissance Foundation arranged for field visits and subsequent seminars and document translations that were facilitated by Prof Bohdan Krawchenko, Director, Institute of Public Administration, Council of Ministers, Government of Ukraine.

During the first mission, members participated in a seminar on July 7, 1992, to discuss 15 background reports that had been prepared by Ukrainian consultants. Titles of the reports and their authors are listed in the bibliography. The background reports provide an invaluable base for understanding and analyzing social sector issues in Ukraine.

Basil Kavalsky, Director, Europe and Central Asia Department IV, led discussions of the draft report with government officials, February 1-5, 1993. Mykola Zhulinsky, Vice-Premier, Humanitarian Affairs, coordinated the government's response. Bank staff, which included Michelle Riboud, staff economist, and Mr McGreevey also met with members of Parliament and the press.

The report was prepared under the general direction of Robert Liebenthal, Chief, Human Resources Development Division, Europe and Central Asia Department III. Russell J. Cheetham was the department director when work began; Mr Kavalsky became director prior to discussion of the report with government. Susan S. Sebastian prepared the manuscript for publication with the assistance of other support staff in the PHN Department of HROVP, including Wendy Cagen, Amelia V. Menciano, and Otilia Nadora. Marilou Abiera, Rozena Ochoco, and Suman Rajpal, EC3/4HR support staff, contributed substantially to the report preparation. Nicholas Burnett, Estelle James, Bruno Laporte, Maureen Lewis, and Alexander Preker were the peer reviewers.

CURRENCY EQUIVALENTS

Currency Unit-Karbovanets (Krb)

Exchange Rates: KRB per $
(End of Period)

December 1992	715
March 1993	2000
April 1993	3000
September 1993	10,000

WEIGHTS AND MEASURES
Metric System

GLOSSARY OF ABBREVIATIONS AND ACRONYMS

AIDS	Acquired Immune Deficiency Syndrome
BCG	Tuberculosis vaccine
BMW	Bavarian Motor Works
CEM	Country Economic Memorandum
CSFR	Czech and Slovak Federal Republic
DPT	Diphtheria, pertussis, and tetanus vaccine
EC	European Community
ES	Employment Service
FY	Fiscal Year
G7	Group of Seven (highly industrialized countries)
HIV	Virus hypothesized to cause AIDS
IAS	Industrial Adjustment Service
ILO	International Labor Organization
IMF	International Monetary Fund
MOE	Ministry of Education
MOF	Ministry of Finance
MOH	Ministry of Health
MOL	Ministry of Labor
MOS	Ministry of Statistics
MSW	Ministry of Social Welfare
OECD	Organization for Economic Coordination and Development
R	Ruble
SDR	Standardized Death Rate
SSR	Soviet Socialist Republic
SSUZ	Technical college
UN	United Nations
UNDP	United Nations Development Program
UNFPA	United Nations population Fund
UNICEF	United Nations Children's Fund
USSR	Union of Soviet Socialist Republics
VUZ	Universities
WDR	World Development Report
WHO	World Health Organization

FISCAL YEAR
January 1 to December 31

EXECUTIVE SUMMARY

INTRODUCTION

1.   This report lays out a strategy for Ukraine to make the transition to a market economy in the social sectors, taking into account the widespread system of benefits and the high spending on education and health inherited from the former Soviet Union. A central part of this strategy is the need to protect vulnerable groups during the transition, but within a financially sustainable framework. After a description of social conditions and social protection in Chapter 1, the report considers the shift of the labor force from a command to a market economy; second, it examines the advantages of converting the current system of social protection to a poverty-focused, sustainable safety net approach, including support for labor-force reassignment; and third, it explores opportunities for enhancing the efficiency and quality of social service, education, and health programs. Key elements of these programs must be maintained through the transition as part of a safety net and as a cornerstone of policies encouraging economic growth investments in human capital.

2.   The introduction of effective macroeconomic policies, reform of the enterprise sector, price reform, and financial restructuring all require an effective social safety net. Social policies, the subject of this report, cannot be neglected or deferred. The social costs of adjustment must be anticipated and, to the extent possible, provided for.

CAN UKRAINE AFFORD ITS PROGRAM OF SOCIAL PROTECTION?

3.   In 1992, the overall cost of social protection (pensions, allowances, subsidies, and social services) was budgeted at more than 40 percent of GDP, or two-thirds of consolidated

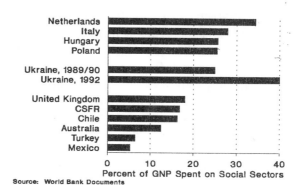

Figure S.1: International Comparison of GDP Devoted to Social Sector Spending

spending by Ukraine's state, social funds, and oblast budgets, which exceeded significantly the estimated 25 percent of GDP allocated to social spending in 1989-90. Virtually no other government in the world bears such a burden (see Figure S.1). This high share results from two main factors. Most significant has been the collapse of output in state enterprises, and thus the lowering of GDP, since 1989. At the same time, the government decided to protect the real value of pension benefits paid to 13.5 million recipients, stipends and in-kind assistance for 11.4 million students, and salaries paid to the nearly 6.0 million employees from state and oblast budgets, over half of whom deliver education and health services. The burden of providing benefits or wages to nearly two-thirds of the population, while only one-third works in directly productive activities, has grown to exceed any possibility of being financed by the economy and government.

4.   This report seeks to identify a basic safety net that can protect those most in need of it. It also seeks ways of reducing public outlays to those beneficiaries who can manage without being subsidized--at least until the transition to a market economy is well advanced and the economy has been stabilized.

5.   Public social spending depends on economic output, which can be expected to change substantially over the next several years. Between 1990 and 1991, GDP declined by about 15 percent, and there was a further 14 percent decline between 1991 and 1992. If the economy contracts further in 1993, social sector spending (for pensions, allowances, and wages for education and health workers) will also have to contract. Otherwise, production of goods and services will not be sufficient to support current wages and consumption. Looking further into the future, once the phase of output expansion begins, resources for the social safety net can grow with the rest of the economic system.

6.   In 1992 there was a notable increase in the *share* of public resources allocated to social protection and social services (see Table S.1); if this level is unsustainable, as is argued later in this summary and in this report as a whole, some principles must govern the means by which the obligations of the state are trimmed back to a level that can be financed. A principle that has guided analysis in other countries of Eastern Europe and the former Soviet Union is that those who are poor, or who are likely to be made poor by the events associated with the collapse of output, must be *protected fully* against the erosion of their levels of living with adequate subsidies and social services. A first step in articulating this principle is the establishment of a realistic poverty line, which may be considerably lower than the level of living that the government might currently wish to protect. At least one report of the Government of Ukraine recognizes that "payments are made even to the wealthiest strata of society." The government regards as essential the concentration of resources on poor and vulnerable groups. Early in 1993, financing difficulties led the government to propose cutting

the number of family-allowance recipients down to 2 million from what had been 20 million families. This step would require that the government provide some means to identify poor and vulnerable groups, building on demographic characteristics, such as family size, structure, and composition (including features of residence, disability, and dependency on friends or relatives outside the household), and also building on economic means that include the ability to work and to earn from past savings. The identification of those who are sufficiently poor and vulnerable to require public assistance will change over time, perhaps dramatically, if unemployment strikes specific regions or single-industry towns. With this in view, the government must have the capacity to monitor continuously and reshape its policies. Once the groups and their needs are identified, the government must establish benefit levels that will keep those at risk out of poverty. As prices continue to rise, benefits would have to be adjusted periodically to support the principle that those at risk be fully protected.

7.   A second principle is that all benefits above the poverty line should be continued only to the extent that resources permit. The collapse in output, should it continue into 1993 and beyond, would severely limit the state's capacity to make its transfer payments to retirees, the disabled, and other pensioners, as well as to Chernobyl victims, workers on sick leave, families with minor children, and, most notably, unemployed and displaced workers. Available resources may be driven down, for a time at least, to a level that would permit no payments (even those to which the government was obligated) beyond social protection for the poor and vulnerable. At that point, the government would have to make hard choices that would distinguish falling into poverty from maintenance of a reasonable standard of comfort. Inaction, or lack of a clear policy choice in favor of protecting those at greatest risk, would probably result in acute misery for a significant share of the poorest, particularly the rural elderly living alone and children in single-parent households.

8.   A third principle is that reforms must increase the efficiency of social spending over the longer term.

9.   A strategy to reduce social sector spending substantially in 1993 and to return to a sustainable level by the following year would include three key features:

•   Shift resources to favor cash benefits for vulnerable groups, training for displaced workers, curriculum development in technical training, and strengthening of basic maternal and child health services.

•   Reduce public spending on food subsidies, pensions for persons who remain in the work force, stipends for students who can finance their own education, and general family allowances given irrespective of need.

•   Seek efficiencies in social services spending by reducing unnecessary staff,

Table S.1: Past, Current, Suggested, and Sustainable Policy for Public Social Spending

Spending Category	Percent of GDP under Alternative Approaches				Policy Actions Required
	Actual Experience in 1989/90	Budget 1992	Suggested Program for 1993	Sustainable Program Beyond 1993	
Employment and Labor Market Policies	---	0.8	2.4	3.7	Expand active policies by strengthening Employment Service; all cash benefits at single rate near minimum wage
Pensions	8	13.9	11.3	7.7	Flat-rate pension for 1993 near minimum wage; introduce personal saving accounts in 1994; gradually raise retirement age beginning in 1993
Family Allowances	1	8.8	6.2	3.4	Target on single parents and families with three or more children, and elderly living alone
Consumer Subsidies	8	5.1	3	0	Reduce in 1993 then eliminate all untargeted subsidies after 1993
Education	5	7.8	7.0	6.0	Reduce unnecessary staff by attrition; eliminate stipends for foreign students; reform vocational training to support active labor policies
Health	3	7.7	7.0	6.0	Reduce hospitalizations and staff with out-patient care; cut numbers of new medical students; expand imports and production of selected essential drugs
Total	25.0	44.1	36.9	26.8	Introduce budgeting by objective in selected ministries

Note: The line "Employment and Labor Market Policies" describes current, suggested, and sustainable spending in these areas, as a percentage of GDP, for the years 1992, 1993, and beyond 1993, respectively. This is followed by a summary of policy actions required in these areas. This line appears in Chapter 4 as the bottom line of Table 4.2, which provides further details on spending and policy actions that are discussed in this report. Table S.2 offers details on a possible program of external technical and financial assistance that could support government policies in these same areas. This same approach (summarizing policy action required, and possible external technical and financial assistance) is followed in each area reviewed for this report.

Source: See Tables 4.2, 6.4, 7.3, 8.8, and 9.4 for sectoral details for 1992 and beyond. Estimates for 1989/90 are based on IMF, World Bank, OECD and EBRD (1991).

introducing innovative approaches such as outpatient treatment in health and computerized learning in education, and expanding the role of private providers who can cut costs but maintain quality.

10.   The government's strategy should not only reduce low priority expenditures but should also increase the resources allocated to priority tasks. One means of assuring that programs improve social conditions and provide social protection is to introduce a systematic budgeting arrangement for all social spending. Budgeting by objective is one approach to consider. Such a technique requires that all users of public social funds present their program goals and intended approaches for central budget review, usually by the Ministry of Finance. Allocations then depend on the importance of the goals and the cost-effectiveness of the approaches.

11.   Private sector development in support of the social safety net will depend on the creation of a sound legal framework. The government must provide both laws and detailed regulations that clarify the rules for such new undertakings as tax accountancy, privately provided training, and a structure of fees and prepayments for health care services. Progress will be slow until the framework for private initiative is in place.

THE PROBLEM OF EMPLOYMENT

12.   The command economy, based on state orders, did not force high-cost producers to cut costs to be competitive, or to respond to consumer demand by combining low price and high quality in order to win markets. With the change to production driven by consumer demand, the structure of output and the demand for labor will also change dramatically. As workers move into new productive activities, especially in the private sector, some periods of unemployment for millions of workers are almost inevitable.

13.   The structure of the economy's labor force is decidedly different from that of high-income (OECD) and upper-middle-income economies. A larger share of Ukrainians work in agriculture and industry, and a smaller share in services (see Figure S.2). Even in the

services sector there are significant distortions

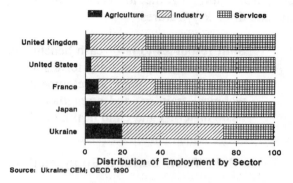

Figure S.2 International Comparison of Employment by Economic Sector, Late 1980s

that have led too many into public employment and too few into the service occupations that are usually found in the private sectors of developed economies. Overall, a third of Ukraine's labor force will probably need to switch from primary and secondary to tertiary service activities by the end of the transition to a market economy. Active labor market policies (see para. 16 below) will be needed to support this shift.

CONFRONTING UNEMPLOYMENT

14.   All OECD countries combine, in different measure, *active* and *passive* labor market policies (see Figure S.3)[1] and spend in a range from less than 1 percent of GDP to more than 5 percent. (Chapter Notes appear at the end of the text). Sweden, which is in the middle of the range, relies on active labor market policies; the United States favors passive income support, and most other countries blend these approaches. Since March 1991, Ukraine's Employment Fund, managed by the Employment Service (ES) of the Ministry of Labor, finances both active and passive policies. In 1992, active labor market policies were budgeted to use 62 percent of Employment Fund resources, 28 percent were to go to passive policies, especially cash benefits to laid-off workers, and administration was to absorb the remaining 10 percent. These services are financed by a 3

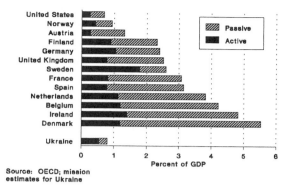

Source: OECD; mission estimates for Ukraine

Figure S.3: Percentage of GDP Spent on Active and Passive Labor Market Policy in OECD Countries and Ukraine, 1992

the negative impacts of unemployment and also

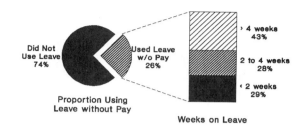

Source: Survey of 333 Enterprises

Figure S.4: Industrial Employees on Leave without Pay, 1992

percent payroll tax on enterprises that provided 18.8 billion rubles to the Employment Fund in 1992. The total cost was 0.8 percent of GDP in 1992, excluding the three-month severance pay that enterprises must give to redundant workers. When unemployment eventually rises, more resources will be needed. General revenues may therefore be needed for employment services, if higher payroll tax is to be avoided.

15. The illusion of full employment is beginning to disappear. A survey by the Ministry of Labor's ES asked 333 firms that employ nearly half a million people how many workers were on unpaid leave. About a quarter of all workers were on unpaid leave in the first half of 1992 and many were on leave for a month or more (see Figure S.4; Chapter 2 offers further details, and data are summarized in Annex Table 1.80). Today's hidden unemployment would become open if enterprises lose access to credit and their managers sense an irreversible collapse of demand. The social and political costs of mass layoffs are high, and government will probably put them off as long as possible. In Eastern Europe, about two years elapsed between the start of adjustment and the point at which unemployment began to rise. On the basis of that experience and the 25 percent decline in output to date in Ukraine, there may be 3 million unemployed (about 12 percent of the labor force) by 1995. Chapters 3 and 4 consider measures that can be taken to reduce

examine ways in which the transition can enhance Ukraine's productivity.

Active Labor Market Policies

16. Expenditure on active policies is divided equally between job matching (creation) and training/retraining. Worker retraining and job and skills matching for the unemployed can pay for themselves and can be a cost-effective solution to rising unemployment as command economies undergo the transition to a market economy. A policy of equipping displaced workers with new skills can increase their employability and facilitate their movement into new jobs. In 1992, the ES retrained only 2,500 of some 30,000 unemployed workers. If unemployment rises substantially, the ES would face a considerable challenge to expand its active labor market policies. With adequate external technical and financial assistance, it can meet this challenge. The ES needs to automate its job-matching service; to develop system software; to train its staff; and, perhaps most important, to reform worker training programs, which must be made much more flexible to deal quickly with the needs of the large numbers of displaced workers. Private-sector, enterprise-based training programs, where skill requirements are well understood, have proved to be the most successful training programs. Experience in OECD countries suggests that early interventions in cases of mass layoffs can shorten the period of unemployment and bring

about reemployment. Assistance to the unemployed to create small enterprises and to purchase raw materials and production tools can increase the productivity of those displaced workers who are willing to become self-employed. Such programs, which may be suitable for 2 percent to 3 percent of all displaced workers, must include complementary services of technical assistance in production, marketing, accounting, and management. Finally, policy changes are needed to enhance labor mobility. In particular, restructuring the labor force will require abandoning the system of resident permits and the practice of imposing a tax on the employer or employee when a permit is issued (the *propiska* system).

17.   Eighty percent of workers who find a new job do so via informal contacts, and make no use of the ES. In view of this, a main task of the ES is to *facilitate* the informal labor market. Beyond that, active labor-market policies can help address unemployment and should not be crowded out by the need to provide unemployment benefits. Training enables displaced workers to find new jobs; spending on an active ES that counsels workers may lead to a more rapid transition to a new work environment; and a job-matching program can facilitate job search. Nonetheless, mass layoffs will put a premium on spending Employment Fund resources on immediate cash benefits, which may be essential for social protection but which may do little to put workers in new jobs. This conflict between these two uses of a single source of money suggests that separate financing may be necessary. A solution may be to guarantee that not less than half of Employment Fund resources are assigned to active labor market policies. For example, if the need for cash benefits exceeds half of Employment Fund resources in any three-month period, this need should be financed from general revenues of the state budget.

Passive Policies: Unemployment Benefits

18.   Enterprises must pay 100 days of wages from the date of notification of layoff, according to the March 1991 Employment Law. Thereafter, the dismissed worker reports to the local employment office and is eligible, after a ten-day waiting period, for cash benefits, which are 75 percent of the worker's past average wage for the next three months and 50 percent of the average wage for the following six months but are never less than the minimum nor more than the average wage.

Design of the Unemployment Benefit

19.   With millions unemployed, it would be simpler to pay all claimants the same benefit, regardless of past wages. To scale payments individually would swamp the accounting capacity of the ES. (In Poland, an earnings-based system proved too expensive and complex.) An alternative would be to set two or three payment levels depending on age and experience. Additional cash benefits based on family size should be eliminated as they are inconsistent with the principles of an insurance system. There is little justification for giving benefits to voluntary quits, school leavers, and other new entrants to the labor force. The current cost of benefits would be cut 16 percent by excluding these claimants. Money saved from unnecessary benefits can be devoted to training and finding jobs for the unemployed.

Passive Policies: Wage Subsidies

20.   Some employment offices use Employment Fund resources to pay wage subsidies to selected state enterprises to induce them to keep redundant workers; such subsidies will slow the pace of adjustment. International experience suggests that the costs of such subsidies far outweigh any benefits, because the unemployment of one group is merely substituted for that of another and because the subsidies go mostly to labor-intensive enterprises that hire unskilled workers even without subsidy.

Employment Program Administration

21.   The ES staff is adequate to handle the 1993 year-end estimates of 400,000 unemployed. Mass layoffs may not occur at all in 1993, and substantially higher unemployment could be forestalled until 1995. Thus, there is time to adequately address the problem. The preparation for this will require four steps:

•**Training.** Train ES staff in the management and provision of the active labor-market services of job matching, early intervention in mass layoffs, training program development and management, and administration of a cash-benefits system.

•**Procurement.** Procure essential equipment and software to support staff work and training.

•**Infrastructure.** Develop training-program infrastructure in cooperation with the Ministry of Education and private entities that can offer training.

•**Monitoring and Analytic Capacity.** Enhance the capacity to monitor and respond to the changing labor market, to both mass layoffs in failing state enterprises and new employment opportunities in the private sector.

22. The Ministry of Labor must shortly begin to reassign staff and train them for work in the ES; it must also acquire a management information system and related equipment to support staff work. The ministry has a management plan for this area of its work and has itemized its needs for staffing, technical assistance, and training, some of which will require substantial external assistance.

SOCIAL PROTECTION

23. Social protection under socialism included labor pensions, related to labor or labor service, and social pensions, paid to the dependent or disabled. The basic legislation regulating cash transfers includes the 1956 all-Union law on pensions for workers and employees, the 1965 all-Union law on pensions for collective farmers, and the 1990 pension law, which provided that cash-transfer payments, at a base rate of 55 percent of pre-retirement wages, are not taxable and are paid regardless of other income. The 1990 law considerably increased the cost of benefits and the numbers receiving benefits; there were then 9.7 million old-age and disabled pensioners in Ukraine, and the number had grown to 13.5 million by the middle of 1992, including 362,000 people in the security sector (see Figure S.5).

24. Recently, over half the population received one or more cash benefits. A quarter of the population received disability, retirement, or survivors' benefits; 20 percent received student stipends and related free board and room; over half received family allowances for children under age 16; more than 10 percent received Chernobyl Fund payments; and a small percentage received unemployment benefits. The state subsidizes food, transportation, and shelter. Education and health care are provided at no cost at the point of service; enterprises provide day care services for children under age six, paid maternity leave for three years, and vacation sanatoria for employees. Periodic wage adjustments and expansion of the numbers of pensions and family allowances are recent steps taken to insure against declines in real incomes, even for those well above poverty levels. A major issue is whether income smoothing can be pursued simultaneously with social protection for the poor and vulnerable during conditions of extreme austerity.

25. In the longer run, the principles of risk sharing, social insurance, and earnings-related benefits should gradually be restored as the economy becomes stronger and public obligations no longer constitute a threat to macroeconomic stability. Unemployment insurance and workers' compensation are prepaid benefits with fee schedules that vary by industrial group according to risk in many OECD countries. Successful social insurance schemes protect members of many societies from income loss associated with illness and aging and protect against the risks of high costs for health care where private medicine prevails. Government can create a regulatory framework that will encourage saving, so that individuals and families will self-insure for their old age and for other financial needs and risks that differ widely from person to person. All these steps require a broad legal framework that will define private-sector development and its responses to the demand for financial services that help reduce social risks. The experience in Eastern European countries in recent years indicates that false steps in these areas, particularly in the design of unemployment and health-insurance schemes, may prove costly and that such schemes must be carefully worked out prior to

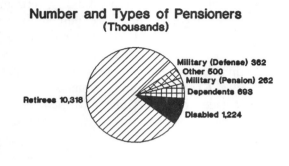

Number and Types of Pensioners
(Thousands)

Military (Defense) 362
Other 500
Military (Pension) 262
Dependents 693
Retirees 10,318
Disabled 1,224

Source: Ministry of Social Welfare

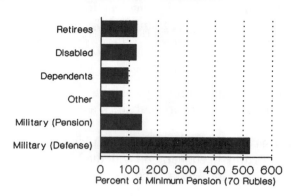

Relative Size of Pensions

Retirees
Disabled
Dependents
Other
Military (Pension)
Military (Defense)

0   100   200   300   400   500   600
Percent of Minimum Pension (70 Rubles)

Figure S.5: Pensioners and Their Benefits, January 1, 1992

implementation.

Retirement, Disability, and Survivors' Benefits

26.   Pensions, the largest component of the social safety net, are essential to the well-being of millions of the elderly poor and disabled. At least several million people live on the edge of poverty in rural areas, often alone and with no relative to provide any means of support. Eight million of the pension beneficiaries have incomes so low as to qualify them for low-income allowances. Data from the 1989 census show that 10.9 million people have passed the retirement age of 55 for women and 60 for men; their numbers are projected to be 12.3 million in the year 2000 and 12.6 million in 2010, with a consequent increase in the demands on pension fund resources.

27.   There are anomalies in the pension law. Benefits are not provided to the elderly because they retire: they are provided automatically when the recipients reach retirement age. Thus as many as a quarter of the 11 million recipients of retiree pensions are also earning wages. A quarter of disability pensioners may also be employed because once the pension is awarded it is permanent, and many of those declared disabled subsequently recover and return to work. Some workers, among whom miners are perhaps the largest group, can begin receiving a pension on the basis of 20 (for women) or 25 (for men) years of service completed, which

may occur well before pensionable age is reached. About 7 percent of workers retire early on this basis. Reducing some of the payments to some of these recipients would probably not cause them to fall into poverty.

28.   There may be ways to reduce pension payments while maintaining benefits for those who need them. One option is to allow inflation to erode the real value of pensions to a level that can be financed. The burden of that policy would fall mostly heavily on those least able to protect themselves against price increases--the poorest members of society. A second option, and the one recommended here, is to eliminate benefits to those who do not urgently need them. Several measures could, when taken together, result in significant reductions in payments while still protecting poor and vulnerable groups:

- **Retirement Age.** Raise the normal retirement age to 62 or 65 for both women and men. Men have a life expectancy of 72.4 at age 60; women's life expectancy is 79.5 at the same age, so there is little justification for earlier retirement for women. The reduction in the dependency burden is shown in Figure S.6 for the years 2000 and 2010. Retirement age could be raised by one year for each of the next two or five years for men and by one year for each of the next seven or ten years for women, and current beneficiaries would not lose their entitlement. By the year

Retirement-Age Population

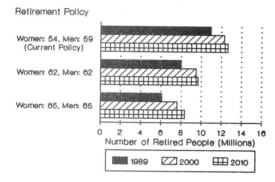

Dependency Ratios

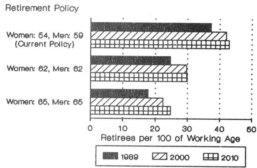

Source: World Bank Projections

Figure S.6: Effects of Alternative Retirement Age Policies on Number of Retired and Dependency Ratios, 1989 through 2010

2000, pension payments would be 20 percent lower than they would otherwise have been which is equivalent to about 3.5 percent of GDP.

- **Benefits.** Reduce the benefits of the 25 percent of elderly and disabled pensioners who continue to work, thereby saving up to 19 percent of total pension spending.

- **Early Retirement.** Abolish the option of early retirement, thereby saving up to 5 percent of total pension spending.

Raising the retirement age would yield no immediate savings, since it would have to be phased in over a number of years. It might also be inappropriate to cut all benefits to those still working or those who retired early. The Government of Ukraine is reviewing its options but does not expect to raise retirement age immediately.

Personal Security Accounts

29.   An option being considered in the Ministry of Social Welfare is the institution of a system of personal-security accounts that would permit a more flexible approach to retirement. Able-bodied workers could continue to work as long as they wished, with related provisions for many means of transferring pension rights to third parties or of using them for such purposes as financing private annuities or other expenses that do not interfere with the income-security provisions of pension law.[2] Personal accounts could be built initially with the distribution of ownership rights in mutual funds made up of publicly distributed shares of privatized state enterprises. Retirees' claims to such shares could be designed as annuities that, like current retirement benefits, terminate with the recipient's death, with the shares then reverting to the Pension Fund for subsequent distribution to new claimants. Identifying practical designs for such a scheme would merit high priority in any program of external technical assistance.

30.   To reduce pension spending along the lines suggested for 1993 in Table S.1--that is, to reduce the share of GDP allocated to pensions from 13.9 percent of GDP in 1992, to 11.3 percent in 1993, and to 7.7 percent beyond 1993--would require immediate measures on an emergency basis: a *unitary benefit* would be introduced for all pensioners at a level that would fully protect pensioners against the risk of acute poverty. This flat-rate benefit would prevail only until the economy improved. Such a measure could result in savings equivalent to about 30 percent of total pension spending-- about 4 percent of GDP. The cuts would fall on those best able to absorb them; they would leave a program that should improve the safety net for the most vulnerable pension recipients.

31.   Table S.2 suggests key areas of external technical and financial assistance that would be

required to strengthen pension programs. These would include advice on data collection and analysis to define more accurately the characteristics of the recipient population by age, sex, income, residence, family size, support systems, and other features that would give the Ministry of Social Welfare information on the needs of the beneficiary population. The ministry and the pension fund will also need advice on how possible changes in benefits would affect individuals and groups in the population. In addition, in view of the heavy responsibilities placed on these agencies, management and administrative capability will need to be strengthened.

Allowances and Benefits

32.   In 1992 Ukraine offered over 60 cash allowances and assistance programs: some aimed at low-income and vulnerable groups, others designed for the general population, and still others targeted to Chernobyl victims. The last accounted for 39 percent of social assistance spending; aid to vulnerable groups accounted for 37 percent; and allowances available to the general population accounted for 23 percent. Many allowances did not differ substantively from one another; they are funded, administered and distributed by several agencies, while others are funded by one agency, administered by a second, and distributed by a third. According to Table S.1, these programs now require 8.8 percent of GDP. If they are to be reduced because of the resource limits of government, the reduction should respect the need to protect vulnerable groups and other claimants to state support. The following suggestions point to programs that deserve priority and others that may be candidates for reduction:

- **Protect Important Benefits.** Allowances for sick pay, maternity leave, and short-term disability, and benefits to Chernobyl victims, should be generally protected.

- **Shift the Burden of Sick Pay.** Enterprises should be held responsible for sick pay and at least some portion of short-term disability pay to avoid overburdening the sickness fund.

- **Retarget Other Benefits.** Most other benefits should be offered only to families in specific vulnerable groups.[3]

Savings from these measures could be as much as 25 percent of total allowance spending in the first year that they are implemented. (Details of recommended changes appear in Chapter 7.) A reduction of spending in this area from 8.8 percent of GDP in 1992 to 6.2 percent of GDP in 1993, and 3.4 percent thereafter would be in the right direction of fiscal balance while protecting the needs of vulnerable groups. Early in 1993 the Government of Ukraine was already moving in this direction by reducing the number of benefits and targeting the remaining benefits on vulnerable groups. Government spent less on family allowances in the past, while the costs for Chernobyl allowances were shared among several republics of the former USSR.

33.   There is considerable need for technical assistance to support reforms in this area. The most important objective would be to help the government reorganize and rationalize its many programs. Budgeting by objective could be a useful management tool to combat the likely waste that may have emerged over time in the proliferation of programs.

Consumer Subsidies[4]

34.   Consumer subsidies, especially those for food, were meant to compensate for the immediate price increases expected in January 1992; the government proposed to abandon them thereafter. In any event, consumer subsidies cost 5.1 percent of GDP in 1992. There is general agreement that such subsidies are inefficient as a means of social protection; their elimination could save 5 percent of GDP. Part of those savings could supplement family allowances and assistance for pensioners living in poverty. Elimination of all subsidies may not be possible in 1993, for which year 3 percent of GDP might still be required for that purpose (see Table S.1). Thereafter, efforts should continue to eliminate consumer subsidies entirely.

Table S.2: Technical and Financial Assistance Requirements for Execution of Social Sector Reform Program, 1993-1995.

Category	Principal International Technical and Financial Assistance Needed	Principal Sources of Assistance
Employment and Labor Market Policies	Machinery and equipment to strengthen the Employment Service; development of training programs and curricula appropriate to market economy; advice on handling mass layoffs; management of program to select and develop labor force concepts and definitions that are consistent with international standards; develop administrative sources of institutions	Labor ministries, ILO and related UN and regional agencies; agencies with experience in OECD countries; international financial institutions
Pensions	Training for pension-fund management; actuarial analyses of projected fund balances; planning and evaluation support on benefits and allowances	Social security agencies in OECD countries; international financial institutions
Family Allowance	Advice on restructuring benefits to fit needs of poverty and vulnerable groups	Welfare ministries in OECD countries
Consumer Subsidies	--	--
Education and Training	Curriculum development for vocational and technical training and technicums to strengthen private-sector response;	Education ministries in OECD countries; international financial institutions
Health	Assess capacity of local pharmaceutical industry; international procurement of essential drugs; hospital management reform; strengthening of maternal and child care and related outreach; health education and communications reform	Health ministries in OECD countries; WHO, UNICEF, UNFPA, and UNDP; international financial institutions
Overall	Introduce budgeting by objective in selected ministries; analysis of the political economy of alternative responses to unemployment and spending cuts	International financial institutions

PUBLIC SOCIAL SERVICES

35.   The Government of Ukraine finances and provides the key social services of education and health, and the budget needs of these essential activities should be protected and their quality enhanced where necessary. These programs were expected to cost 15.5 percent of GDP in 1992, far more than the 8 percent (5 percent for education and 3 percent for health) typical of the 1980s. Employment in these sectors has grown much faster in the past decade than in other sectors. Teachers and health workers now seek salary parity with the industrial sector where wages have traditionally been 50 percent higher. Increasing costs of imported pharmaceuticals, and the need to absorb the additional costs of converting to Ukrainian as the language of instruction, have placed added strains on these services. A major challenge is to maintain quality while reducing future spending in these areas to the level, as a share of GDP, that prevailed before the current crisis.

EDUCATION AND TRAINING SERVICES

36.   Ukraine has a large and diversified educational system. Its coverage is extensive from preschool through secondary education, and enrollment rates at the post-secondary level compare favorably with those in countries with similar income levels. The dropout rate is negligible and the repetition rate is very low.

Teacher qualifications are high, with most teachers in urban areas having several years of post-secondary education. There are 10.9 million full-time students, and hundreds of thousands of part-time students, enrolled in 47,500 establishments employing 1.8 million, of whom 1.1 million are teachers, resulting in an overall student/staff ratio of 5:1. In higher education, Ukraine's student/teacher ratio is but a third to a tenth of the level prevailing in most countries. In the 1980s, the number of teachers' college graduates nearly doubled, while education graduates at higher-level institutions increased by 60 percent. But there are now too few complementary resources for the education system to be able to maintain the level of quality already achieved.

37.   Chapter 8 briefly describes the levels of instruction and some of the key issues at each level. The most serious problem is that resources are needed to introduce innovations in teaching, such as the use of computers, modern software, new texts, and teaching materials that can raise the quality of instruction. Staff reductions, perhaps by attrition, could help solve the resource problem. While it is vital to reform and strengthen education, these objectives must be sought within the financial resources that will be available to the sector over the next few years. The Law on Education provides that 10 percent of GDP should be allocated to education, and other recent legislation proposes that teacher salaries should be made equal to salaries in manufacturing. Neither condition is feasible during this era of budgetary stringency.

38.   Education spending, 7.8 percent of GDP in 1992, should probably decline to 7 percent in 1993 and 6 percent thereafter, to what would be a sustainable level (see Table S.1, and, for details, Table 8.8 in the main text). Staffing ratios are high in comparison with other countries, suggesting some possibility of saving on staff costs. UNESCO data show that developing countries spend 3.8 percent of GDP on education and developed countries spend 5.8 percent. The former Soviet Union spent roughly the same share as developed countries. Comparisons across countries and across time suggest that 6 percent of GDP for public

education spending may be sustainable. These changes would be accomplished through the adoption of several measures:

- **Staffing.** Reduce staff to levels commensurate with the student/teacher ratios observed in other countries; cut the number of new teachers coming out of the pedagogical institutes and schools.

- **Technical Curriculum.** Reform vocational and educational training and the technicums to make them better able to serve the needs of displaced workers who need retraining.

- **General Education.** Speed reforms of general education by introducing lycees, magnet schools, optional courses, and other innovations that are already proving to strengthen education.

- **Day Care.** Assist private sector efforts to replace the declining role of enterprises in the provision of day care.

39.   There is an urgent need for a careful study of how many teachers will be required at each level, from preschool to higher education, and in the various sub-specialties of education. In the aggregate, raising student/staff ratios to the average level in developed countries would cut personnel costs by 44 percent and total education spending by 24 percent, to under 6 percent of GDP. Such a change could not and should not be accomplished overnight, but 1 million productive former education staff could produce an additional 4 percent of gross product. The net gain to aggregate output could exceed 5 percent by the year 2000.

40.   Along with staff reductions, education authorities could seek alternative means to finance education, including voluntary contributions, parental in-kind assistance in labor and goods, and, especially at higher levels of education, the introduction of tuition fees. Specific actions might include the following:

- **Complementary Services.** Save up to 4 percent by targeting the recently enacted free lunch for preschoolers to needy families; provide free textbooks, student stipends, and room and board only to students from poor families.

- **Foreign Student Subsidies.** Save 5 percent of the Ministry of Education budget by the gradual attrition of the 20,000 foreign students now being supported and by suspension of any new invitations for costly, subsidized study.

- **Language of Instruction.** Introduce Ukrainian-language texts at a pace consistent with normal replacement to cut out extra printing costs.

- **Vocational Schools.** Eliminate some of the 1,242 vocational schools that cannot adapt to training for a market economy.

- **Displaced Workers.** Seek donor assistance, such as that provided by Germany, that addresses training needs for displaced workers.

From 1993, the Government of Ukraine has started taking a number of these steps. The Government will undertake more intensive study of key sector issues following up on the major conference report, "Ukraine Education in the Twenty-First Century," now being prepared.

HEALTH SERVICES

41. Life expectancy at birth in Ukraine was 70.5 years in 1990, well below that of most of its European neighbors. The infant mortality rate is higher than in the rest of Europe, although infectious and communicable diseases have largely been brought under control. The greatest loss of life in Ukraine, with males and females considered together, is from circulatory and respiratory diseases, neoplasms, and injuries (see Figure S.7). Much of this can be attributed to smoking, high cholesterol and fatty diets, alcohol consumption, and lack of exercise. Emphasis on curative medicine may be leading to misplaced priorities; more attention needs to be given to preventive medicine. Abortion is the principal form of birth control; modern contraceptives that have not been available can prevent unwanted pregnancies at considerable

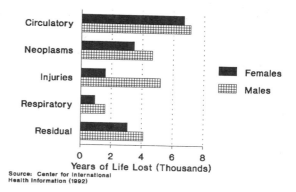

Source: Center for International Health Information (1992)

Figure S.7: Potential Years of Life Lost by Cause of Death

savings. Hospital costs of treatment for the complications of abortion have been estimated at 3 to 4 billion rubles in 1991 (see Box 1.1 in the main text and the related discussion of maternal and child health). Only 30 percent of contraceptive needs are being met; adequate services would cost a quarter of what is presently spent on hospital care for the treatment of post-abortion complications. A reorientation of disease priorities could provide a basis for considerable savings and for greater effectiveness in the pursuit of the goal of the Ministry of Health to reduce the principal causes of death and extend useful life.

42. Health care spending accounted for 7.7 percent of GDP in 1992, two-thirds of which was allocated to hospital costs (see Figure S.8). While pharmaceutical prices have risen faster than those of almost any other input, it has become extremely difficult to obtain drugs; hence, spending on that essential input declined. Construction declined from 5.2 percent of total spending in 1989 to 0.1 percent in 1992, reflecting the fact that the state has no resources to maintain its facilities.

43. The Ministry of Health could improve sector efficiency and bring down somewhat the high level of public spending on health. Spending could be brought down from 7.7 percent of GDP in 1992 to 7 percent in 1993 and 6 percent in subsequent years--which is a level substantially higher than that prevailing in

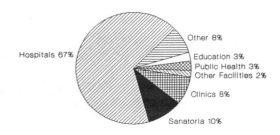

Source: Draft 1992 Budgets

Figure S.8: Distribution of Public Spending on Health Services

the 1980s (see Table S.1 and, for details, Table 9.4 in the main text). Sector objectives would be served by the following steps:

- **Admissions.** Reduce hospital admissions by one-third, treating many conditions on an outpatient basis, along the lines already adopted in OECD countries; reduce hospital bed supply, making comparable reductions in staff; withdraw unnecessary hospital beds from service, preferably by closing whole wards in order to gain the full impact of staffing reductions.

- **Preventive Care.** Focus staff resources and additional financial resources outlined in Chapter 9 on preventive care, especially communicable disease control, and maternal and child health programs. Develop health education and communications programs promoting a more healthy diet, less smoking, lower consumption of alcohol, and beneficial exercise.

- **Management.** Strengthen sector management capability by clarifying the functions of all levels of government within a decentralized system.

- **Pharmaceutical Production.** Enhance the capacity to import and produce essential drugs.

- **Health Finance.** Consider options for health insurance, prepayment systems, and other innovations that can reduce services and improve the quality of services. These steps would shift emphasis to the basic health care needs of all the population.

Health Sector Human Resources

44.   From 1993 there will be a reduction in the intake of first-year students by 500 per year for a period of three years to achieve a norm of 32 physicians per ten thousand population. Some medical schools have been considered for closure to take into account what is now seen to be an oversupply of physicians. There are plans to decrease first-year intakes and close some nursing schools.

Pharmaceutical Production

45.   The extreme scarcity of essential medicines and the lack of certain equipment available only in the West create serious immediate problems for health care in Ukraine. The breakdown of exchange within the former Soviet Union has left manufacturers in Ukraine without some key inputs. About one-third of the medicines of the former Soviet Union are produced in Ukraine, mostly by 50 state-owned enterprises that had an aggregate pharmaceutical output of R1.2 billion in 1990 and R1.8 billion in 1991. The industry faces a serious deterioration of its equipment and plant, and production is near collapse for lack of key inputs. Options for the use, production, and importation of essential drugs and medical equipment are under review.

46.   Drug shortages at hospitals have become common; barter among health care facilities was used to obtain required drugs. Extensive substitution of drugs considered non-optimal is common. Urgent needs include insulin, oral anti-diabetics, hormones, syringes, needles, cold-chain equipment, medical and surgical supplies, insulin purification equipment, and sterilization supplies and equipment. There is an immediate need to finance imports of essential drugs and supplies and for pharmaceutical production. Steps to address these needs were

already under way early in 1993. External technical and financial assistance could be useful to support an essential drugs program, given the considerable experience of international agencies such as WHO and UNICEF, and the health agencies of the OECD countries. Tables S.1 and S.2 summarize some priority areas for such assistance. There is also considerable interest in developing a health insurance scheme, to mobilize more resources health care and to widen the range of choices for consumers. Technical assistance by knowledgeable international experts on this topic is badly needed, because the introduction of health insurance is extremely complex and can lead to problems with the efficiency and equity of service delivery.

EXTERNAL ASSISTANCE

47.   Table S.2 indicates technical and financial assistance requirements for social sector programs. Government can make effective use of assistance only if the move to sustainable social programs is part of an overall restructuring of the role and obligations of the public sector in the economy of Ukraine.

48.   Each of the areas of expenditure and public action discussed in this report could benefit substantially from external technical and financial assistance; the brief descriptions of such assistance in Table S.2 summarize lengthier discussions in the body of the report. In general terms, this assistance would have three aims: first, to modernize the systems that manage programs offering cash benefits and social services;   second, to achieve significant efficiency gains in the systems of public finance and delivery of these benefits and services; and third, to develop mechanisms that can assure that those in the greatest danger of poverty and its ill effects are protected to the extent possible.

49.   These aims and priorities are shared by the Office of the Vice Premiere for Social Rehabilitation, which now sets social sector priorities.   The resulting requirements for international technical and financial assistance can be summarized as follows by ministry.

50.   *Ministry of Labor*

Information system for development of job-loss documentation; training and on-the-job training, and purchase of equipment and applied computer programs.

Training and retraining centers for employees being released as a result of unemployment.

51.   *Ministry of Education*

Definition of educational levels and their integration into international standards.

Curriculum development for professional training programs.

Procurement of foreign hardware, software, and computer control systems.

Labor demand and training analyses, including study of international experience in specialist training under market-economy conditions.

Development of a certification system for educational institutions, including study of certification experience in selected OECD countries.

Creation of an information-and-analysis data bank on educational institutions.

52.   *Ministry of Social Welfare*

Computer system for the compilation and analysis of information to define categories of citizens for whom social assistance is needed; development of a system of state support for such citizens, including documentation development, on-the-job training for staff, and procurement of equipment and software.

New technologies for modern prosthetic devices and invalid rehabilitation, including the development and acquisition of new technologies, their implementation, and the training of personnel in their use.

Social program management, including the creation and maintenance of a Cabinet-level administrative office for strategic management with appropriate related units in oblast administrations, including the development and implementation of essential information systems, conducting of seminars, and symposia.

53.   *Ministry of Health*

Implementation of health insurance, including the development of the documents needed for analysis of international experience, personnel training, and the setting up and equipment of private insurance companies.

Strengthening of the system of immunization and vaccination, including scientific research, and purchase of technologies and germ cultures.

54.   Assistance is also needed in the reform of education and worker training programs which would include, *inter alia*, merging some higher-education institutions; initiating structural changes of some professional training to improve response to the market economy; reducing subsidies to evening and correspondence courses by 50 percent now and eliminating them over

five years; giving higher-education institutions greater control over admissions and budgets; and permitting them to charge fees as appropriate.

55.   The Ministries of Labor and Education will revise the qualification requirements for specialists and employees on the basis of a new multilevel system of specialists' preparation that can lead to attrition in the number of higher-education, subsidized students.   The ministries would then upgrade capacity to meet the needs of regional employment centers with financing provided from the Employment Fund.

56.   Several governments are already actively discussing areas in which they can be of help, including labor-market analyses, health-care financing, effective pension and allowance schemes, and overall financial management and budgeting.   Various modes of coordination need to be considered for social protection as a whole, and in each of the specific areas considered in this report.

57.   The government might consider periodic meetings of interested donors and agencies that would review progress in social protection and the complementarity of donor assistance.   Such reviews could provide one means of setting goals and checking on their achievement; they can also invigorate external assistance by restatement of priorities.   The meetings could also confirm the efficacy of donor assistance or point to ways in which new assistance may play a useful role.

1
SOCIAL CONDITIONS AND SOCIAL PROTECTION

INTRODUCTION

1.   As part of the former USSR, Ukraine participated in a socialist society that tried to guarantee universal access to a minimum standard of living. Two statistics often used to assess the standard of living are life expectancy and infant mortality: on these indicators, Ukraine stood, on the eve of its independence, well below the West (and East) European countries but somewhat above middle-income countries from other parts of the world (see Table 1.1). Some analyses show that the former socialist countries fell behind Western Europe on these indicators in the past score of years, with adult mortality having risen perceptibly because of the higher incidence of circulatory and respiratory diseases, which were being brought under control by modern preventive medicine in the West. Ukraine was probably somewhat better off in terms of schooling attainment, ranking nearer its European neighbors and performing well in international competitions. An extensive system of day care facilities may have assisted early learning, in addition to permitting very high levels of women's participation in the labor force.

2.   The system of social protection included state-provided education and health; pension benefits for the elderly, disabled, orphans and widows; family allowances and student stipends and subsidies for basic food and services that lowered living costs for all consumers. The cost was about 25 percent of GDP (8 percent each for social services, pensions, and food subsidies,

Table 1.1: International Comparison of Social Indicators
(most recent year available)

Country	Population (Millions)	GDP Per Capita (Dollars)	Life Expectancy at Birth	Infant Mortality Per Thousand Live Births	Total Fertility Rate
Ukraine	52	n.a.	71	20	1.9
Turkey	56.1	1,630	67	60	3.5
Poland	38.2	1,690	71	16	1.8
Chile	13.2	1,940	72	17	2.5
Mexico	86.2	2,490	70	39	3.3
Hungary	10.6	2,780	71	15	1.8
CSFR	15.7	3,140	72	12	2.4
Australia	16.8	14,360	77	8	1.9
UK	57.2	14,610	76	9	1.8
Italy	57.5	15,120	76	9	1.3
Netherlands	14.8	15,920	77	7	1.5
France	56.2	17,820	77	7	1.8
Germany	80	20,440	75	8	1.4
USA	248.8	20,910	76	10	1.9

Sources: WDR 91, 92; IMF et al. 1991 report on USSR for Ukraine, 1989; and Poland social sector study (World Bank).

and 1 percent for family allowances; see Table 1.2 and Executive Summary Figure S.1). About 40 percent of all Ukrainians were entitled to one or more cash benefits at the time of independence.

3.   The collapse of output in the state enterprises, combined with the urgency of maintaining the real value of cash benefits and public salaries, led to a crisis in 1992 in which programmed spending for social protection reached an inordinately large proportion of a shrunken GDP. A major issue is how to continue to provide for social needs despite the extreme scarcity of resources. To help address that issue, it is helpful to review the basic demographic structure, how the labor force is deployed, what the safety net now provides, and what vulnerable groups require priority attention.

Population Size and Structure

4.   Ukraine's population is 51.8 million, making it one of the larger countries of Europe, and growing over the past decade by about 0.3 percent per year. Two-thirds of the population is urban, and one-third is rural. The three largest of the 26 oblasts are highly industrialized: D o n e t s k (5.3 m i l l i o n), Dnipropetrovsk (3.9 million), and Kharkiv (3.2 million). The smallest are the western oblasts of Chernivtsi (0.9 million), Volyn (1.1 million) and Ternopil (1.2 million) (see Table 1.3).

5.   The age structure of Ukraine is very close to that of Portugal with 21.4 percent of the population less than 15 years of age, 66.4 percent between 15 and 64, and 12.1 percent 65 or more years of age. The population is somewhat older than that of Europe as a whole or the neighboring countries of Belarus and Poland, or North American countries such as Canada, but is younger than that of the United Kingdom or Sweden[5]. This

structure has several implications for social programs. First, the demands of the elderly are substantial and growing, particularly because women receive pensions beginning at age 55 and men at age 60, with some workers eligible for an even earlier pension entitlement. (Continuing to work does not reduce pension rights.) The

Table 1.2: International Comparison of Public Spending on the Social Sectors, 1989-1990

	Percent of GDP Spent on Social Sectors[1]		
Country	Welfare[2]	Education and Health	Total[3]
Ukraine	9	8	25
Turkey	0.9	5.6	6.5
Poland	16.1	8.3	24.4
Chile	11.1	5.2	16.3
Mexico	2.4	2.9	5.3
Hungary	19.6	6.1	25.7
CSFR	15.5	1.3	16.8
Australia	7.9	4.6	12.5
UK	12	6	18
Italy	18.5	9.4	27.9
Netherlands	22.1	12.3	34.4
France	17.3	11.9	29.2
Germany	14.3	5.5	19.8
USA	6.7	3.4	10.1

Notes: 1.   Excludes state and local government spending for most countries, which distorts comparisons by making large federal systems, like the US, appear small.

2.   Includes housing, amenities, social security and welfare.

3.   Ukraine includes 8 percent of GDP in general consumer subsidies

Sources: WDR 91, 92; IMF et al. 1991 report on USSR for Ukraine, 1989; and Poland social sector study (World Bank).

pension-eligible population will grow from under 11 million in 1989 to over 12.2 million by the year 2000; there were 37 retirees for each 100 people of working age, and there will be 42 per 100 at century's end. The resource requirements for retirement benefits will grow accordingly, unless steps are taken to raise the age of retirement, now 55 for women and 60 for men, to the level of most OECD countries, which is 65 for both sexes. Second, the requirements for heavy spending on child health and education so familiar in developing countries should pose less of a burden. As evidence consider the high labor-force participation rate of about 50 percent. Only 40 percent of the population in most countries, both richer and poorer, are working; women in Ukraine usually have one birth or two (the total fertility rate is 1.9) and with maternity leave and day care are able to continue in their working careers. With relatively fewer children than most middle-income countries, the requirements for education spending could also be less burdensome. Finally, the mature demographic structure implies a more mature labor force that should as a result be more productive than one dominated by youthful and inexperienced workers. The age structure differs by oblast; those with the largest proportion of persons 60 or more years of age are Chernihiv (24.7 percent), Poltava (22.7 percent) and Cherkasy (22.5 percent) while those with the smallest proportion are Zakarpattia (12.6 percent), Kiev city (12.7 percent) and Crimea (15.0 percent).

Ratio of Females to Males

6.   Ukraine has a high female-to-male ratio. There were 116.7 females per 100 males reported in the 1989 census, a markedly larger ratio than 105.2 in Poland in the same year, reflecting losses during the Second World War. This ratio is more pronounced with increasing age and in certain oblasts. In Ukraine as a whole, 22.4 percent of women are 60 or more years of age compared to 12.8 percent of men, while in oblasts like Chernihiv, Poltava and Sumy, 28-31 percent of women are 60 or more years of age compared to 15-17 percent of men.

One in ten women in the country as a whole is 70 or more years old. One in seven is 70 or older in these three latter oblasts. The largest number of women 60 or older is found in Donetsk, Dniropetrovsk and Kharkiv, the largest oblasts.

7.   A World Health Organization (WHO) report estimates that 2 million pensioners in Ukraine live alone. Many of them are likely to be elderly women living without spouses, alone and in rural areas. Of the 0.5 million pensioners estimated to require daily social or medical assistance, only a third receive such care, much of it in hospitals and smaller health facilities. Health-service institutions care for the lonely elderly who cannot care for themselves. Elderly women make up a vulnerable group that is growing and deserves priority for social and health support programs. Dislocations expected during the transition to a market driven economy will add to the difficulties faced by this group in the future.

Life Expectancy

8.   At birth, life expectancy in Ukraine was 70.5 years in 1990, up from 69.7 in 1981, but significantly below the target of 75 years set by the European Regional Office of WHO for its region (WHO/EURO) and actual experience in Europe. The average life expectancy at birth for 27 countries in Europe in 1989 was 74.0 years and for European Community countries in 1988 was 76.2 years. From birth, males had a life expectancy in 1990 of 65.6 years, an 87.9 percent chance of surviving to age 45 and a 59.7 percent chance of reaching age 65. From birth, females had a life expectancy of 74.9 years and chances of survival to ages 45 and 65 are 95.2 percent and 81.7 percent, respectively. This

Table 1.3: Population Growth, Ukraine, 1981-1992 (in Thousands)

	1981[1]	1985	1990	1991[2]	1992
Total	50,169.8	50,914.1	51,636.8	51,745.8	51,801.9
Male	22,954.3	23,402.9	23,884.1	n/a	n/a
Female	27,215.5	27,511.1	27,752.7	n/a	n/a

Sources: 1.   Years 1981-1990 WHO/EURO-ESR Unit May 19, 1992 Mid Year Estimates
               2.   Years 1991-1992, MOH. Ukraine 1992 is as of 1st January

survival pattern to ages 45 and 65 is marginally worse than in neighboring Belarus and Poland, and much worse than in Portugal, the United Kingdom, Sweden, and Canada (see Table 1.4).

Vital Events

9.   Since 1983 the birth rate in Ukraine has been falling more quickly than the death rate, which showed a relatively sharp upswing in 1990. Data for 1991 and the first quarter of 1992 show a net natural decrease in the population of -1.1 and -3.1 per hundred thousand population, respectively.   The total fertility rate fell from 2.1 in 1985-86 to 1.9 in 1990; the net decrease in population is also linked to a deterioration in the health status of mothers and infants during the economic crisis (see Health Annex Tables 5, 6 and Figure 3). The collapse of output and declining incomes in 1991 and 1992 undoubtedly led to deferral of marriages and births. Ukrainian authorities fear that this demographic reversal of normal

conditions (births exceeding deaths) will have negative implications in the longer run.

IMPLICATIONS OF DEMOGRAPHY FOR HEALTH

10.   The demographic picture of an aging population with growth rates below natural replacement has important implications for the health system.   There is a critical need to develop family planning policy that responds to the social and other factors contributing to demographic losses. A shorter-term need is to improve the care of mothers and infants. And, as in the industrialized countries, Ukraine must redirect its health system to respond to present and new needs in the next decade arising from an aging population and greater numbers of adults of working age.   The redirection will affect the training of health care workers, the present structure of different levels of health facilities and their roles and locations.

Table 1.4: Life Expectancy and Survival by Gender, Ukraine and Selected Countries

	Ukraine 1990		Belarus 1990		Poland 1990		Portugal 1990		United Kingdom 1990		Sweden 1988		Canada 1989	
Males	L	S	L	S	L	S	L	S	L	S	L	S	L	S
Age														
0	65.6	100.0	66.2	100.0	66.5	100.0	70.1	100.0	73.0	100.0	74.2	100.0	73.7	100.0
1	65.6	98.5	66.1	98.6	66.7	98.2	70.0	98.8	72.6	99.1	73.7	99.3	73.3	99.2
15	52.2	97.6	52.6	97.8	53.1	97.6	56.5	98.0	58.9	98.7	59.9	99.0	59.6	98.8
45	25.8	87.9	26.2	88.4	26.1	89.7	29.3	91.5	30.4	95.3	31.5	95.2	31.5	94.5
65	12.5	59.7	12.9	60.7	12.5	61.8	13.8	72.4	14.2	78.2	15.0	80.3	15.3	78.4
Females	L	S	L	S	L	S	L	S	L	S	L	S	L	S
Age														
0	74.9	100.0	75.8	100.0	75.6	100.0	77.3	100.0	78.7	100.0	80.1	100.0	80.6	100.0
1	74.8	98.9	75.5	99.0	75.6	98.6	77.0	99.0	78.2	99.3	79.5	99.5	80.1	99.4
15	61.2	98.3	62.0	98.5	61.9	98.2	63.4	98.5	64.4	99.0	65.7	99.3	66.3	99.1
45	32.6	95.2	33.2	95.6	33.1	95.6	34.6	96.0	35.3	97.2	36.6	97.3	37.3	97.1
65	15.8	81.7	16.5	82.8	16.2	82.8	17.0	86.6	18.1	86.3	18.8	88.9	19.8	87.9

Note: L: Life Expectancy at Age X. For example, a male age 0 has a life expectancy of 65.6 years in Ukraine; a male age 65 has a life expectancy of 12.5 additional years.

S: Percent of the Population Surviving to Age X. For example, 98.5 percent of males survive to age 1 in Ukraine; 59.7 percent survive to age 65.

Source: 1991 World Health Statistics Annual, WHO Geneva 1992

11.　　The relatively poor health status of people in Ukraine compared to other European countries demonstrates the effects of age and chronic conditions. It also points to the need to deal with communicable diseases, to ensure safe food, water and air, to provide for ongoing acute care needs, and to meet the needs unique to the ecological conditions of the country.

MORTALITY AND HEALTH STATUS

Mortality

12.　　The leading causes of death in Ukraine are much the same as for the OECD countries. Over 75 percent of deaths are from diseases of the circulatory system (44.9 percent M, 60.0 percent F), malignant neoplasms (19.1 percent M, 13.5 percent F) and injuries, adverse effects, homicide and other violence (14.4 percent M, 3.8 percent F). Respiratory diseases are the fourth leading cause of death. The crude mortality rate is 1,219 per 100,000 (1,246 for males, 1,196 for females).

13.　　The Standardized Death Rate (SDR) for Ukraine, 1,142 per 100,000, is comparable to Poland but 6 percent higher than Belarus, 20 percent higher than Portugal, 30 percent higher than the European average, and 57 percent higher than Canada. The SDR for circulatory diseases is 45 percent greater than Portugal's and two times the rate for Canada. The cerebrovascular SDR is particularly high, 29 percent higher than Belarus', 2.6 times the rate in Poland and 3.7 times the rate in the United Kingdom. Mortality from malignant neoplasms was the third highest in the former Soviet Union including trachea, bronchus and lung cancers, and has been increasing. Mortality rates from ischemic heart disease, injury and poisoning and motor vehicle injury are relatively high and are increasing.

14.　　Infectious disease continues to cause avoidable deaths. The SDR for infectious diseases is 55 percent higher than in Belarus, 33 percent higher than in Poland and three times as high as in the United Kingdom. About 4,500 people died of tuberculosis in 1990. Except for persons 75 and older, age-specific SDRs for tuberculosis in Ukraine are greater by two to

nine times than in Poland, which is generally acknowledged as having one of the significant tuberculosis problems in Europe (see Health Annex Tables 7, 8, 9). The World Bank's *World Development Report 1993*, "Investing in Health," gives special emphasis to tuberculosis control as one of the highest priorities and most cost-effective, public health interventions.

HEALTH OF MOTHERS AND CHILDREN

Infant Mortality

15.　　Infant mortality has been gradually decreasing over the past decade and reached a low of 13.0 per thousand live births in 1990, but then began a sharp upward swing reaching 15.0 in the first quarter of 1992. This high rate is still well within the WHO/EURO Region target of 20 per thousand live births and is 25 percent less than Poland, but it is 25 percent higher than Belarus and Portugal and more than twice as high as Canada and Sweden. Some local studies, e.g., in Ivanofrankiusk, have shown rates well above 20.

16.　　Infectious and parasitic diseases, respiratory infections, and birth defects are the main causes of infant mortality in Ukraine. The SDR for infants (less than one year old) from infectious and parasitic diseases was 82.5 per 100,000 for males and 64.6 per 100,000 for females in 1990. This was better than Poland, worse than Belarus, and worse by a factor of 8-9 than Canada, where the 1989 rates were 8.9 for males and 6.3 for females per 100,000. The SDRs for diseases of the respiratory system are twice the level of infectious diseases: 162.3 per 100,000 for males and 136.4 for females. Two-thirds of the rate is due to pneumonia. Canadian rates for respiratory diseases were 15.5 for males and 12.5 for females, per 100,000. Most infant deaths, however, were from congenital malformations, birth trauma and conditions originating in the perinatal period. These birth defects account for two-thirds of all infant mortality on a standardized basis. One quarter of all mortality is from congenital birth malformations (414.4 M and 355.5 F per 100,000). Mortality from birth defects in Ukraine is generally comparable to Belarus, better than Poland, but much worse than

Portugal, the United Kingdom, Sweden or Canada. The SDRs for the United Kingdom for congenital birth deformations, for example, are 173.9 for males and 139.8 for females, per 100,000.

Maternal Mortality

17. The maternal mortality ratio was 32 deaths per 100,000 live births in 1990, the same as that for Belarus and an improvement from 44.5 in 1980. The rate is well above the WHO/EURO target of 10 and is triple the rate in Poland, four times the rate in the United Kingdom, and eight times the rate in Canada. Approximately 45 percent of maternal mortality is caused by obstetrical conditions and abortions. Age-specific abortion mortality rates are comparable to Belarus but higher than Poland, four times as high as Portugal and the United Kingdom, and significantly higher than Sweden and Canada (see Health Annex Figures 5,6,7).

18. Maternal and infant health remain poor despite the fact that all births occur in hospitals, and primary and secondary care services are widely available. Improvements are necessary in laboratory and technical equipment for diagnosis of prenatal and perinatal conditions.

Abortion and Contraception

19. Abortion is the principal form of contraception due to lack of information and access to modern contraceptives. Estimates indicate that up to two-thirds of the population is uninformed about modern contraceptives. The incidence of contraception for women of fertile age (15-49) including abortion, oral contraceptives and intrauterine devices (IUDs) is 17.9 percent and varies among oblasts from a high in Zhytomyr of 31.0 percent to a low in Lviv of 4.9 percent. The incidence of abortion as the sole means of contraception for Ukraine is 8.3 percent and ranges from 14.2 percent in Zaporizhzhia to 3.7 percent in Lviv. Ukraine does not produce its own contemporary contraceptive products. Access to contraceptives will deteriorate with price increases and curtailment of imports in the transition to a market driven economy. The abortion rate was 155 per 100 live births in 1990, among the

highest of former Soviet Union countries. The rate has been increasing since 1987 when it was 145. This is equivalent to 82.6 abortions per thousand women in the fertile age and compares to 55.7 live births per thousand women in the same age. The total number of abortions has decreased from 1.66 million in 1986 to 1.02 million in 1990, but the number of live births and females of fertile age has also decreased. Many women have multiple abortions.

20. The impact of abortion on the health of women and on health system costs is significant. In Ukraine 30 percent of women who had an abortion suffered from subsequent inflammatory diseases of internal genital organs, 50-60 percent from secondary sterility, 50 percent from complications of pregnancy, 22 percent from miscarriages and 13-15 percent from uterine bleeding during deliveries. Because of these complications of abortion, the health system must provide added numbers of gynecological beds and resources for treatment that would be unnecessary with fewer abortions. Hospital costs of treatment for complications of abortion have been estimated at 3-4 billion rubles in 1991 (see Box 1.1).

Table 1.5: Ministry of Health Estimated Demand for Contraceptives for 1991

Denomination	Number	Value in Million Rubles	$US (Million)
Condoms	468 million items	702	14.04
Hormonal Contraceptives	9.9 million packs	114	18.05
Intra-uterine Contraceptives	2.4 million items	39.6	40.32
TOTAL			72.41

Source: Ministry of Health

Family Planning

21. The combination of poor infant and maternal health, the high rate of abortions, and demographic patterns of net natural decrease in

---

Box 1.1: Indicators of Hospital Resource Allocated to Abortion 1991

1.	Supply of gynecological beds (including abortion cases)	37,055
	• rate per 10,000 total population	7.2
	• estimated rate per 10,000 females	13.4
2.	Excess average days occupancy of gynecological beds over average occupancy of total beds	6 days
3.	Number of women undergoing abortion	957,000
4.	Cost of an abortion in Kiev	650 rubles
5.	Percent and number subsequently treated for complications of inflammation disease as a result of abortion	30 percent
6.	Proportion and number that can expect to be cured with one treatment	half
7.	Proportion and number requiring treatment for resulting chronic condition	half 143,550
8.	Average number of courses of treatment for chronic condition	5-6
9.	Average courses of treatment	21 days
10.	Average 1991 cost per treatment	3,505 rubles
11.	Number of women undergoing treatment for infertility (largely associated with complications of abortion)	52,161

Source: Khodorovsky, G., 1992

---

the population indicate a need to make family planning policy an important social priority. Progress towards a national program is slow, indicating insufficient government support. A priority within the new policy must be to ensure access to modern contraceptives as an alternative to abortions. Family planning services need to be strengthened. They are available in theory in marriage counseling centers and from health workers, but their focus is on diagnosis and treatment of infertility rather than on the provision of advice on family planning methods. Only 30 percent of contraceptive needs are being met. The Ministry of Health estimated the cost of meeting the contraceptive needs of the population at 846 million rubles in 1991, significantly less than the 3-4 billion rubles estimated as the cost of hospital care for treating post-abortion complications. A decrease of 14 percent in the total number of abortions between 1986 and 1990 is attributed to the greater availability of contraceptives. This trend needs to be supported by further increasing the availability of contraceptives and family planning services (see Table 1.5). External technical and financial assistance could play a critically important role in providing such services until the availability of foreign exchange eases with the expansion of export earnings.

MORBIDITY

22. More than for mortality, interpretation of data on morbidity is difficult in Ukraine, as in other former Soviet Union countries. An all-union institute in Moscow developed norms for supply and utilization of facilities and services. Expectations were clear that the norms should be met. Politically safe morbidity data often followed, resulting in information that now presents an ambiguous picture of the use of health services. Based on the number of outpatient consultations and admissions to hospitals, the estimated rates for morbidity

reported in Ukraine are among the highest in the former Soviet Union. Incident and prevalent cases of respiratory disease account for the largest proportion of reported morbidity, 53.5 percent and 33.9 percent, respectively. Incidence of diseases of the nervous system and sense organs is next highest (8.1 percent), followed by diseases of the skin and subcutaneous tissues (5.5 percent). For prevalence, circulatory system diseases are next, (16.3 percent), followed by diseases of the nervous system and sense organs (9.3 percent).

23.   WHO reports that circulatory disease morbidity accounts for 21 percent of all adult morbidity, the highest in the former Soviet Union, similar to Belarus. Respiratory morbidity in children accounts for 60 percent of childhood diseases and 25 percent of adult diseases. Since the accident at Chernobyl, the incidence of certain respiratory diseases, particularly pneumonia and asthma, has reportedly been increasing. Children suffer at the highest rate of congenital anomalies among the former Soviet republics. There is particular attention paid to the diagnosis, monitoring and treatment of increasing thyroid-related pathologies, cancers, related hematological diseases and genetic defects in newborns of parents at risk. Reports indicate that 60 percent of children have some degree of thyroid modular hyperplasia, particularly in highly irradiated areas of the country.

Infectious Diseases and Immunization

24.   Mortality from infectious and parasitic diseases is about twice the European Community (EC) average. Diarrheal diseases are reported on the increase partially due to the decreasing quality of the water supply. According to WHO, diarrheal diseases caused by bacterial infections are rarely diagnosed. A UNICEF/WHO mission in early 1992 estimated the real coverage for infants in 1991 by vaccination for DPT is 75-79 percent rather than the much higher reported levels. Coverage was 89 percent for measles in children under age two, and 81 percent for poliomyelitis for infants. BCG, measles, and DPT vaccines were found to be in short supply. WHO standards on cold chain maintenance were not always met.

25.   An increase of 29 percent in reported Hepatitis A is one indicator of poor sanitation and hygiene conditions. There is a risk that Hepatitis B may be transmitted through inadequately sterilized syringes that are reused. At the end of 1991, 257 HIV positive cases were reported and identified; 8 cases of AIDS have been documented, which have resulted in 6 recorded deaths. Authorities believe there are some 500 HIV infected individuals in the country.

Selected Risk Factors

26.   Incidence of alcoholism in Ukraine was the second highest in the former Soviet Union republics, 136.4 per 100,000 in 1990. Incidence of drug abuse was also the second highest at 7.1 per 100,000. There is concern at the Ministry of Health about levels of tobacco use but apparently no survey data. Interest is emerging among the international tobacco industry firms in marketing tobacco products in the country and exploiting Ukrainian-produced leaf products. These developments could pit the health of the population against immediate economic gain for a few. The government should develop public health policies to limit tobacco use by means of education, limits on advertising, and other measures to convince the young not to start smoking. If they are successful, thousands of lives could be saved a dependence on a disease-causing product avoided.

27.   Food consumption patterns in Ukraine traditionally relied on satisfactory levels of cereals, potatoes and meat; diets were relatively high in dairy products and sugar. Price increases and shortages are distorting these patterns. In 1991, reports indicate people ate 5-8 percent less meat, milk and eggs than in the previous year and the consumption of fruits and vegetables dropped by 20-30 percent. Health promotion requires an effective nutrition, food, and health policy. Changing to a healthier diet with less fat and cholesterol but more fiber, fruits and vegetables could solve the current high levels of adult mortality caused by stroke, heart attack, and cancer.

OCCUPATIONAL INJURY AND POLLUTION

28.   High rates of occupational injury are documented most notably among miners in Donetsk oblast. Occupational diseases are under-reported, but pneumoconiosis, chronic dust bronchitis, and other occupational diseases are documented, mainly in coal miners.   A large secondary lead smelter in Konstantinovka accounts for the very high exposure of its 1,600 workers, and many of the city's residents, to lead   poisoning.   Other   heavy-metal   and chemical- exposure-related incidents and illness have been reported in industrialized areas.

29.   High concentrations of pollutants in ambient air, including dust, oxides of nitrogen, and carbon monoxide, are documented in concentrations considerably higher than the guidelines of the former Soviet Union and of the United States would permit.   Metallurgical plants in a number of cities account for most of their total air pollutants. Resultant illness, such as exacerbation of chronic lung disease or occurrence of lung cancer, cannot be readily documented with public health statistics.   The Ministry of Health, however, reports that morbidity from oncological, skin, blood and urinary-system diseases is higher than average in certain cities, suggesting that illness may be attributable to elevated levels of industrial pollutants.   The rate of spontaneous abortions (miscarriages) in two industrial cities with high air pollution has been found to be twice the rate of a clean control city.   The rate of congenital anomalies was found to be three times the control rate in the same study.

30.   Apart from reported increases in thyroid cancers, and an indication of increased mortality and morbidity of congenital defects over the past few years, data from the Ministry of Chernobyl has not yet revealed clear-cut evidence of health effects from the Chernobyl disaster.   More time will be required before there are sufficient statistical data to relate leukaemia and various cancer incidents to the release of radioactive materials.   A recent *Lancet* editorial dated October 3, 1992, reviewed 30 scientific studies of mortality and concluded that "environmental pollution is unlikely to result in gross excess mortality, and, therefore, cannot be responsible for   variations   in   death   rates   between populations."[6]

LABOR FORCE

31.   About half of the population of 52 million work, a fifth in agriculture, over half in manufacturing and a quarter in services.   This structure   differs   considerably   from   other countries and may be expected to change along lines suggested in Chapter 2 below, with serious implications for problems of labor productivity and unemployment.   If consumer demand, in contrast to state orders and spending on the security forces, is permitted to manifest itself, about a third of all workers might shift out of agriculture and manufacturing into services, with many complications and costs of disruption if the process occurs quickly.

32.   A mature population, one in which births   are   roughly   equal   to   deaths,   also approximates a situation in which new entrants to the labor force equal the number exiting into retirement.   The potential labor force includes all persons aged 15 to 65 years: each year, about two percent enter as youths and 2 percent exit as elderly retirees.   Thus in 1993, for example, about half a million new entrants will seek jobs, many of them in the nascent private sector, especially in service activities.   Of the half-million retirees, many will leave farming occupations and perhaps even more will be leaving   declining   defense-related   industries. Thus, a substantial part of the transformation of the labor force can occur with no one losing a job or being unemployed.   The movement into service-sector employment of one-third of the labor force could occur in 17.5 years, i.e., by the year 2010, with no one changing jobs, but just as the result of natural labor-force turnover. These considerations may help demonstrate that structural   change   need   not   be   a   socially disruptive process.   On   the   other   hand, government must take care not to block these natural processes with inhibiting regulations. For example, the system of *propiska*, which severely limits internal migration, may already be blocking the transformation of the labor force by keeping potential movers out of major cities.

32.   In virtually all countries, most working-

age males are in the labor force. Ukraine is distinctive because of the high participation rates of working-age females. The benefits from wage incomes are probably offset in some measure by lost leisure time and less parental attention to child raising, but there are no studies that analyze this feature of work. Many enterprises are beginning to abandon their past support of day care facilities for minor children. This change may have significant negative effects on women's option to work.

THE SOCIAL SAFETY NET

33. At the time that the Soviet economy was beginning to fray at the seams in the 1980s, there was a growing awareness that social protection under socialism fell short on objectives of fairness and equity. The Soviets divided cash transfer payments (*pensiya* in Russian) into two kinds: labor pensions, which are either directly or loosely related to labor or labor service; and social pensions, which are paid to disabled individuals with no labor service. The basic legislation regulating cash transfers includes the 1956 all-union law on pensions for workers and employees, the 1965 all-union law on pensions for collective farmers, and the 1990 pension law, which provided that cash transfer payments, at a base rate of 55 percent of pre-retirement wages, are not taxable and are paid regardless of other income.

34. This legislation considerably increased the cost of benefits, and the numbers receiving the benefits. By the beginning of 1993, about two-thirds of all persons in Ukraine were receiving one or more cash benefits: a quarter of the population receive disability, retirement, or survivors' benefits; 27 percent receive student stipends and related free board and room; 25 percent receive family allowances for children under age 16 and special allowances from the Chernobyl Fund; and a small percentage receive short-term assistance from the sickness fund to pay for lost work time, or from the Employment Fund in the case of unemployment. The state also finances massive subsidies that wax and wane with administratively determined prices for food, transportation, and shelter, and that reached 8 percent of GDP in 1992. Education and health care are provided to all at no cost at

the point of service; enterprises are required to provide day-care services for children under age six, and paid maternity leave for three years, but they are increasingly failing to meet this obligation. The social safety net was stretched to cover a majority of the population as 1993 began, but it was, as a result, failing to provide adequate assistance for the minority of the poor and those most in need.

RETIREMENT, DISABILITY, AND SURVIVORS' BENEFITS

35. In 1990, there were 9.7 million old-age pensioners in Ukraine, receiving an average monthly pension of 109.69 rubles. The minimum pension was 70 rubles, and 3.6 million elderly pensioners, 37 percent of all old-age pensioners, received only the minimum benefit. For each full year of work beyond 25 years for men and 20 years for women, the pension was increased by 1 percent of earnings, thus raising the maximum replacement rate from 55 percent to 75 percent of highest-ever earnings. About a quarter of both disability and elderly pensioners continued to work with no reduction in benefits. There were 1.3 million disabled receiving benefits ranging from 47 to 127 rubles per month in 1990 (for background on the USSR cash-benefit system see Chapter 5).[7]

36. The number of pensioners had grown to 13.5 million by the middle of 1992, including 362,000 people in the security sector (see Table 1.6). The average pension was 22 percent above the minimum, but Pension Fund payments to military pensioners exceeded the minimum by 144 percent, and pensions issued by the Ministry of Defense averaged 5.2 times the minimum.

ALLOWANCES AND BENEFITS

37. This paragraph describes the allowances that prevailed in the middle of 1992. Family assistance programs were substantially revised early in 1993 with the objective of focusing cash benefits on fewer and needier groups. In 1992, Ukraine offered a large number of cash allowances and assistance programs, some aimed at low-income and vulnerable groups; others designed for family assistance to assist child-

rearing among the general population; and those targeted to Chernobyl victims. Allowances accounted for 20 percent of social sector spending in 1992 and about 8.8 percent of GDP. About 47 percent of total allowance funding was derived from general government revenues, 38 percent from the Chernobyl payroll tax, 11 percent from the social insurance fund, and 4 percent from the pension fund. Benefits targeted to Chernobyl victims accounted for 39 percent of social assistance spending; aid to vulnerable groups, 37 percent[8]; allowances available to the population as a whole, 23 percent.

- **Chernobyl.** About two-thirds of *Chernobyl* allowance spending goes to wage bonuses to workers in areas of radiation contamination. Housing and relocation benefits account for about 9 percent of Chernobyl-related allowance spending; disability and death compensation, 9 percent; supplemental family allowances, 4 percent; food provision, 4 percent; and other allowances, 6 percent.[9]

- **Food Allowances.** Allowances to low-income families for the purchase of food products accounted for 48 percent of spending on low-income and vulnerable groups. This benefit was paid monthly for each child under 18 and pensionable age and ranged from 30-40 percent of the minimum wage. Allowances to compensate for increases in children's clothing prices accounted for 24 percent of vulnerable groups' allowances, and were also introduced to protect families from price decontrol; non-cash benefits to the infirm elderly accounted for 10 percent of funding; stipends to low-income families with children from age 3 to age 6, 6 percent;[10] additional allowances to low-income families and single mothers, 8 percent; and maintenance of

orphanages, 4 percent.

- **Consumer Subsidies.** Assistance to the general population and specific non-vulnerable groups includes stipends to all families with children under age three, (41 percent of this category); sick leave and short-term disability pay, 27 percent; benefits for the disabled, 11 percent; [11] recreation benefits, eight percent, maternity benefits, six percent; and other benefits, seven percent. The Social Insurance Fund pays for 42.5

Table 1.6: Pensioners and Their Benefits, January 1, 1992

Pensioners	Number in Thousands	Percent of Total	Average Pension as a Percent of the Minimum Pension[1]
Pension Fund Supported	12,997	97	122
Retirees	10,318	77	125
Disabled	1,224	9	123
Dependents	693	5	96
Other[2]	500	4	75
Military	262	2	144
Military Paid from Ministry of Defence	362	3	522
Total	13,359	100	133

Notes: 1. Figures do not reflect July and October 1992 increases.

2. People who never worked including those disabled from childhood and hobos.

Source: Ministry of Social Welfare

percent of non-targeted benefits; state and local general revenues, 40 percent; and the Pension Fund, 17.5 percent (for details see Chapter 7).

There were over 60 allowances and benefits, many of which did not differ substantively from one another.[12] Many allowances were funded, administered and distributed by several agencies; others were funded by one agency, administered by a second, and distributed by a third.[13] There are special benefits for servicemen's families, cars (or the cash equivalent) for some disabled persons, telephone service for veterans, and free access to vacation camps. Early in 1993, government officials were in the midst of a serious effort to redefine and limit benefits to those in greatest need. The results of their efforts remain to be determined in the future.

POVERTY GROUPS

38.   Official estimates of the former Soviet Union placed the share of the Ukrainian population living in poverty at about 8 percent in 1988, which was above the Soviet average. Assuming the poverty level in 1990 was 100 rubles, then poverty increased to 11.3 percent of the Ukrainian population. The true poverty line for 1990 is unknown, but there are data on the distribution of income for 1988-90. There are no data on the characteristics of households living in poverty, but they would include aged rural people living alone, orphans, the seriously disabled, families with three or more children, single parents, and pensioners receiving less than 1.5 times the minimum pension. These groups constitute from 10 to 20 percent of the population. The numbers living in poverty have undoubtedly risen in the past two years of economic crisis. An unpublished study based on a special survey in the Russian Federation found that 36.7 percent of population is below the poverty line. Characteristics of households that appear to be associated with poverty are the presence of children under age six in the household and the presence of an unemployed or handicapped person (Popkin, Mazhina and Baturin 1993, Table 1). As Russia and Ukraine have both suffered from the decline of trade

---

Box 1.2: Key Issues for the Social Sectors

Three major issues confront Ukraine in assessing its inherited program of public social spending. First, what share of GDP can the government afford to devote to social compensation? Ukraine's stabilization will not accommodate so large a share of GDP as 41 percent. Reduction to almost 20 percent, at most 25 percent of GDP is probably required.

Second, on what basis will the Government make the choices of allocation of social spending within the several components of pension benefits, food subsidies, family allowances, unemployment compensation and training, and the social services of education and health? These choices need to be informed by two kinds of concerns:

- That public resources be efficiently used, and

- That the implicit and explicit subsidies provided by government go preferentially to those most in need.

These changes would require reducing general subsidies, a step already taken, rescinded, and taken again by the government in the difficult policy environment of 1992 and 1993. Government officials have also recognized the need to concentrate limited resources, especially family allowances, on vulnerable groups, including inter alia single-parent families and the rural poor.

Third, how will the Government strike the balance between spending that supports current well-being and spending that builds capacity for future productivity, such as education, health, and training services provided by government? In difficult times, such as those faced now by Ukraine, there will be a bias against investment and in favor of spending for current benefits. This bias ought to be the subject of continuing review to assure that government invests enough in children, in their good education and health, and in the equipment, pharmaceuticals, textbooks, and other inputs that, in difficult times, are put off in favor of protecting current benefits, such as salaries, pensions, and family allowances.

within the former Union, the incidence of poverty and related problems may be similar.

39. Women may constitute a vulnerable group that is susceptible, under various circumstances, to falling into poverty. Even at current low rates of unemployment, the number of unemployed women is nearly double that of men. Single women heading households are likely to be poor (see background papers by Pirozkhov and Lakiza-Sachuk; Libanova; and Khodorovsky, all prepared in 1992). Unavailability of family planning and complications of abortion frequently endanger the reproductive health of women of childbearing age. Although earlier retirement is an advantage women enjoy over men, women's longevity often leaves them as unsupported

Table 1.7: Income Distribution, 1988-1990

Income Class (Rubles Per Capita Per Month)	Percent of the Population		
	1988	1989	1990
Under 75	8.1	6.0	2.7
75-100	16.8	14.2	8.6
100-150	38.5	37.2	31.2
150-200	22.4	24.5	28.0
over 200	14.2	18.1	29.5

Source: Braithwaite (1992).

widows with inadequate pensions. The onset of crisis has led many enterprises to cut back on day-care services essential to women. Finally, maternity leave and other benefits have the effect of raising the relative cost of hiring women, thus potentially aggravating their employment problems during periods of labor shedding.

MAIN ISSUES FOR SOCIAL PROGRAMS

40. This review of social conditions and social protection raises a number of issues that will be addressed in succeeding chapters. The most general issue is that resources available to the government during this period of crisis seem totally inadequate to meet the vast responsibilities bestowed on the state by its predecessor. The productive economy has

shrunk owing to the shock of the dislocation of the integrated system of the former Soviet Union, and the available resources of social protection have shrunk as well. In the competition for program survival, the government is trying to spend more than it has available, thus contributing to inflation. Unless managers set priorities for the distribution of benefits, there will surely be considerable waste, inefficiency, and payment to many who may not be absolutely dependent on assistance for their well-being (see Box 1.2). Setting priorities, which is the subject of much of the rest of this report, can help to ensure more effective use of limited resources.

41. There is a risk that open unemployment will rise, and it is probable that there is already considerable hidden unemployment in many state enterprises, as shown in Chapter 2. What actions should the government take to address the problem of unemployment? The next three chapters of this report offer a number of suggestions.

42. The government has more obligations to its citizens than it can serve: How then can the government trim back those obligations and still attend to the most basic social assistance needs of pensioners, families, students, and the poor? Chapters 4 through 7 address the many aspects of the match between needs and program assistance to try to find the least painful way to bring resources and obligations back into balance.

43. Social services, particularly education and health, are essential components of social well-being. Sustainable development will depend on providing adequate social services as they promote productivity. Currently available programs are acknowledged by their managers to be inefficient. Chapters 8 and 9 summarize current issues in each area and summarize areas in which efficiency improvements, most of which are contemplated for introduction by managers of public education and health services, could reduce spending yet maintain the quality of services. Regrettably, resources did not permit this study to include related social sector ministries that support programs of culture, youth and sport, and smaller

components of the aggregate public effort to provide for the broad range of social needs. In reviewing a draft of this document, the authorities asked for follow-up studies that could include this broad range of programs. Certainly those areas of responsibility that are adjacent to education and health are at considerable risk of budget reductions, and an analysis of highest priority services needs to be made in conjunction with an overview of sector needs.

REASON FOR HOPE

44.   Recent surveys in Russia, Bulgaria and Czechoslovakia indicate that a mood of pessimism is more deeply embedded in the first country, (Rose 1992). Ukraine may share Russia's mood of uncertainty about the economic and social future. A major objective of social protection must be to protect vulnerable groups and bring the country out of a process of transition into a better condition than that which prevailed before the commitment to independence and restructuring. No one should suffer unnecessarily in this process. The collapse in economic output imposes nearly impossible conditions on a government intent on protecting its population; nonetheless, sound priorities, especially a determination to attend to the needs of those most vulnerable during the next year or two, coupled with timely external financial and technical assistance, should be adequate. The following chapters review in more detail how a bias for hope can build a framework for continued dynamic economic growth while limiting the social costs of adjustment. There are ways to reduce public outlays among those current beneficiaries who can get along without subsidy, at least until the transition to a market economy is well along and the economy has been stabilized. At the same time, there is space within the safety net to accommodate those who might, through no fault of their own, fall into unemployment and who need social protection and assistance in the shift to new lines of work.

SOURCES AND USES OF FUNDS FOR THE SOCIAL SECTOR, 1992

45.   Today, the state is trying to protect pension benefits of 13.5 million recipients,

family allowances for a broad spectrum of recipients, stipends and in-kind assistance for 11.4 million students, and real salaries among the nearly 6 million employees paid from state and oblast budgets, over half of whom deliver education and health services as part of the social safety net. If to these are added a potential 3 million unemployed, then 34 million persons, or 65 percent of the population, will be beneficiaries or workers in the system of social protection. It seems unlikely that the productive economy can readily support such a large burden; thus, this report seeks to identify a basic safety net that might stretch to accommodate that smaller share of the population that is most in need (see Box 1.2 on key issues for the social sectors).

Sources of Funds

46.   The social sector budget for 1992 was set at R1.2 trillion in June of that year. According to budgets made in May and June 1992, general revenues from state and local governments would account for 53 percent of total sources of funds; earmarked payroll taxes, 43 percent; and enterprises and individuals, 3 percent (see Figure 1.1).

47.   General revenues were to be derived primarily from a value-added tax (VAT) and an enterprise income tax. The VAT could account for about 45 percent of general government revenues in 1992; the enterprise income tax, 29 percent; the personal income tax, 10 percent; and excise and trade taxes and non-tax revenues, 16 percent.

48.   Payroll taxes, at 53 percent of gross wages, even though reduced from the 84 percent that prevailed in the first quarter of 1992, remain among the highest in the world. The pension and social insurance taxes, 37 percent of wages, feed into the Social Insurance Funds. A 1 percent tax is levied on employee earnings and accrues to the Pension Fund. The Chernobyl tax is 12 percent of the wage bill, down from 19 percent in spring, 1992. The Employment Fund tax is 3 percent of wages. Moreover, the enterprise profits tax partially includes salary expenses as income.

Uses of Funds

49.   In July 1992, social spending was forecast to reach 44 percent of GDP; by February 1993, most analysts thought such spending had indeed exceeded 40 percent of GDP in 1992.

Sector Budgeting Issues

50.   The preceding description shows that the means to finance and provide social protection is

there may be considerable inefficiency emerging from the lack of central control. Allocations for the social funds may have been correct in the past, but they may now need to be increased (as with employment services) or decreased (as with resources for the sickness fund) depending upon changing national priorities.

51.   Succeeding chapters discuss current and emerging issues that could lead the government to set new priorities for its social programs. For example, the hardening of budget constraints for

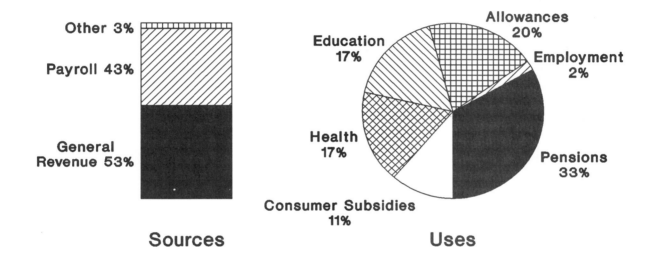

Source: Mission estimates based on
Information from government sources in
July 1992.

Figure 1.1: Percentage Distribution, Sources and Uses of Funds in the Social Sectors, 1992 Budget

extremely complex. Certain legislation earmarks funds for specific purposes, such as the wage taxes paid into several funds that in turn pay for pensions, allowances, sickness, and employment services, according to specified rates set by the government. Other programs depend on general revenues; these include most spending for education and health. Some programs, especially preschool and some health services, have been financed on a voluntary basis by enterprises out of their profits. Because this complex system of finance has no central focus,

state enterprises may lead to labor redundancy and unemployment, which will require an active response of job matching and training, as well as resources to pay unemployment benefits (see Chapters 2, 3, and 4). The resources to support such new programs may have to come from scaling back somewhere else. Pensions and family allowances (Chapters 5, 6, and 7) offer some opportunities for selected spending reductions that do not reduce effective social protection. The principal public social services offered in the areas of education, training, and health require continued support, but they may also offer some opportunities to achieve efficiencies while expanding some key areas (pharmaceutical availability, retraining for redundant workers, and education for nation-building) deemed essential by government and society (Chapters 8 and 9).

52.   One means to assure that programs improve social conditions and provide social protection is to introduce a systematic budgeting arrangement for all social spending. Budgeting by objective is one approach to consider. Such a technique requires that all users of public social funds present their program goals and intended approaches for central budget review, usually by the Ministry of Finance. Allocations

then depend on the importance of the goals and the cost-effectiveness of the approaches offered. A periodic publication by the Brookings Institution in Washington DC, *Setting National Priorities*, a review of the USA federal budget, offers an interesting example of how a budget can be reviewed against national objectives. Given the importance of social protection in Ukraine, and the substantial public resources allocated to achieving improvements in social well-being, the government might wish to consider this approach as a means to bring social spending under control yet ensure that social protection is maintained. It could help ensure that limited resources contribute as well as they can to meeting diverse, important objectives of social protection.

THE LABOR MARKET IN A COMMAND ECONOMY

1.   Several features distinguish the command economy with central planning from a market economy; a number of those features affect the labor market.   First, the command economy operates the entire economic system as if it were a single firm. Coase (1988) has shown that the size of firms in a market economy is determined by the relative costliness of acquiring each particular commodity or service needed by the firm through internal, non-price acquisition, or through purchase in the market. In a command economy, however, there is no market discipline and the various branches of the single firm acquire inputs from each other at centrally determined rates in physical, not necessarily in price, terms. Similarly, the firm acquires labor in an environment without market discipline so that the price paid is set overall by the single firm that is the state.

2.   Because the goals of each enterprise are set in physical terms as outputs (of tons of steel or coal, for example), and because over time soft budget constraints came to characterize the operating environment of enterprises, there was no signaling mechanism that gave enterprises incentives to use labor efficiently.   Labor hoarding is a term used to describe the enterprises' tendency to overuse labor.[14] Because wages are set overall in the command economy, individual enterprises offer extensive nonwage compensation (free housing, child care, paid vacations, education and health services) to attract and retain workers. Coexistence of labor hoarding and labor scarcity is thus a chronic condition in the command economies of Eastern Europe and the former Soviet Union (Kornai 1980).   School leavers normally had jobs arranged prior to graduation and there has been no visible unemployment in these economies.

3.   Certain additional distortions of the labor market of the USSR derive from the Marxian labor theory of value, from differential treatment of productive and nonproductive labor, and from systematic undervaluation of services directed at the management of capital assets.   The labor theory of value, in contrast to classical and neoclassical economics, attempted to identify the value of all production as a direct or indirect result of labor inputs. No productive value was associated with capital except insofar as it is "congealed labor."   As a result, the price of waiting goes unpaid and the productivity of capital as waiting goes unrewarded. Prices of the factors of production do not reflect their true scarcity and productivity values, and there is as a result chronic underinvestment in capital goods, such as housing, that were inconsistent with the aims of central planners. The Marxian theory of value came over time to undervalue so-called nonproductive work; the measurement of net material product, for example, excludes many services, notably those provided by state employees of education and health services.

4.   The Marxian system recognizes three classes as they relate to the means of production: peasants, workers, and the intelligentsia.   These groups are broadly consistent with the neoclassical division, usually attributed in this century to the empirical work of Colin Clark and Simon Kuznets, of primary, secondary, and tertiary workers.   The Marxian system, however, has had an ideological bias favoring workers, a tolerance for peasants, and a certain tradition of skepticism about the contribution of the intelligentsia. This bias was reflected in the relatively high (as percentage of the average) wages of certain segments of the working class (miners, transport and construction workers). Nonetheless, the evolution of demand in any economy that experiences a rise in per capita output is toward a decreasing application of resources in primary activities; growing efficiency in secondary activities that permits an eventual reduction of resources applied there,

and the growth of tertiary or support services.

5.   This evolution created a tension in the Soviet economy because the system emphasized secondary work (mining and manufacturing), yet many nonpecuniary rewards derived for many labor force participants from becoming part of the intelligentsia and the service sector. In Ukraine, for example, the education and health sectors have absorbed a far larger share of the labor force than is typical of OECD countries, let alone the middle-income countries around the world that apply even fewer of their labor-force participants to these activities. The lack of alternative lines of work, particularly in the management of the economy's capital assets, has led to an overuse of service-sector workers in the provision of social services.

LABOR MARKET STRUCTURE

6.   Ukraine is characterized by a comparatively high level of economic activity within its population, a typical feature of Eastern Europe. More than 50 percent of the population is employed somewhere, whereas in Western Europe the number is about 40 percent. As far as the structure of employment is concerned, by Western European standards, and by standards of other middle-income countries, Ukraine has a high share of employment in agriculture (19.8 percent) and manufacturing (53.8 percent), and a very low share in services (26.4 percent), in particular in the banking and insurance sector (0.5 percent). Comparative evidence is shown in Table 2.1. However, the Ukrainian employment structure is similar to that of other Eastern European countries. A comparison of the dynamics of Ukrainian employment with Western European employment shows that the Ukrainian employment structure changed much less than that of Western Europe in the 1970s, and hardly changed in the 1980s, when the Western European employment structure shifted remarkably toward services.

7.   The division of labor among agriculture, manufacturing, and services broke down to some extent in response to demand for service work

associated with the growing complexity of the Soviet economy. Many workers in Ukrainian agriculture and manufacturing do service work, such as equipment repair, cleaning, and materials supply. Differences in labor-force structure between Ukraine and developed OECD countries are real, not just a statistical artifact, for several interrelated reasons. First, the structure reflects the priorities of the Soviet system. Investment decisions in the USSR were biased towards investment goods. There was a self-reinforcing process in that the production of investment goods was raised so as to have more fixed capital, which had to produce investment goods that contributed in turn to the growth of fixed capital. This spiral advanced, resulting in more investment and more fixed capital.

Table 2.1: Employment by Sector in International Perspective

	Ukraine	United States	United Kingdom	France	Japan
Agriculture (Primary)	19.8	2.9	2.3	6.8	7.9
Manufacturing (Secondary)	53.8	26.9	29.6	30.3	34.1
Services (Tertiary)	26.4	70.2	68.1	62.9	58.0

Sources: For Ukraine, 1989 census data. For other countries, OECD, Labor Force Statistics, 1990.

8.   Second, the manufacture of tangible material goods was viewed as the productive sphere, and the provision of most services as a nonproductive sphere of economic activity. The nonproductive sphere was neglected because of lack of private producers where the sovereignty of consumers prevails in Western countries through market reflection of consumer demand. Moreover, a lack of democratic procedures made impossible the existence of political parties that otherwise would have been willing to vote the sums to developing public services.

9.   Third, defense policies favored big, new installations and the arms industry; it was easier to build a new factory than to properly maintain the existing one. The phenomenon was not confined to material production, and diseconomies of scale are also visible in the service sector. The authorities attempted also to

create better wage and labor conditions in the defense industry. Two decades ago wages of scientific personnel in the defense industry in the USSR were higher than those of their civilian counterparts by up to 50 percent, but over time this advantage has been decreasing (see Oxenstierna 1990, pp. 146-147).

10.   Fourth, productivity in agriculture was very low and hence an unusually large share of the labor force had to be retained in the primary sector of production to supply basic consumer demand for foodstuffs. Related agricultural processing industries are also low in productivity compared to European or even middle-income countries, so these areas of manufacture require more workers than would be the case if normal levels of productivity were to be obtainable in these activities.

11.   Despite high demand, queuing, shortages and waiting lists, levels of consumption by individuals in Ukraine (as in the whole Soviet Union) lag behind consumption by those living

Table 2.2: An International Comparison of Car and Telephone Density

	Number of cars per 1,000 inhabitants, 1987	Main lines per 100 inhabitants 1986
West Germany	462	
Switzerland	418	
Italy	392	
Norway	387	
Spain	251	25.2
Greece		33.0
Cyprus		24.7
Ireland		21.2
Bulgaria	127	15.1
Czechoslovakia	174	12.5
East Germany	209	9.8
Poland	111	7.0
Soviet Union	44	9.0

Source: Kornai (1990, pp. 304-305)

production and weaponry, in which investment in military hardware was given priority over consumption. The population was compelled to sacrifice present consumption to investments that support military policy. Table 2.2 and Figures 2.1 and 2.2 presents differences in density of cars and telephones between the Soviet Union and other countries; these differences demonstrate how completely the demand for private consumption has been suppressed. Once effective consumer demand becomes the main determinant of what is produced, employment will shift to a pattern more like that of other market economies.

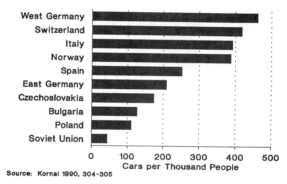

Source: Kornai 1990, 304-305

Figure 2.1: International Comparison of Density of Automobile Ownership, 1987

OPEN AND HIDDEN UNEMPLOYMENT

12.   The rate of unemployment in Ukraine was negligible, around 0.15 percent, in July 1992 and continues to be low, though rising slowly, early in 1993. The number of unemployed has more than tripled since the first quarter of 1991. Of this number almost 70

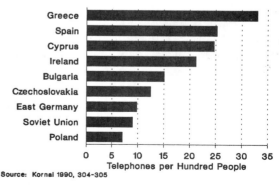

Source: Kornai 1990, 304-305

Figure 2.2: International Comparison of Density of Main Telephone Lines, 1986

under capitalism. The lag is greater in consumption goods than in production goods, a result of the strategy of accumulation for

percent are white-collar workers, and more than 70 percent are women. The unemployment rate in July 1992 varied from 0.01 percent in Vinnytsia oblast to 0.56 percent in Ivano-Frankivsk oblast. About one-third of the unemployed lost their jobs owing to liquidation or reorganization of state enterprises. There are reports of a widespread practice of cutting working hours in the enterprises and keeping labor idle. Credits from the state budget enable the enterprises to go on paying wages without producing, thus avoiding layoffs. The resultant public deficit and inflation lead to the conclusion that this arrangement must eventually collapse. Unemployment may accelerate in an unmanageable way, and the steps undertaken to prepare for it may prove insufficient.

13.   Historically, since the late 1950s, labor hoarding has prevented any major manifestation of open unemployment in Ukraine. As in other countries in Eastern Europe, labor hoarding was accompanied by labor shortages. Labor shortages prevented firms from firing unnecessary workers, yet numerous workers on the payroll were underemployed. In the period 1970-1989, when employment growth slightly exceeded labor force growth, the number of vacancies was consistently much higher than the small number of registered unemployed. This pattern was typical of Eastern Europe, indicating an excessive demand for labor, which even accelerated in the late 1980s owing to relaxation in monetary and fiscal policy. A majority of vacancies have been for blue collar male workers. In July 1992, the number of vacancies was still higher than the number of unemployed (see Annex A.61 and A.62).

14.   As a result of the disruption of the economy, price liberalization, imbalance between orders and available raw and technical materials, the breakdown in trade with Eastern Europe and the Baltics, and a decline in state orders for various types of production, Ukraine is experiencing a collapse in output. Most managers believe the drop in the volume of production will be temporary. Anticipating a renewal of economic ties and an increase of demand, managers continue to hoard labor. There has been a sharp increase in the incidence of extended administrative leave without pay,

transfer to jobs with shorter working hours, discontinuance of shift work, and related changes that reduce hours worked while disguising the reality of unemployment. This process has become prevalent in all branches of the economy, as the following evidence, partly based on surveys, and partly anecdotal, will indicate.

15.   Based on a sample survey conducted by local employment centers in 333 enterprises in Ukraine, the incidence of leave without pay has affected 26.3 percent of the average monthly employment; 29.5 percent of leave takers were on leave up to two weeks, 27.7 percent between two and four weeks, and 42.8 for percent over a month (see Figure S.4 in the Executive Summary and the Statistical Annex). Some were on indefinite leave. Casual observation and occasional surveys provide various examples of temporary layoffs associated with lack of raw materials. The Gorlovska knitted textile factory, with 2,420 staff, worked only one day in 1992 until March 1, 1992; the Kiev "Ukrkabel" plant had 1,350 people working a 32-hour week. For the same reasons, in February, 1992 the Zaporozhska textile/garment factory went through a 17-day stoppage, with 645 workers affected, and the Mukachevska textile/garment factory with its 723 employees stopped for almost a month. Both the Uzhgorodskoe footwear company, with 2,000 workers, and "Elektrodvigatel" with its 1,004 employees, had stoppages of two weeks. The Kharkov "Malshieva" factory worked a shorter hour week, with its 3,000 employees; the Rovno radio plant, with its 7,165 workers; and textile/garment factory, with its 1,400 workers, also worked short hours. Following the disruption of economic ties, partly with Russia, the "Tos" factory in Yvano-Frankovskoi oblast expects a R7-8 million decline in its output, and a 130 person layoff. Both 463 workers in the "Elektrobitpribor" Troskianeykom factory and 270 workers in the Belopolski tool-machine factory (Sumskaia oblast) were given a leave of two months. The Ternopol baking plant closed for almost two months. In Donetsk oblast, owing to shortages of power and raw materials, lost working time increased by 2.3 times in January 1992 in comparison with January 1991.

16. A survey of 13 state enterprises employing 65,000 workers in Kiev found that they cut employment by 13 percent in 1992, much more among producers of civilian goods (25 percent) than military goods (10 percent, with two large firms having no layoffs). Interviews with 350 of the laid-off workers showed that most got new jobs, the exceptions being workers over 50 years of age. Over half the redundant workers under age 35 got jobs in the private sector (Simon and Ustenko 1993, reported in Financial Times, February 14, 1993). These findings suggest that the labor market can absorb younger, male (women fared less well than men in the search for new jobs), big-city workers in the burgeoning private sector of major cities. But for older workers in single-industry towns far from cities, the prospects remain bleak.

17. As there has been no unemployment in the past, there are no statistical systems that study it. In the future, Ukraine will need to develop a systematic approach to gathering unemployment data so that effective policies can address employment problems when and where they arise. For the present, policy data are far from adequate to design effective responses as problems emerge.

LABOR MOBILITY AND MIGRATION

18. Labor mobility is constrained by the system of residence permit, (propiska), the lack of affordable housing, and the rigid and overspecialized education system. The tightness of the Ukrainian labor market varies across regions. Opportunities for work are weakest in the eastern region, in particular in the cities of Donetsk, Krivoy Rog, Dnepropetrovsk, and Kharkiv where a huge concentration of mining, metallurgy and machine-building industries exist, the bulk of them being part of the defense complex, and where mass layoffs can be expected in the future. The Odessa region (in particular its southwestern part) suffers from disguised agricultural unemployment. The situation is better in the western region, where the number of new openings in the private sector is the highest, and where excess labor travels informally to neighboring countries.

19. An additional strain on the Ukrainian labor market may come from international migrants. Ukraine has experienced net in-migration since 1985, mainly from Crimean Tatars who are returning to Crimea, and refugees from Armenia, Azerbaijan and Moldova. This immigration may adversely affect local labor markets, as the migrants cluster in some regions with few job opportunities. The government is beginning to develop international agreements on migration with neighboring countries.

WAGES AND INCOMES

20. In the Ukrainian Soviet Socialist Republic, wages and employment were strictly controlled. Wage setting was based on a tariff system. In addition to tariff wages set centrally, most employees were earning bonuses, which were determined and allocated at the enterprise level. Tariff wages were based on skill scales reflecting differentials relative to the least skilled. There were basic rates for the least skilled, and additional coefficients for arduous work.

21. Throughout 1991 the old system of wage setting was still in place, although beginning in March, enterprises could set their own tariffs, subject to ministerial approval. All wages were adjusted for inflation through changes of the minimum wage when the monthly price rise exceeded 5 percent. Wages lower than twice the minimum wage were fully indexed, wages of two to three times the minimum were increased by 50 percent, and those higher were not indexed at all. Up to the end of 1991, indexation was mandatory for both government and enterprises.

22. Earnings by sector used to be unrelated to the workers' educational attainment by sector, perhaps indicating that monetary returns to education are low. For instance, the three lowest paid sectors were education, culture, and health in which the number of university graduates was the highest. The two highest-paid sectors were construction and industry, where the majority of the work force had no secondary education. This anomalous situation is changing with banking and insurance earnings overtaking

all others. Wage differentials among managers, specialists, and workers vary by sector, but are low as well. In the government sector, according to salary schedules, specialists earn 25-30 percent more than workers; managers, 80-100 percent more. The rules for indexation of government workers' salaries have compressed salary schedules; unless the rules change, the compression is going to deepen with inflation. Early in 1993, the Government's Plan of Action provided for significant changes in wage policy. With inflation near 30 percent per month, wage adjustments were seen to be essential. At the same time, it was clear that across-the-board increases exacerbated inflation. Some enterprises were raising real wages. Government policy sought to cap enterprise wage bills to keep real wages from rising beyond productivity increases and hence help to suppress inflation. The effectiveness of these policies remains uncertain.

COLLECTIVE BARGAINING AND UNIONS

23.   In the long run, in an open European economy, the collective bargaining scheme may enhance or impede productivity growth and development. The current Ukrainian system impedes wage setting in the enterprises by making wages subject to collective agreements at the industry level. There are 33 such agreements in the country, some of them very detailed, specifying various obligations of employers not mentioned elsewhere. Since Ukraine is a large country, the Swedish-type setting of collective bargaining, based on centralized relations between government and union representation, does not seem appropriate; agreements at the enterprise level could suit the country better. Such a system would contain wage pressure and involve trade unions in anti-unemployment actions consistent with the market economy, allowing for a more serious involvement of trade unions in supplementary unemployment compensation, industrial relations improvement, and labor productivity issues.

UNEMPLOYMENT FORECAST

24.   Projections of high unemployment at the end of 1992, which were made in March and April of that year, were not confirmed. This

experience suggests the need for a different estimating procedure. A simple unemployment forecast for Ukraine can be done on the basis of the assumption that Ukraine is going to follow the Eastern European path of adjustment. Table 2.3 shows proportions between the GDP drop and unemployment rise in Eastern European countries and compares those data to Ukraine's situation.

25.   Across Eastern European countries, the elasticity of unemployment to GDP in the third year of recession varied between -0.33 and -0.58, and, excluding Germany, between -0.46 and -0.58. In Ukraine unemployment has not responded to the drop in output, which raises two important questions: (1) Why does labor hoarding persist in Ukraine? and (2) How long will it persist? For the first question, note that in Ukraine the first year of output decline was 1991. The Eastern European experience of 1989

Table 2.3: GDP Drop and Unemployment Rates in Selected Eastern European Countries and Ukraine, 1988-92

	GDP Drop compared with 1988 (Percent)	Unemployment Rate (Percent)	Proportion Unemployment Rate : GDP Drop
Bulgaria	32	13	0.46
Czechoslovakia	15	7	0.47
E. Germany	42	14	0.33
Hungary	13	7	0.54
Poland	19	11	0.58
Ukraine	9	0	0

Sources: For Eastern Europe, National Official Statistics. For Ukraine, IMF Economic Review, April 1992.

and 1990 shows that labor shedding does not start together with *any* recession but only when recession is caused by a *demand shock*. For instance, Poland had zero unemployment until December 1989, although industrial output in

1989 was already falling and GDP stagnated. But the drop in 1989 was, similarly to Ukraine in 1991, influenced primarily by the supply shock resulting from a break-up of economic ties with the other Comecon countries. In January 1990, when a huge demand shock occurred, labor shedding began. Therefore, it is reasonable to expect acceleration in unemployment in Ukraine as soon as the demand shock comes into the picture.[15]

26. For the second question the relevant observation is that expected GDP for 1992 stabilized in some countries (Hungary, Poland) or dropped slightly in others (Bulgaria, Czechoslovakia), indicating that reform-induced recession lasts three to four years. In Eastern Europe recession started in 1988 or 1989; one may expect Ukraine to reach the Eastern Europeans' situation in 1994 or 1995. A GDP drop of one-quarter, coupled with an employment elasticity of -0.5, would yield an unemployment rate of 12.5 percent in 1994-95, about 3 million people. The Eastern European experience shows that the higher open or depressed inflation is at the outset of a stabilization program, the larger will be the following GDP drop (compare Poland and Bulgaria on one hand and Czechoslovakia and Hungary on the other). In Ukraine, inflation in 1993 is already running above 20 percent monthly, which may indicate that GDP could decline even more than one-quarter from its late 1980s peak before rising again. Therefore, the working assumption of 3 million unemployed for 1995 may be justified. Succeeding chapters consider what policies can most effectively address the challenge of unemployment and economic revival to find new jobs for all workers.

3
POLICY RESPONSES TO EMPLOYMENT PROBLEMS

INCOMES POLICY

1. In January 1992, the government liberalized wages and wage-setting in state-owned enterprises but imposed a new salary scale for budget employees, those employed and funded from government revenues. Periodic minimum wage adjustment, with less-than-equivalent percentage changes for all wages above the minimum, was the main tool to adjust wages to inflation. The level and distribution of income changed in 1992; the minimum wage fell behind price increases in the early months of the year, but wage increases in most state enterprises, and even for budget employees, overtook price increases. In May 1992, the average wage in the economy was R3,052.4, 88.4 percent more than in January, when it had been R1,655.9. Prices of the minimum basket of goods, the only proxy for a true consumer price index, rose by 59 percent. The minimum wage was increased by a factor of 2.25, from R400 on January 1, to R900 on May 1, 1992.

2. In principle, according to the government's law of October 1991, indexation of wages and social benefits should be a second instrument of adjusting incomes. The law provided for a sliding scale of index compensation that varied according to the relationship of income to the minimum wage. Automatic indexation would be 100 percent for that part of wages up to twice the minimum wage, and 50 percent for the amount between two and three times the minimum wage. There would be no automatic indexation for that part of wages above three times the minimum wage. Such adjustments would be obligatory for wages in the government sector and for social benefits, but would be indicative for the enterprise sector, where wage determination has been freed. Indexation is supposed to be enacted only in those months when the minimum wage remains unchanged. These policies were overtaken by the reality of virtual hyperinflation. Special

compensation for children and pensioners was tried for several months then abandoned as inflationary and too costly early in 1993.

3. Incomes policies are in flux: Parliament introduced requirements that teachers' and health workers' average wages must equal the average wage in industry; average wages in the culture sector must equal the average wage in the economy. A tax-based incomes policy was introduced on July 1, 1992, that allowed for tax-free wage increases in proportion to output growth at the enterprise level. Increases above this threshold resulted in an increase in the rate-of-profit tax by two to five times depending on the level of excessive wage-bill growth. Provisions for an excess-wage tax were strengthened early in 1993. These measures may be inconsistent with the objective of balancing the supply and demand for labor in the various sectors of the economy.

ACTIVE LABOR MARKET POLICIES

4. Active labor market policies can increase the productivity of workers, enhance their employability, and improve the operation of labor markets. These policies facilitate labor mobility in a market economy as workers respond to changing economic opportunities. Examples of active labor market policies that increase productivity include retraining and small enterprise development; policies that improve the operation of labor markets include the delivery of employment services, the development and dissemination of labor market information, and mobility assistance. Active labor market policies work in combination with passive labor market policies that protect the incomes of workers displaced from their jobs by economic adjustment, while encouraging their movement to new employment. Unemployment benefits and separation payments play this passive role.

5.   Industrial countries differ in how they combine active and passive labor market policies. Sweden, which has had one of the lowest unemployment rates in Western Europe, relies on active labor market policies; the United States favors passive income support, and most other countries blend these approaches (see Figure S.4 in the Executive Summary, which shows the share of GDP spent on active and passive labor market policies in Ukraine and selected OECD countries). Evaluations of various active labor market policies show that these policies can produce savings in passive income support that exceed their cost by reducing the time required to move displaced workers to new employment. The policies can pay for themselves and be a cost-effective response to rising unemployment.[16] Ukraine has both types of labor market policies, but spends a smaller share of GDP on them than OECD countries, but for the obvious reason that the command economy leaves almost no one unemployed.

RETRAINING

6.   The transition to a market economy will mean a decline of employment in some economic sectors and growth in others as employers adjust to market-driven demand instead of the system of state orders that drove the command economy. New technologies and methods of production will be introduced that will change skill requirements. Wages will rise or fall for specific skills in proportion to the balance of their demand and supply. These features of a market economy will mean a displacement of workers in some jobs and a subsequent expansion in others. Displaced workers, however, may not possess the skills needed for employment in growing sectors of the economy. A policy of equipping displaced workers with new skills can increase their employability and facilitate their movement into new jobs. The pace at which this job shift occurs determines the cost of the transition in lost income for workers and their families and the foregone production and potential social disruption.

7.   Resources for retraining displaced workers are located in the Ministry of Labor in the Employment Service (ES). The ES controls expenditures of the Employment Fund which can be used to procure skills training for displaced workers. This Fund was created by the Ukrainian Law on Employment of 1991. During its first year of operation, the Fund was used to retrain 2,500 workers (1 in 12 of the unemployed) nationally at an average cost of 10,000 rubles. The ES used the Fund to purchase training from vocational schools in the Ministry of Education, from other ministerial training programs, including city training centers, and from special training institutes attached to enterprises or sectors of the economy. The Fund gives the ES flexibility in the choice of training provider and the type of skills training purchased.

8.   The Ministry of Labor is considering establishing its own retraining centers. Four or five regional administrative centers would be established, each with a cluster of local training centers. Approximately 600 to 700 training centers would be established with some existing centers taken over by the Ministry of Labor. A second option under consideration would continue the present procurement of skills training from existing schools and training centers and create a smaller number of Ministry of Labor training centers for areas of special need.[17] The best choice will depend on which option can meet the needs of displaced workers flexibly. International experience shows that displaced workers have different training needs from youth seeking training for their first job. Older workers may lack basic computational and communications skills and require upgrading. Displaced workers may be at different stages of job readiness and need training that allows them to enter at different levels of proficiency. The timing of displacements, which cannot be expected to fit traditional school openings and closings, requires training that is flexible with regard to entry and exit. The opportunity cost of time spent in training for displaced workers in lost incomes creates a need for training that allows trainees to accept jobs when competency goals are reached rather than when a fixed amount of time is spent in training.

9.   A city-owned training center in Kharkiv offers skills training of very high quality for a

broad spectrum of occupational specializations in the command economy. Simulators are in use where trainees practice their theoretical skills in such trades as elevator repair, crane operation, and building engineering. Repairs and operating conditions could be simulated and trainees tested for situations that would not be easy to replicate on the job, except at considerable expense. The learning environment is attractive. Classrooms are clean and well lighted, and libraries are stocked with current trade publications. Recurrent budgets showed 80 percent of expenditures for salaries and the balance available for supplies and other teaching materials. Over 90 percent of graduates were immediately placed in employment. The annual capacity of the training center is about 12,000 trainees.

10.   This training center may be above average; it serves the needs of the command economy very well with its predictable flow of trainees and demand for skills but may do less well in serving a new market economy and displaced workers. The center lacks flexibility in adjusting to market demands for skills. Its heavy investment in simulators in the short run locks it into training for certain skills. The simulators were designed for a specific technology, as monopolistic closings and restructuring state enterprises produce only one elevator system or type of crane. A market economy will quickly increase the number of producers, domestic and foreign, and the technologies in place. Training in such centers will need to become more general, leaving specific skills to be learned on the job with particular equipment or in supplier training programs. Although it is theoretically possible with simulators, competency-based training was not employed, nor was training packaged in modules for flexible entry and exit.

11.   This was not the only mode of training offered, however. The center offers training in more than 300 specializations with some of the training delivered in enterprises outside the classroom and laboratory. Curricula were taken from Moscow. The large number of occupational specialties is an indicator of its job-specific nature.[18] This degree of specialization is perhaps appropriate for an economy where expected labor mobility is low and the need for workers to adapt to different jobs and technologies is limited. In this environment, general skills are less important. Ukraine's transition to a market economy, however, will increase the demand for general skills.

12.   Training is closely linked to employers. Some centers are tied to particular sectors, such as the Aviation Institute, while others are connected with state enterprises. Most training is paid for by enterprises, thus directly regulating the balance of demand and supply. In other cases, as mentioned above, training is paid for by the ES from the Employment Fund with the training theoretically tied to actual job listings. Trainees in a small number of cases may pay for their own training. These arrangements appear to be both effective now and promising for the future.

13.   Ukraine is approaching a period of adjustment and mass layoffs with limited capacity to offer training that is suitable to the needs of a market economy and displaced workers. Solutions could include reforming components of the existing training system or establishing a new system within the Ministry of Labor. For the near term, with projected closings and restructuring of state enterprises and their attendant labor displacement, there is a threat to the state's ability to finance this training. Reform issues will have to address the inflexibility of the current system, its focus on job-specific rather than general skills, and its ability to meet the special needs of older workers displaced from jobs in the command economy.

GRANTS FOR THE UNEMPLOYED

14.   Retraining displaced workers is one type of active labor market policy that increases the productivity and employability of workers. Another is the granting of credit to the unemployed to create small enterprises by capitalization and prepayment of unemployment benefits. The ability to purchase raw materials, production tools, and other productive resources can increase the productivity of the displaced worker who is willing to become self-employed. The start-up of small enterprises can create new

jobs for other displaced workers and provide important goods and services to consumers. Although the new employment law permits the ES to provide unemployed workers with grants for this purpose, such grants have not yet been made.

15. Experience in a wide range of industrialized and developing countries indicates that grants or loans often result in fraud and abuse. The failure rate of small business start-ups is very high. Few of the unemployed have the aptitude for self-employment and the ability to produce a marketable product. The availability and cost of space are major constraints to private employment expansion. Excessive regulation and taxation constrain small-enterprise development still further. Libanova (1992) reports an active black market for labor providing services in construction, trade, food products, health care, and even private tutoring. In other economies, this is recognized as the informal sector. It is a vibrant, active source of employment absorbing many of those unable to find work in the regulated sector of the economy, the so-called modern or formal sector. Faced with regulation and taxation, enterprises remain small and hidden under the surface of the economy, thereby limiting their expansion and contribution to employment and public revenue. A survey of 223 enterprises in April 1992 found that high taxes and regulatory instability are perceived as the principal obstacles by entrepreneurs.

16. In most industrialized countries, small enterprise development programs are suitable for less than 5 percent of displaced workers. The ES role is best limited to that of screening displaced workers for their suitability for this service. In other countries, non-governmental organizations, representing private or non-profit enterprises, are more effective in delivering a package of small enterprise development services. The ES role is usually that of procuring these services and screening displaced workers as clients. It is premature to consider such programs in Ukraine.

WAGE SUBSIDIES

17. Wage subsidies should be avoided as they can slow the pace of the transition in the economy. Officially, the Employment Fund can pay wage subsidies, but the ES is not doing so. However, anecdotal evidence based on field visits in Ukraine indicates that some employment offices use Employment Fund resources to pay wage subsidies to selected state enterprises to induce them to keep redundant workers. Wage subsidies paid to enterprises to retain workers impede adjustment by slowing the pace at which workers are encouraged to look for alternative productive employment. International experience with wage subsidies suggests their costs far outweigh any benefits. When given to specific groups of workers, such as unemployed youth, the subsidies tend to substitute the unemployment of one group for that of another, encouraging the hiring of youths in preference to the hiring of adults who are ineligible. The net job-creation potential is modest; subsidies go mostly to labor-intensive enterprises that hire unskilled workers even without subsidy.

PUBLIC WORKS

18. The ES is authorized to use the Employment Fund to create public works and jobs for the unemployed. Like grants for the unemployed and wage subsidies, public works have been used only on a small scale and should continue to be avoided. Public works projects are a counter-cyclical employment tool and a source of employment-of-last-resort for disadvantaged workers. The share of the unemployed provided with jobs, however, has been small. Wages are set below market wages for unskilled workers to encourage self-targeting. That is, workers who elect employment in public works are those unable to find jobs for higher wages elsewhere. Potential public works projects include flood control, care and maintenance of public grounds and facilities, and community public health projects which would not compete with private market provision of these goods. The ES in Kiev has used public works on a small scale for unskilled workers. It has contracted with a firm that places unemployed workers in jobs in grounds and maintenance work. To use the program

successfully, the ES will need to work closely with local community governments that are best equipped to identify public works projects. Delivery of these works may be contracted out to non-governmental organizations or local governments. It is unlikely that public works can be used as an active labor market policy because their labor-intensive nature rarely offers extensive opportunities for skills training.

EMPLOYMENT CENTERS

19.   Ukraine's employment centers deliver a wide array of services to job seekers through a network of 636 local offices at city or local (*raiyon*) level that report to 27 regional offices. Regional centers provide retraining for the unemployed, occupational testing, and assessment. The local offices receive notices of vacancies from enterprises; the Employment Law requires they be notified two months in advance of any dismissal of employees and that vacancies be listed with the office. The mandatory listing of vacancies and the absence of private employment agencies make the local offices the sole labor exchange; still, 80 percent of hiring is done by enterprises themselves at the factory gate, through referral of their own workers and in other informal ways. The predominance of informal job change suggests that policies should facilitate informal job search whenever possible. The ES should concentrate on the most difficult cases--older workers and mass layoffs in single-industry towns. The state Employment Service gives priority to its labor-exchange function: job matching is its primary mission. Before the passage of the March 1991 employment law, staff worked mostly with the "5 percent quota" groups --special categories of hard-to-place workers, such as alcoholics or ex-convicts --for whom enterprises are required to reserve 5 percent of vacancies. Since the command economy was characterized by labor shortages, most other job seekers found work by themselves. Only a small percentage of workers who left their previous jobs voluntarily used the system.

20.   The Employment Service system has expanded its offices and staff to meet current conditions and handle the expected influx of job seekers. The ES unemployed: has 11 staff for each 100,000 population performing both the Employment Service and unemployment benefits functions, and can increase to 16 staff per 100,000 population in the near future. Local offices authorize retraining programs through the regional retraining centers; a laid-off worker seeking a job, retraining, or benefits visits the same location for assistance. Policies of the Employment Service should leave ample space for informal job search.

UNEMPLOYMENT BENEFITS

21.   Most industrialized nations have a system of income support for the unemployed; Ukraine's system was enacted in the March 1991 Employment Law, which provides earnings-based benefits that differ according to separation reason or labor status. The most generous benefits are reserved for so-called "Category One" unemployed: persons dismissed from employment owing to layoffs, bankruptcy, or closure of the enterprise. They receive one month's severance pay in advance for the first month of unemployment and then receive two additional months of 100 percent pay, paid for by the enterprise. Thus the enterprise is responsible for the first three months of assistance. During these months, the dismissed employee has not achieved the status of unemployed and does not count in the unemployment statistics.

22.   At the end of three months, the dismissed worker must report to the local employment office to register for benefits by making a joint application for benefits and for job-matching assistance. The local office has ten days to match the applicant with a suitable vacancy before benefits start. Applicants must follow the instructions of the office staff as to job referrals and can reject a job offer if the wage level is below the prior wage or the job is beyond traveling distance. Two refusals of work trigger sanctions or disqualification.

23.   Unemployment begins officially if the worker is not employed prior to the end of the ten-day, job-matching period, that is, 100 days after the last day of actual work in the former employer's enterprise. As long as job search requirements are met, workers will receive 75

percent of their average wage for the next three months and 50 percent of their average wage for the following six months but in no case less than the minimum wage nor more than the average wage, between 900 and 2,010 rubles in July 1992. The upper ceiling is lifted in the case of unemployed persons entering professional retraining programs as an incentive to enter re-training.

24.   The law provides for somewhat lower benefits for other categories of unemployed, while the ten-day waiting period and job search requirements remain the same.   Voluntary quits, and those who have only worked in 9 out of the last 12 months, receive 50 percent of average salary for six months (with the previously described minimum and maximum applied). They will also be eligible for another period of three months in year two and three months in year three, so that they also get twelve months of assistance, but not in one year. New entrants receive 75 percent of minimum wage for six months.   Higher-education graduates and servicemen (non-officers) receive 100 percent of the minimum wage.   An additional benefit of 50 percent of the minimum wage for each dependent is available upon application up to twice each year.   This provision is not widely used as yet, as is illustrated by the fact that for the first six months of 1992, 44,000 persons received benefits but only 2,058 applied for and received this benefit.

25.   Unemployment benefits are administered by the Ministry of Labor, which uses the regional and local offices of the Employment Service described above. Of 700 offices in the system, 636 city and local-level offices actually work with clients. Payment is by check and is given in person and cashed at a bank. The claimants are given a choice of frequency of payment: weekly, bi-monthly or monthly. Regardless of frequency of payment, claimants must see their inspector once a week at his or her discretion, based on local labor market conditions. Only 400 of the 700 offices of the Employment Service have computers; some do not even have one computer on which to calculate benefits, maintain case records and vacancy lists, match recipients and other job-

seekers with available vacancies, or collect aggregate data for statistical reporting and management information. Where computers do exist, the ES has developed the capability to calculate benefits based on the category of unemployment, the application date and the average wage, as certified by enterprises in each worker's employment book.   Written applications are filled out by the claimant, since Ukraine courts require written documentation of legal transactions.   Claimants must sign an acknowledgement of rights and responsibilities and must sign for each check and each refusal of an offer of employment.

Financing Labor Market Policies

26.   Forecasts for benefits and services to unemployed people call for this category to account for about 2 percent of social sector spending and slightly less than 1 percent of GDP in 1992.   According to Ukrainian law, unemployment benefits are to be funded by enterprises directly, with a 3 percent payroll tax and government contributions of 3 percent of state and local revenues. Nevertheless, owing to the economic crisis and the slower-than-anticipated growth in explicit unemployment, the government did not contribute to the fund in 1992. Final figures were not available in time for this report; the projected sources appear in Table 3.1.   These numbers have been made obsolete by inflation and the switch from the ruble to the coupon.

27.   The payroll taxes from enterprises are collected at the local level and 80 percent of funds are retained for local use. The remaining 20 percent are sent to the Employment Service, where they are used to fund administrative costs (including the purchase of computer equipment for the local offices) and also as a reserve to subsidize offices in areas of particularly high unemployment. This reserve will be crucial as unemployment grows, since areas that experience the greatest number of enterprise failures will have lower Employment Fund revenues to retain at the local level.

28.   In July 1992, the ES estimated that cash benefits to unemployed workers (passive labor market policies) would require about 28 percent

of total funds; active labor market policies, 62 percent; and administration and overhead expenses, 10 percent (see Table 3.2). While cash benefits are available to a number of different groups, including first-time job seekers and people who voluntarily left their employment, 84 percent of cash benefits will go to workers who lost their jobs owing to restructuring or the bankruptcy of their employer. Active labor market policies spending is divided almost equally between job creation and training/retraining (see Table 3.2).

29. Local offices receive an allowance from the state office to cover their administrative costs. Their active and passive labor market policies are funded from the revenues they receive from the 3 percent payroll tax levied on enterprises in their area and local government payments. The state office also may use its 20 percent share of collections as a reserve to subsidize local offices in areas of particularly high unemployment. While all local employment offices must pay benefits based on norms established at the national level, spending on active labor market policies is at the discretion of the local office.

30. The combination of financing for active and passive labor market policies in the Employment Fund could pose a potentially serious problem when mass layoffs begin in the Ukrainian economy. Unemployment benefits will consume the funding available for active labor market policies. Enterprise contributions to the fund will fall once hard budget constraints are imposed and supplier credits disappear. The failure of some enterprises and the downsizing of others will lower the tax base. In a period of reduced aggregate demand and falling output, it will be all the more difficult to raise the enterprise tax rate to produce additional revenues. Cash benefits will

draw down the resources of the Employment Fund at the expense of retraining. International experience suggests that a third of displaced workers may qualify for existing jobs and that two-thirds will need retraining and assistance for self-employment. In some instances, this training may be as simple as on-the-job or job-search training, but in other cases it may require a more costly investment. To control this cost, the ES will need to develop its diagnostic capacity for skills assessment and build an effective job bank to match skill needs with existing jobs. Other countries have addressed this problem by separating the funding for active and passive labor market policies.

STATISTICAL INFORMATION

31. The currently available statistical information on unemployment in Ukraine comes from administrative records based on the employment office registers of the unemployed. Other labor market data, such as the number, educational level, or age status of the jobless, are collected from administrative sources. The monitoring and evaluation of labor market trends and developments rests primarily with the Ministry of Labor (MOL) and the Employment Service. To the extent that labor-market issues

Table 3.1: Sources of Funds for Unemployment-Related Activities, May 1992 Projection for Full Year

	Total in Million Rubles	Percent of Total	Percent of GDP
Employment Fund	20,322	93.5	0.7
Enterprise Payroll Tax	18,870	86.8	
State Government	1,000	4.6	
Surplus from 1991	452	2.1	
Est. Enterprise Direct*	1,407	6.5	0.1
Total	21,729	100	0.8

Note: * Payments to workers for the first three months of their joblessness at a 100 percent replacement rate would cost approximately 1.4 billion rubles in 1992. This estimate is based on the pension fund's May 1992 estimate of the total number of laid off workers in 1992 and their average wage. An adjustment was made for the assumption that some workers would find employment before their three months of benefits had expired.

Source: Employment Fund 1992 Budget (May Draft) and mission estimates.

touch on the overall socio-demographic and economic structure of the country, the Employment Service depends on supplementary data from the Ministry of Statistics (MOS) such as the population census, or sector information, included in the Ministry's routine analytical work and reporting.

32.   The MOL receives information in a summary form from its 25 oblasts and two city employment offices, based on primary information coming from enterprises through local employment centers. Any discrepancies detected in the reporting are resolved over the phone, which occasionally results in further distortions owing to the poor communications system. There is no quick and reliable communications system for data transmission

between the MOL and the oblasts. While this information channel has remained unchanged since the past, the data requirements have recently grown substantially and changed qualitatively. Computer equipment in the oblasts is used more on an experimental than a routine basis, since many offices have only one computer (there are 400 computers and 700 centers) and few staff are trained to use them.

33.   In terms of its experience and organizational structure, the Ministry of Statistics is better equipped for data collection and processing than the MOL but nonetheless lacks the equipment and staff skills usually found in OECD countries. The 1989 Census provides fundamental information on employment structure, labor force participation, and labor-

Table 3.2: Uses of Funds for Unemployment-Related Activities

	Total 1992 in Million Rubles	Percent of Total	Percent of GDP
BENEFIT PAYMENTS	6,142	28.5	0.2
Restructuring/Bankruptcy[1]	5,152	23.9	
Labor Force Returnees	405	1.9	
First Time Job Seekers	223	1.0	
Voluntarily Left Job	211	1.0	
Fired from Job	41	0.2	
Other[2]	49	0.2	
Additional Benefits for Needy	62	0.3	
ACTIVE LABOR MARKET POLICIES	13,354	61.9	0.5
Job Creation[3]	5,921	27.5	
Training and Retraining	6,919	32.1	
Job Information System	274	1.3	
Public Works	234	1.1	
Labor Market Mobility/Other	5	0.0	
ADMINISTRATION/OVERHEAD	2,068	9.6	0.1
Maintenance of Centers	993	4.6	
Building Acquisition	797	3.7	
Fund for Local Centers	505	2.3	
Research and Staff Training	53	0.2	
Deduction by MOF	-281	-1.3	
TOTAL	21,564	100	0.8
SURPLUS	165	0.8	

Notes: 1.   Includes mission estimates of direct employer payments.
        2.   Includes wives of returning military personnel, refugees and people newly released from prison or institutions.
        3.   Includes reduction required by Ministry of Finance.

Source: Employment Fund and Ministry of Finance May and June 1992 draft budgets for the Employment Fund and mission estimates.

force supply by oblast. Labor resource balances, with employment coefficients, are prepared twice a year, by oblast and branch. Computation and data processing are done by the internal computing center, equipped with slow Russian computers, while much routine work is done by hand, and typed. The low capacity of the statistics print shop is a bottleneck in data dissemination.

34.   The MOS is considering steps to reform its organization, switch to innovative methods of data collection, such as sample surveys, and improve the speed and quality of its work. Contacts with Eurostat, the United States Census Bureau Center for International Research, and the International Labor Organization will contribute to the reform program.

35.   Administrative records, though less costly than other forms of data collection, are insufficient for the purpose of labor market information.   More detailed information is needed on the incidence of joblessness and unemployment than is available from the employment registers. Those who have not filed with the employment services and undertake a job search on their own are uncounted. There may also be some double-counting, when a

registrant finds a private sector job and fails to report this to the Employment Service. Private-sector reporting, though mandated by the law, will be increasingly difficult to maintain as employment there expands. The monthly and quarterly labor market reports sent to the Employment Service from regional offices need several improvements. They lack information on the length of the unemployment spell, characteristics of the unemployed, such as age, educational level, and skills of the affected workers.   Left out as well are pensioners seeking employment. Those without a job for over a year are grouped together with those who, for personal reasons, did not hold a job. No information is given on hidden unemployment, such as leave without pay, shorter working week, and incidence of voluntary shorter hours, e.g., by women with small children. Labor-resource balances, with employment coefficients, though prepared twice a year, are not done on the branch/town level, which would be more helpful operationally. It is expected that the incidence of unemployment will be disproportionately high in the single-industry towns once the main employer closes down. Clarification as to the composition of various subgroups, such as homemakers or private agriculture, is needed.

4
RESHAPING LABOR MARKET POLICIES

1.   This chapter considers policies to address employment problems associated with converting a command economy to a market economy. It suggests some necessary changes in incomes policies; labor market policies that could pay for themselves by speeding the conversion of workers to market-based production; effective approaches to mass layoffs; design of cash benefits that can minimize the degree to which they inhibit or slow the conversion process; and the means to strengthen the capacity of labor markets to adjust and keep on adjusting to the changes that are characteristic of market economies. It presents recommendations for improving labor statistics and discusses policies that inhibit labor mobility and exacerbate the problems likely to arise in smaller, single-industry towns that may be faced with mass layoffs and nowhere for the work force to go. It ends with suggested investments in labor market policies expenditures and how these can be complemented with external technical and financial assistance.

INCOMES POLICIES

2.   The type of indexation the government introduced in July 1991 was inflationary and inefficient; it was abandoned in 1993 in favor of ad hoc adjustments to protect in real earnings yet avoid fueling inflation. Incomes policy now caps wage growth to block monopoly price gauging. A maximum rate of wage increase is now linked to a price index; enterprises that exceed this rate are subject to a substantial financial penalty. A case for an incomes policy can be made for socialist countries on *a priori* grounds (see Box 4.1[19]); however, it is not clear-cut. World experience with incomes policies is mostly negative, or mixed at best; the lessons, however, are instructive for Ukraine (see Box 4.2).

ACTIVE LABOR MARKET POLICIES

3.   Active labor market policies cannot solve the problem of unemployment produced by insufficient aggregate demand for goods and services. The only solution to that problem is sound macroeconomic management of the economy. In the near term, unemployment will come from insufficient aggregate demand when public expenditures are cut to conform to revenues and to stabilize the economy. As private investment begins to emerge and replace the public sector, labor market policies can encourage human capital formation and the mobility of labor to new employment produced by this spending. Improving labor mobility with policies that increase the productivity of labor and improve the operation of labor markets will reduce the social cost of economic adjustment in foregone production, income, inflation, and social turmoil.

INTRODUCING FLEXIBILITY IN RETRAINING PROGRAMS

4.   The Ministry of Labor should use the market procurement model and the financial leverage of the Employment Fund to increase the flexibility of retraining programs. As a national training authority, the MOL can introduce procurement policies that require the delivery of modular, flexible, competency-based training for displaced workers. This recommendation places the Ministry in a policy role rather than a delivery role for training. Instead of producing its own captive capacity for retraining, the MOL would rely on the supply response of existing and new training capacity that would emerge in response to the market it creates through the resources of the Employment Fund.

5.   This approach has numerous advantages. Ukraine can draw on the experience of more

than 50 industrialized and developing countries that have created training funds to encourage skills training. By opening competition to include training offered by private employers and training centers, the MOL can induce state training centers to compete for the delivery of skills training and encourage greater efficiency in the delivery of these services. With competition, training costs can be reduced and quality improved. This approach would ensure that training is linked to actual jobs, that it is demand driven. Changes in market needs for skills training identified by the Employment Service can be quickly addressed through the procurement process.

HANDLING MASS LAYOFFS

6.   Ukraine has no specific law governing

massive layoffs by state (or private) enterprises, although the Employment Law does anticipate this eventuality in several ways. The Employment Service has the authority to contact an enterprise that has announced a layoff to offer partial wage subsidies from the Employment Fund for up to six months where this intervention would provide the time or resources for the enterprise to achieve stability. Another state fund provides similar subsidies and incentives in the case of new enterprises.

7.   Other industrial countries have established comprehensive programs to deal with mass layoffs; Ukraine could consider some of the tools employed in dislocated worker statutes in the West:

• **Advance Notification.** The current

Box 4.1: The Theory of Incomes Policies

The traditional case for an incomes policy is as an instrument to break inflationary expectations and a persistent wage-price spiral, thus reducing the dependence on deflationary fiscal and monetary policies. Various forms of incomes policies have been used for this purpose, but with mixed or no success. However, there may be a stronger case for incomes policies in reforming socialist economies. The potential pressures for wage inflation are especially strong in such economies, given:

- A lack of an effective advocate for the interests of owners of capital as long as there is pervasive state ownership of enterprises.

- The fact that, at least initially, unemployment is low and cannot act as an intrinsic moderating force on wages.

Yet the links between wage inflation and problems with macroeconomic adjustment are particularly strong in reforming socialist countries for several reasons:

- As enterprise taxes account for a large share of revenues and public sector wages for a large share of expenditures, higher wages have a strong distorting impact on the budgetary balance.

- With domestic market structures frequently still monopolized, domestic price competition is a fairly ineffective brake on price increases.

- Import competition is typically low and only gradually growing, providing little counterweight to conventional mark-up pricing that accommodates wage increases.

- In the run-up to privatization, managers and workers could easily be tempted to decapitalize enterprises by paying themselves high wages and deferring necessary investments and adjustment measures.

All of these problems suggest that an incomes policy *may* be an important element of macroeconomic measures taken during the transition. Implementing an incomes policy may be difficult, however (see Box 4.2).

requirement of two months' notice of a pending dismissal or layoff is definitely on the short end of the practice of OECD countries. Too long a period is counterproductive, but more than 2 months is justifiable when more than 50 percent of an enterprise's workforce, or 20 percent of the labor force of a labor market area, is affected by the layoff or closure. This extra planning time would allow for other interventions to ease the transition of workers into new jobs.

- **Rapid Response and Local Area Involvement.** One successful model of this approach is Canada's Industrial Adjustment Service (IAS). The IAS involves the workers, employers and local officials in the design and delivery of services. The IAS and some state dislocated-worker programs in the United States are organized to move rapidly into a community and arrange for donated resources from the affected enterprise, employee trade unions or other employee organizations and the local community. Affected workers are counseled to minimize misinformation and panic, and are informed about their benefits under the employment law, labor-market conditions, and opportunities for retraining. Some dislocated-worker programs open offices or worker-assistance centers on or adjacent to the grounds of the enterprise (on property or with funds donated by the enterprise) to provide ongoing support and assistance to affected workers. These centers operate best when staffed jointly by agency staff and staff trained from among local workers, since trust is an important element when dealing with a crisis.

8. The Employment Service needs a mass layoff unit to plan programs of on-site, locally-delivered services in instances of mass layoffs, which will ease the burden of the existing local office. Special legislation could provide for additional notice in mass-layoff situations and could provide a package of interventions from among the options above.

DESIGN OF THE UNEMPLOYMENT BENEFIT

9. The government should consider the temporary use of a flat-rate benefit scheme to cope with the financial burden of rapidly escalating unemployment likely during the shift to a market economy and until it is able to fully automate local employment offices. The benefit structure as it now stands is certainly well within the range of practice in industrialized countries, but the complexity of benefits and the financial cost in a time of rapid growth in unemployment would argue for a simplified system.

10. MOL officials have expressed concern about the effect of a flat rate system on their strong desire to differentiate benefits between Category One (dislocated workers) and other unemployed persons. It would be possible to meet this commitment to maintain higher benefits for employees who lose their jobs through no fault of their own (bankruptcies, mass layoffs) through a two-tier benefit system, or by eliminating lower-priority categories, such as high school and university leavers and other new entrants. The eligibility of such persons for unemployment benefits is inconsistent with practice elsewhere that new entrants not receive benefits.

11. Flat-rate benefits would ease administration, since calculation of earnings-based benefits can be very cumbersome in offices that are not computerized. Experience in Estonia and Poland, where such schemes were recently implemented, shows that there are overall benefit savings as well as administrative savings. In Poland, in particular, an earlier earnings-based system proved to be too expensive and complex for the period of adjustment from a command to a market economy. After a period of stabilization, it would be possible for Ukraine to return to the earnings-based system.

12. Many industrialized nations disqualify voluntary quits; the Employment Fund could save some money by following such a policy. The elimination of first-time job seekers, labor-force returnees without recent work experience and voluntary quits, would result in a 16 percent reduction in current costs for unemployment

benefits. This percentage would decline with mass layoffs where Category One claimants would predominate.

13.   The recent reconciliation of an inconsistency between the Employment Law and the Labor Code in favor of the Labor Code's automatic entitlement to three months of 100 percent pay without registration with the Employment Service is also unfortunate. Experience worldwide shows that earlier intervention significantly reduces the duration of unemployment and will result in savings. Even though the benefit for the first three months is paid by the enterprise, the government would save by enforcing the earlier provision that the unemployed register with the ES within ten days of dismissal in order to receive benefits.

FINANCING LABOR MARKET POLICIES

14.   The Government of Ukraine should guarantee funding for active labor market policies (see Box 4.3) and should fund any additional unemployment benefits from general revenues. Eventually, the unemployment compensation program should be funded by a payroll tax on enterprises modeled after options to be found in OECD countries.

Box 4.2: The Practice of Incomes Policies

Various forms of incomes policies were used by Western industrialized countries during the 1960s and 1970s, and they have also been used by several developing countries as a part of so-called "heterodox" stabilization programs. The experience of both groups of countries has been at best mixed. The two main lessons generally drawn from these country experiences are that (a) incomes policies can be effective *only* as a complement to, not as a substitute for, deflationary fiscal and monetary policies; and (b) the policies tend to fail, given the numerous incentives for non-compliance and the enforcement difficulties that accompany them.

Most Eastern European economies in transition have adopted incomes policies as part of their stabilization programs. Bulgaria imposed ceilings on individual wages, while the Czech and Slovak Republics and Hungary imposed ceilings on the total wage bill. Poland first introduced a ceiling on the wage bill and after one year changed to ceilings on the average wage. Apart from Bulgaria, which used administrative controls, countries have implemented their incomes policies through the imposition of an excess wage tax (wage increases above the ceiling are subject to a certain penalty tax). Poland has set the ceiling on wage growth as a percentage of the current rate of inflation, while the other countries have linked wage ceilings to target rates for inflation. In most cases the private sector has been exempted.

An important argument for ceilings on the average rather than the total wage bill is that ceilings on the average bill avoid taxation of employment. Firms that have growth potential can expand. However, because of the overstaffing of most state enterprises, there is a case for applying the ceiling initially to the total wage bill and switching later to ceilings on average wages (as Poland has done).

Tax-based incomes policies offer several advantages over a direct regulatory approach. Tax-based policies tend to infringe less on free bargaining between employers and unions. They add some flexibility by providing enterprises with the option of exceeding the general wage growth target as long as they are willing to pay the tax. Tax-based approaches cut administrative costs, as they can be enforced through the existing tax system rather than through separate institutional arrangements. These additional tax revenues can offset the negative impact of excessive wage growth profit tax revenues. However, the effectiveness of taxes, like that of fines or any other financial enforcement mechanism, is greatly reduced if firms can simply incur arrears on these or other taxes or borrow to pay the taxes. The Polish experience has shown that many firms choose to pay the tax.

The experience of Western market economies suggests that, even more than any particular formal enforcement mechanism, the support of governmental incomes policies by employers and unions, preferably in the form of a tripartite social consensus, can increase the probability of broad-based compliance substantially. Austria and Sweden are examples of countries where incomes policies have been implemented successfully through social contracts.

Box 4.3: Financing Labor Market Policies

All OECD countries combine, in different measure, active and passive labor market policies. Sweden, which has one of the lowest unemployment rates in Western Europe, favors active labor market policies in the absolute share of GDP spent on these policies, 1.8 percent. Passive policies dominate spending in countries like Denmark, Ireland, and Belgium, partly in response to higher unemployment (see Figure S.4 in the Executive Summary). Ukraine, which has not yet experienced mass layoffs and unemployment, spends only 0.25 percent of its GDP on passive policies providing incomes support for the unemployed. The demand for this spending will increase as unemployment begins to rise with economic reforms, placing pressure on Ukraine's low level of spending on active labor market policies.

Research in OECD countries shows that effective employment programs combine active and passive measures (U.S. Department of Labor, 1986). Although active programs are more expensive per participant per month than are passive programs, they can effectively shorten the duration of an unemployment spell enough to make them cost effective (Scherer, 1990). Passive policies can actually increase the duration of unemployment without leading to higher wages through extended job search (Hamermesh, 1992:18-19).

Active employment programs are normally publicly financed from general tax revenues (Fretwell, 1992, p. 39). Some countries rely on the private sector to help their redundant workers directly. The United States and Japan rely heavily on the private sector and non-financial means of public action. In contrast, unemployment benefits are customarily funded through a payroll tax. Only Italy and the United States (except for three states) do not tax employees. Japan taxes all covered wages, the United Kingdom applies its employer tax to all wages, and Italy taxes all wages above an exempt amount. The others have ceilings on taxable wages. All six nations tax more of their wages than does the United States.

In Ukraine, both active and passive labor market policies are financed from the same source, the Employment Fund. Because unemployment benefits are not financed independently from active labor market policies, Ukraine faces the danger that, as unemployment grows, active labor market policies would be crowded out by unemployment benefits.

---

15.   The Employment Fund resources should be committed preferentially to active labor market policies. The support of this Fund should come from enterprises and the state budget contributions that are already part of the annual Fund revenues. Training resources could be found by shifting portions of the recurrent budgets of existing state training centers to the Fund, which would then commission training linked to jobs identified by the ES. These training centers would then be expected to compete for training contracts, much like the model of Sweden mentioned earlier.

16.   The MOL is considering a social-insurance concept for financing unemployment benefits that would require an employee contribution to the system, as in Germany, where employer and employee contributions are split 50/50; Canada, where employee contributions cover 42 percent of benefits; and Japan, where employee contributions cover 37.5 percent of benefits (see Table 3.1). Establishing an employee contribution would increase

revenues, but contributions by employees are not necessary to establish an insurance concept, which bases benefit entitlements on previous work experience and amounts on past wages. Payments are financed out of wage-linked contributions; Ukraine's current system is based on the insurance principle. Some countries use assistance-type schemes characterized by such features as general revenue funding and means-testing, rather than wage-based benefits. Most OECD countries have a mix of insurance-based and assistance schemes where payroll taxes cover a fixed duration of unemployment after which an assistance scheme, funded from general revenues, extends benefits when general macroeconomic conditions are adverse. The use of an employee contribution would be more appropriate in a system where the economy has stabilized and where unemployment is more of a shared risk between employer and employee. The economic transition in Ukraine is not one where it would be expected that the individual would share some degree of responsibility for the risk of unemployment. In such a case of widespread structural unemployment, an employee contribution would be premature.

EMPLOYMENT PROGRAM ADMINISTRATION

17. The government's staffing pattern seems adequate to handle 1993 estimates of as many as 400,000 unemployed persons. However, the maximum current authority for Employment Services staff increases is approximately 8,300. If, for instance, unemployment rises above 10 percent in the following year, each worker would be responsible for handling the cases of 300 unemployed persons, which compares with 100 in Portugal or Greece and about 50 in other OECD countries (see Table 4.1). This potential staff shortage is made more acute by the lack of adequate equipment. The ES has developed and installed some impressive computer programs for the handling of benefit administration. The system contains case records, calculates benefits according to priority category, average wage and date of application, tracks disbursement of benefits, and matches job specialties to computerized lists of vacancies. Yet the agency has only 400 computers for 700 offices. Given the need for computers for statistical reporting and management information at the Republic and oblast levels, most smaller offices do not yet have computers. The MOL estimates a minimum need for 1,500 computers and wants to install 5,000 computers. There is also a need to standardize the computer programs in use, as some oblasts are working with different programs from others, where local staff have developed their own. The MOL has made an impressive start with scarce resources, but this is an area in which they need help and an area in which international agencies may offer significant assistance, beginning with an assessment of needs in the computerization field. Assistance would include consultant services on the design of a rational, standardized system; on the evaluation of hardware needs to determine the proper array of equipment for service delivery; on the use of local area networks, promising savings when compared to current plans to buy individual units; on the purchase of equipment, the setting up of training and support; and on maintenance and ongoing support of the equipment.

18. Since labor exchange and job counseling take place at the same offices as payment of benefits, a period of high unemployment will undoubtedly overwhelm the offices. The concept of a unified benefit/labor exchange office is a good one and the government has moved to specialty workers for each function. Officials must be prepared to facilitate, and not try to compete with, informal, private-sector mechanisms for job search. If unemployment rises, the "employment office" will quickly be turned into the "unemployment office." Job matching could fall victim to the pressing demands of benefit administration.

MONITORING LABOR MARKET ADJUSTMENT

19. The MOL should improve the collection and reporting of unemployment statistics from administrative sources, and, in the medium term, begin development of enterprise, household, and labor force surveys. This effort will require technical assistance in mapping labor force concepts and definitions to international standards and in improving collection and reporting procedures for registered unemployment. It will also require technical assistance and computers for data management and analysis, capacity for conducting a new household labor force survey, and appropriate staff training in each of these areas.

20. A market's efficiency is heavily dependent on the information available to market participants and policy makers; labor markets are no exception. Neither industrialized nor developing economies depend solely on administrative data sources such as the registered unemployed. Countries like the United Kingdom or Germany make effective use of these data but also rely on establishment and household surveys. Canada and the United States have particularly effective systems of labor force statistics and information that should be studied for applicability to Ukraine, along with those of Eurostat as part of the European Economic Community.

TOTAL SPENDING ON LABOR MARKET POLICIES

21. Under a scenario based on Eastern

Table 4.1: Ratio of Labor Staff to Unemployed Workers in Selected Countries, 1988

Country	Staff/Unemployed
Sweden	1:9
Austria	1:33
Germany	1:37
Italy	1:88
United Kingdom	1:98
Portugal	1:120
Poland	1:225[a]
Turkey	1:375[b]
Mexico	1:400[b]

Notes: a. 1990
        b. Staff/applicant ratio, no unemployment benefit system, limited core services and active programs.

Source: Fretwell (1992, p. 42)

European stabilization program experience, unemployment may reach 3 million (about 11.5 percent) in 1995, preceded by a linear trend with 1 million (about 4 percent) in December 1993 and 2 million (about 8 percent) in December 1994. Assuming the introduction of changes described earlier in this chapter, one could expect the following developments:

- **Unemployment Benefits.** In 1993, 0.6

three percent of GDP under present rules. With a flat-rate benefit of six-months' duration at the level close to the minimum wage, unemployment benefits might cost only 0.7 percent of GDP. After 1993, when the number of recipients could rise to over 2 million, it would still be possible to keep benefit payments below 2 percent of GDP with the flat rate.

- **Increased Spending.** Keeping the proportion of unemployed receiving benefits at 50 percent would be possible if workers were to move quickly into new jobs. With efficient training and external technical assistance, labor-market spending in 1993 at the level of 2.4 percent of GDP, and 3.7 percent of GDP after 1993, is well within proportions of Western countries. The Table 4.2 summarizes the above expectations and actions connected with them. Managing labor-market policies, and keeping spending under control, depend on effective macroeconomic, regional, and industrial policies. This issue is not covered in this volume; however, the current "priority development areas" determined by the government according to industrial branches or to the high participation rate

Table 4.2: Current and Suggested Program for Employment-Related Activities

Spending Category	Percent of GDP under Alternative Approaches		
	1992 Budget	Suggested Program for 1993	Sustainable Program Beyond 1993
Benefits	0.2	0.7	2.0
Active Labor Market Policies	0.5	1.5	1.5
Administration Overhead and Other	0.1	0.2	0.2
Total	0.8	2.4	3.7

to 0.8 million unemployed (from the expected proportion between unemployment benefits recipients and all unemployed) would receive benefits costing the Employment Fund more than

of women, will probably have to be replaced by more precise targeting of regions with very high unemployment.

5
CASH TRANSFERS, USSR TO UKRAINE

1.   Ukraine derives its principal social welfare policies from its Soviet experience; cash transfer policy builds on but extends the coverage of the Soviet system, which was not based on means-testing, as in some Western welfare states, but was class-oriented and universal within categories.[20] Lack of means tests had two perverse effects: costs and coverage of those who are not really needy was substantial, yet many indigent or needy persons went unattended. This chapter shows how policies have evolved in such a way as to exacerbate rather than solve the problems inherent in welfare policy under the former Soviet Union.

2.   The Soviet social welfare system addressed the needs of three classes: peasants, workers, and the intelligentsia. (A state-farm employee was a worker, not a peasant.) There was a marked disparity between wages and benefits available to workers and peasants, with peasants receiving very short shrift, especially in terms of cash welfare payments. Up through the Khrushchev years, peasants were ineligible for cash transfer payments from the state. However, this inequity was partially ameliorated by the adoption of an all-union law in 1965 that guaranteed some payments to collective farmers. These cash transfers represented a significant improvement over the pre-1965 situation of no pensions at all. Collective farms were still liable, however, to meet the needs of collective farm retirees and disabled which exceeded all-union norms.

3.   The Soviets divided cash transfer payments (*pensiya* in Russian) into two kinds: labor pensions, which are either directly or loosely related to labor or labor service, and social pensions, which are paid to disabled individuals with no labor service. Since the term "labor pension" covers almost every kind of transfer payment (including disability benefits when the beneficiary has some labor service), it

is probably more useful to divide cash transfers into three distinct groups: work-related pensions, social insurance transfers, and other grants (McAuley 1979).

4.   The basic legislation regulating cash transfers consisted of two all-union "laws on pensions": the 1956 all-union law on pensions for workers and employees and the 1965 all-union law on pensions for collective farmers. With various additions and amendments, these two laws were in force until the adoption of a new all-union pension law in 1990. The 1990 law did not make a distinction between workers and peasants, but included peasants under the regular pension provisions, provided that their collective farm made social insurance payments into the all-union pension fund ("USSR Law on Pensions Published," 1990). The 1990 law was made retroactive, unlike previous legislation, provided that the beneficiary re-filed for the increased benefits within a year of the law's passage. The lack of retroactive provisions in previous legislation, especially as pertaining to collective farmers, can be viewed as the state's attempt to minimize the cost of "providing for the backlog of incapacitated peasants, the consequence of almost forty years of discrimination and neglect" (McAuley 1979, 273). The 1990 law provided that cash transfer payments are not taxable and are paid regardless of other income.

5.   Ukraine began restructuring the social safety net, as an independent state in 1992, making it more generous and, therefore, a heavier burden for the state budget. The expenditures proposed by the government for the social sectors in 1992 **far exceeded** most estimates of government capacity to finance public social services out of the proceeds of general economic capacity, as measured by GDP. In the late 1980s, the USSR offered a more limited menu of social transfers than did its East European neighbors (see Table 5.1),

amounting to about 15 percent of gross income, less than two-thirds of the share of gross income allocated to social transfers in several Eastern European countries.

6.   The share of gross income spent on pensions and family allowances by the USSR government was less half that of its neighbors to the east.   Pressure to expand benefits was coupled with the declining capacity of the central government in Moscow to resist the demands for higher consumption.   Inflation was beginning to undermine the real value of social transfers at the end of the 1980s.   The new duties of an independent government in Ukraine, and the manifest wish of its newly empowered Parliament, combined to create pressures to respond positively to the demand for expanded social protection.   The results of these changes, in terms of increasing demands for public social spending, show up in an enormous jump in *nominal*, projected outlays for social programs in 1992 (see Table S.1 in the Executive Summary and Tables 6.4 and 7.3 in succeeding chapters).

HOW THE SYSTEM EVOLVED

7.   Social insurance transfers for workers and employees were paid out of the Soviet social insurance fund administered by the council of trade unions.   A parallel fund was set up for collective farmers, which received subsidies from the general all-union budget as well as receipts from collective farms.   The 1965 law included all collective farmers in the old-age benefits system, albeit at levels only 50 percent of the benefits received by workers and employees.   Under the old Soviet system, those employed at state farms were considered to be "workers" and received benefits accordingly. The 1990 all-union law raised collective farmers' benefits to the base rate of 55 percent of wages.

8.   The basic structure of cash transfer payments for old age under the Soviet system is presented in Box 5.1.   In 1990, there were 9.7 million old-age pensioners in Ukraine, receiving an average monthly pension of 109.69 rubles. The minimum pension was 70 rubles, and 3.6 million elderly pensioners, 37 percent of all old-age pensioners, received only the minimum

benefit (*Nargos Uk. 1990*, 77-78).   Retirement benefits were paid automatically, without any reduction for other income, at the basic retirement ages of 60 for men and 55 for women, and 55 and 50, respectively, for miners or others involved in hazardous occupations.[21] The base-rate provision of 55 percent of wages was complemented by special rates for hazardous occupations, dwarfs and midgets, mothers with five or more children, women employed in certain occupations, as well as for length of service and other considerations.   For each full year of work beyond 25 years for men and 20 years for women, the pension was increased by 1 percent of earnings, thus raising the maximum replacement rate from 55 percent to 75 percent of highest-ever earnings.[22]

9.   Old-age pensions were paid in full regardless of other income and were not taxable under the provisions of the 1990 law, or of previous laws.   According to a Soviet (Goskomstat) survey, 26 percent of worker and employee old-age pensioners continued to work (*Vestnik statistiki* 9 1988, 69).   Libanova (1992) notes the "high rate" of employment of pensioners, particularly women, and points out that the 1990 labor force exceeded the working-age population by 1.7 million.   Assuming this number is a minimum estimate of the number of working old-age pensioners, the estimated double-dipping rate is 17 percent, which is well below the Soviet all-union rate for workers and employees.   The many non-working spouses and mothers could readily provide the numbers that would lead to a conclusion that in Ukraine, at least a quarter of elderly pension beneficiaries are also current wage earners.

10.   In 1991, many pensioners were not receiving their promised compensation payments.   In Russia, 12 percent of pensioners did not receive their April compensation; in Kazakhstan, 14 percent; in Lithuania, 16 percent; in Moldova, 15 percent; and in Kirgizia, 21 percent. "This was associated with a shortage of funds and weak information for pensioners regarding their rights" (Yakovlev, 1991).   There were also long delays in the administrative process of qualifying for and actually receiving pension benefits.

Disability Benefits

11.   The 1956 pension law recognized three classes of disability.   Class I Disabled need permanent care or supervision or can only work in specially-equipped workshops.   Class II Disabled do not need permanent care, but they cannot work because working would lead to a deterioration in their condition.   Additionally, those with severe visual or mobility impairments are classified as type II, even if they can work. Class III Disabled have suffered a significant loss in capacity so that they must transfer to work of a lower skill level and/or they are not able to acquire new work skills (see Box 5.2).

12.   Disability benefits accrued not only as a

implementation was cut short by the August 1991 coup.

13.   The 1990 all-union law on pensions set the minimum Class I and II Disability pensions as 100 percent of the minimum wage and the minimum Class III benefit as 50 percent of the minimum wage.   In Ukraine in 1990, there were 1.3 million disabled receiving benefits, ranging from 47 to 127 rubles per month (*Nargos Uk.* 1990, 77-78).   For Ukrainian military disabled, benefits were significantly higher, averaging 145 rubles per month.   Full-time attendance in an educational institution is counted as work-tenure for the purpose of assigning disability benefits.

Table 5.1. Social Transfers, Selected Countries, Late 1980s, Percent of Gross Income

Country Benefit	Poland	CSFR	Hungary	USSR
Pensions	15.2	16.5	13.4	8.0
Family Allowance	5.5	5.6	6.0	2.6
Sickness Benefits		3.0	2.0	
Scholarships			0.2	0.3
Others	1.4	0.2	0.8	3.8
Total Transfers	22.1	25.4	22.4	14.6

Source: B. Milanovic (1992), 11.

result of a work-related injury or occupational disease but also from any general illness or congenital condition.   A medical labor commission certified the condition giving entitlement to benefits which were in turn tied to past earnings and seniority.   Disability issues were generally ignored in the Soviet Union, and those with visual or mobility impairments were confronted by urban and rural areas virtually without any sort of handicap-access infrastructure.   In January 1991, the Gorbachev government passed the law on the "Foundation of Social Protection of Invalids in the USSR," which provided for handicap-access designs and facilities in public buildings to be implemented beginning 1992 and 1995.   This law did not change the level of cash benefits, and its

Survivor Benefits

14.   Survivor benefits under the Soviet system were paid to a large range of survivors, including minors, any non-working (dependent) family members, including spouse, parents (if disabled or under pension age), siblings (disabled or full-time child caretakers only), grandchildren, and grandparents (lacking other support).   Step-parents and step-children had the same rights as original parents or natural children.   The 1990 law set the survivor benefit at 30 percent of the wages of the deceased breadwinner, if work-tenure requirements were met.   Benefits from a loss caused by occupational injury had no length of service requirements, while benefits from a loss caused

by general injury were paid in prorated amounts based on length-of-service (following the disability schedule). Families of students, graduate students, and interns who did not work before entering the educational institution were assigned survivor benefits under the same rules as for disability payments.

Family Allowances

15.   The basic Soviet legislation on maternity leave, maternity grants, and additional benefits for single mothers dates back to 1947, but the law was significantly expanded in 1981. Paid maternity leave (at the original salary) was limited to 56 days before birth and 56 days after birth, but leave with full job retention (but

---

Box 5.1: Old-Age Cash Transfer Payments under the Former Soviet Union, 1956-1990

Type of Cash Transfer	1956-1989	1990
Old Age Pensions for Workers	Established in 1956 Law on Pensions. Basic retirement age was 60 for men and 55 for women. Those employed in mining or other specified hazardous occupations could retire 5 years earlier. Sliding scale of payment depending on work tenure & type, from 30 rubles per month to a maximum of 120 rubles per month. Paid to all workers and employees, except for certain white-collar employees. Various supplements depending on work type, number of dependents, etc.	Kept essentially the same retirement age provisions, with similar exceptions for mining and other hazardous occupations, but increased the money amount of the basic benefit to 55 percent of earnings, with a mandatory minimum pension set equal to the minimum wage (in 1990, 70 rubles per month) and a maximum of 75 percent of earnings (this maximum could be obtained by various adjustments to the basic amount, relating to work tenure or number of dependents). Separate legislation and provisions applied to military service personnel.
Old Age Pensions for Certain White-Collar Employees	Established prior to 1956 law on pensions, and recodified in 1959. Old age pensions for teachers, certain medical personnel, certain airline personnel, various agricultural specialists, and for scientific research workers. Although the minimum and maximum pension payments were the same as for workers (30, 120), these long-service pensions were originally to be paid regardless of whether the individual actually retired or continued working. The double-dipping provision was eliminated in 1965, but double-dipping in a different profession was still allowed.	The 1990 law appears to apply to all workers and employees, regardless of profession.
Old Age Pensions for Collective Farmers	No old age pensions were paid to collective farmers until 1965, and then the minimum pension benefit was set at 12 rubles per month and the maximum at 102. In 1971, the minimum pension was raised to 20 rubles per month and a sliding scale based on the same increments as workers' pensions but with the maximum still at 120 rubles per month was adopted.	The 1990 law applies to collective farm members, provided that their farm makes payments to the USSR Pension fund or other social insurance payments. This little-noticed provision eliminated the historic difference between the money amounts of cash benefits to workers and peasants.

Note: Old age pension benefits are not subject to taxation, nor are they to be reduced if the beneficiary earns additional income, under the provisions of the 1990 law.

reduced benefits; a flat 35 rubles/month) could be extended until the child's first birthday. In 1987, paid maternity leave at the original salary was increased to 70 days before birth, and leave with full job retention and 35 rubles/month benefit was extended to 18 months.

16. The original law also instituted a system of one-time maternity grants and continuous maternity grants for four or more children; the 1981 revision increased grant amounts and provided for continuous benefits for three or more children. The one-time maternity grant schedule in the 1981 law was 50 rubles for the first birth (reduced to 30 rubles if the mother was not a full-time student or employed), and 100 rubles for the second and subsequent births. The continuous grants provided for small monthly ruble payments until the child reached the age of 16 (18 for full-time students).[23] Single mothers were entitled to an extra 20 rubles per month per child until the child reached the age of 16 (or 18 for full-time students). Military families received additional small family allowances. The state provided day-care facilities (cost approximately 10 rubles

---

Box 5.2: USSR Disability Cash Transfer Payments, 1956-1990

Type of Cash Transfer	1956-1989	1990
Disability Class I: Disabled individuals who cannot work and need permanent care or supervision. The extent of incapacity is determined by a special commission. Until 1965, collective farmers could not receive any disability payments, and after 1965, they were subject to lower minimum payments.	The regulations are complex; McAuley (1979) summarized them as a minimum payment of 30 rubles and a maximum of 120 per month for this class of workers. Peasants were subject to a minimum of only 15 rubles per month, but this was changed in 1971 to the same system as used for workers. In 1973, the complicated rules were replaced by the formula used in calculating old age pensions.	Disability pensions are now paid to all workers, employees, collective farmers, and to students/children, by a formula designed to take into account labor service and number of dependents. The minimum disability pension for Classes I&II is the minimum wage, and the basic benefit is calculated as 55 percent of earnings. The disability pension is paid in full regardless of wages or other income. For persons with incomplete work tenure, the pension is prorated. If the beneficiary has labor tenure equal to that of the old age pension, then the amount of the disability pension is raised to the level of the old age pension.
Disability Class II: Disabled individuals who cannot work but who do not need permanent (institutional) care. Also covers those with significant motor defects or seriously impaired sight.	McAuley (1979) summarized the regulations as a minimum payment of 23 rubles and a maximum payment of 90 for workers. For collective farmers, the minimum pension was set at only 12 rubles per month. As above, this system was changed in 1971 and 1973.	Same as above
Disability Class III: Disabled individuals who can work, but only at lower skill or reduced skill occupations.	The minimum was 16 and the maximum 45 rubles per month (McAuley, 1979) and until 1967, peasants could not receive Class III pensions. After 1967, Class III pensions were paid to collective farmers only if the disability resulted from an industrial injury. In 1971, the system used for workers was adopted, and in 1973, the old age formula replaced the previous disability formula for calculating benefits.	The minimum payment for class III is 50 percent of the minimum wage, and the basic payment is 30 percent of earnings.

Note: Disability payments are made regardless of whether the disability resulted from a work-related injury, domestic trauma, or a congenital problem. Disability pensions resulting from industrial injury are paid in full regardless of work tenure, while other payments are subject to a sliding scale based on years of labor service. Disability payments are made in full regardless of wages or other income.

per child per month) and low-income families were to be provided with free day care.

17.   Other than the small continuous maternity grants for three or more children (and of course the one-time birth grants), there was no system of family allowances under Soviet law or general practice until the price compensation measures of April 1991. A national law adopted in 1985 enabled a parent to apply for temporary assistance when the other parent refused to pay for child support. The only Soviet family allowance (aside from these maternity grants) was a subsidy paid to low-income families (detailed below). Ukraine enacted a new universal system of family allowances in March 1991, which was not means-tested, as part of its efforts to compensate the population for increased prices. Further changes occurred early in 1993.

Other Transfers

18.   There were three major kinds of Soviet cash transfers not classified above: student stipends, low-income family allowances, and burial grants. Payment for sick and holiday leave was made out of the social consumption fund (financed by enterprise payments and from the general budget), not out of the individual enterprise wage funds. In 1992, student stipends were included in the Ministry of Education budget, and the other transfers are paid from the resources of the social insurance fund.

Student Stipends

19.   Student stipends were paid to most students studying in higher education institutions, and were scaled according to student performance (grades, prizes, etc.) and level (undergraduate/graduate). There were two basic kinds of higher education institutions--the VUZ (basically, universities) and the SSUZ (corresponding to technical colleges). Student stipends were paid to 76 percent of full-time day students in Soviet VUZy and to 74 percent of full-time day students in Soviet SSUZy (*Narkhoz 1989*, 82) during the 1989/90 academic year. In Ukraine, 88 percent of full-time day students in VUZy and 90 percent in SSUZy received stipends during the 1990/91 school year

(*Narkhoz Uk.* 1990, 76). In 1990, the total of all stipends paid amounted to 510 million rubles in Ukraine. Student stipends were revised three times in recent Soviet history and the last revision was in 1987. In 1987-1990, Soviet graduate students received monthly stipends of 130-150 rubles; VUZ students received 100-120 rubles; and SSUZ students received 80-100 rubles. Full-time study is considered to be equivalent to full-time work for the purposes of counting work-tenure (length of service) and other benefits. Students, on ending their studies, are thus considered eligible for unemployment benefits if they do not find a job; most OECD countries do not offer such benefits to graduates.

Low-Income Family Allowance

20.   In 1974, the USSR enacted its sole means-tested cash transfer, a pension for low-income families. Originally, a subsidy of 12 rubles per month per child under eight years old was paid to families with family income of 50 rubles per family member or less. Additionally, families with income under 60 rubles per month were entitled to free day care. In 1987, limited additional benefits to low-income families with three or more children (or to families headed by a single parent) were adopted. These benefits were free school uniforms, free school lunches, and free vacations for both parents (health resorts) and children (summer camps).

Burial Grants

21.   In 1955, a system of burial grants ranging from 5 to 20 rubles was set up for workers, employees, and pensioners; this benefit was extended to collective farmers at rural rates in 1970 (McAuley 1979, 280). The 1990 law, increased the burial allotment to two-months' pension for all pensioners. Anecdotal evidence suggests that these grants are inadequate to finance burial costs, which have come to include significant side-payments to officials and cemetery workers.

PRICE COMPENSATION

22.   The USSR government tried to reduce across-the-board food subsidies on several occasions in the late 1980s but failed to carry

through in the face of public resistance. On February 18, 1991 retail price increases were announced and confirmed a month later in the Cabinet resolution of March 21, 1991, which comprised mostly measures to ensure social protection. Most of the projected state revenues from the increase in prices (some 85 percent) were to be given back to the population in one form of compensation or another: increasing base wages by 60 rubles per month; substantially increasing payments to families with children (see Box 5.3); increasing stipends to higher education students by a maximum of 50 rubles per month depending on performance and type of study; increasing the minimum (base rate) pension by 65 rubles per month; increasing military salaries by 60 rubles per month for enlisted personnel and 80 rubles per month for officers; adding a minimum 50 rubles per month to unemployment benefits, which were tied to the uncompensated minimum monthly wage of 70 rubles; increasing norms for expenditures in hospitals, schools, orphanages, nursing homes, etc.; and increasing salary paid to working prisoners by 60 rubles per month (*Pravda*, March 21, 1991).

TRANSITION TO UKRAINIAN INDEPENDENCE

23. Ukraine had already been following an independent economic course before it declared independence and had seized the initiative to expand the provision of social welfare programs, especially cash transfers, even before the August 1991 coup. This process has continued and accelerated in 1992 to the point where two out of every five Ukrainians receive some cash benefit from the government.

24. What happened to increase the share of social welfare spending from an estimated 25

Box 5.3: New Transfer Payments for Families with Children

One-time allowance at childbirth--250 R

Monthly payments--100 R per child

- for care of infants under 18 months of age to working mothers or full-time students
- for children of military personnel
- for wards of the state or former wards of the state
- for children infected with HIV or ill with AIDS

Monthly payments--90 R per child

- to single mothers of children aged 6 to 18
- for children aged 6 to 18 lacking a source of child support

Monthly payments--80 R per child

- for care of infants under 18 months of age to non-working mothers
- for care of children between 18 months and 6 years if the total income per family member is less than four times the minimum wage
- to single mothers of children under 6
- for children less than 6 lacking a source of child support

Monthly loss-of-breadwinner pensions--65 R increase

Monthly disability pensions--65 R increase

Monthly payments--40 R per child

- for any children under 16 who do not receive other pensions or social security allowances (continues to age 18 for students not receiving a stipend)

Annual payments for poor families (where total income per family member is less than four times the minimum wage)

- for children under 6 years--"no less" than 200 R
- for children 6-13--"no less" than 240 R
- for children 13-18--"no less" than 280 R

Source: *Izvestiya*, 21 March 1991, p. 2.

---

percent of GDP (40 percent of government revenues) in 1990 to a budgeted 44 percent of GDP (75 percent of government revenue) in 1992? A greatly expanded mandate for social programs was enacted in 1991-1992 in response primarily to Ukrainian fears and misunderstandings about the impact of inflation.

25.   Seven steps taken in 1991 expanded subsidies and benefits (see Box 5.4). The March compensation package anticipated the April 1991 price increases. The December social protection package, "Resolution...on Implementing Urgent Measures to Guarantee Social Protection for the Population in Conditions of Price Liberalization," greatly increased the scope of cash transfer payments to protect the general population from the consequences of a transition to freer prices. That the government is responsible for insulating everyone from inflation is an odd notion to a market-system economy but was and is pervasive in Soviet and Ukrainian thinking about macroeconomic policy. The universal entitlement to cash compensation from the government for increased prices underscores the Soviet/Ukrainian social welfare philosophy that benefits should be provided regardless of need.

26.   The March decree, "Social Protection for the People of the Republic in Connection with the Reform of Retail Prices," increased wage rates and transfer payments and created a new cash benefit: payments to families with children under 16 (or students under 19 lacking stipends) who did not already receive cash transfers. (In 1990, there were 11.8 million children under 16.) Three new or expanded cash transfers, for general family allowances, expanded maternity leave and unemployment benefits, provided for monthly payments of 45 rubles to children under 16 who were not covered under the existing maternity grant system and for additional annual supplements of 200 rubles for children under 6 years, 240 rubles for children from 6 to 13, and 280 rubles for children aged 13-18.

27.   The safety net was expanded for maternity leave and grants, providing monthly payments of 85 rubles until the child reached the age of six. Additional monthly grants of 115 rubles were to be paid to children of military personnel, under the care of a guardian, in single-parent families, and children with AIDS or who are HIV-positive. A new one-time grant of 95 rubles (presumably per child) was to be paid to single mothers or to those with a spouse evading child support payments.

28.   The law guaranteed unemployment benefits of 55 rubles per month to those in search of work and enrolled in retraining programs. Cash transfers to single mothers, low-income families, students, survivors, old-age pensioners, and the disabled were increased, and then superseded by subsequent legislation, which increased them further. A December resolution extended maternity leave benefits until the child reached age three and provided additional child-care payments until the child reached age six for families falling under an income ceiling. Most cash transfers were doubled in December 1991 from the July levels. However, old-age pensions were increased as much as 4.5 times, based on length of service and year of retirement (*Demokratichna Ukraina*, December 28, 1991, p. 2). The minimum payments for old-age pensions rose from 221 to 442 rubles by decree of President Kravchuk in 1992.

29.   In January 1992, Ukraine raised cash transfers for military pensions. The Ukrainian Federation of Independent Trade Unions estimated that the poverty level was 2,400 rubles per month as compared to the official October 1991 poverty level of 256 rubles (POSTFACTUM, January, 1992). Since the minimum wage was raised to 400 rubles on January 3, the trade unions concluded that it could only account for one-sixth of the minimum consumption bundle. In February, artistic unions and enterprises (theaters, etc.) were exempted from paying income tax and dues to special funds. In March 1992 government expenditures were projected at a trillion rubles in the popular press.

30.   Also in March 1992, Ukraine adopted increased cash transfers for low-income disabled persons and families (*Pravda Ukrainy*, March 21, 1992, p. 1) and adopted general indexation of incomes for the first quarter of 1992 (*Uryadovyy Kuryer*, March, 1992, p. 2), and President Kravchuk decreed that all savings deposits in the Ukraine savings bank would be increased by 100 percent (*Uryadovyy kuryer*, March 1992, p. 5). The March cash transfers were intended to help the disabled pay for the increased cost of living. These supplemental payments to disabled persons were set at about

800 rubles annually, and each child under 12 was to receive 400 rubles per year. An additional one-time payment of 200 rubles was to be made to non-working pensioners, and to children of low-income families (per child under 12), while a one-time payment of 100 rubles was designated for non-working mothers of children under 3, for the children of military personnel, and for the unemployed (provided an income ceiling was not exceeded).

31. In 1991, Ukraine seized the initiative to rectify perceived shortcomings in the social safety net inherited from Soviet practice. Unfortunately, Ukraine approached this task from a "universal" perspective, instead of a means-tested one. The resulting explosion in transfer payments in 1992 can be partially attributed to the new system of universal family allowances and price compensation measures adopted in 1991.

Conclusion

32. In a sharp break with pre-1991 Soviet precedent, by the end of 1991, Ukraine adopted a system of general family allowances in addition to the means-tested Soviet pension for low-income families. The level of all cash transfers was raised repeatedly during the year, leading to a large expansion in cost. Cash transfers increased from 30 billion rubles in 1991 (for old-age pensions and maternity grants) to somewhere around 440 billion rubles in the June 1992 budget. A large share was due to the new general system of family allowances and price compensation, but the real culprit seems to be an explosion in payments for old-age pensions. In 1990, old-age pensions amounted to 12.6 billion rubles; in 1992, civilian old-age pensions were projected at 253 billion rubles. This increase is partly due to increases in the minimum old-age pension, but the more significant factor seems to be the December 1991, July 1992, and October 1992 increases in length-of-service pensions (pensions exceeding the minimum).

33. Past and prospective policy options are summarized in Box 5.5. By early 1993, the government had taken some positive steps described in succeeding chapters.

Box 5.4: Ukrainian Social Welfare Legislation, 1991

March	Decree of the Uk. SSR Council of Ministers "On Social Protection for the People of the Republic in Connection with the Reform of Retail Prices," No. 72, issued 28 March 1991.
April	Compensation for miners for cost of special food reported to be increased from 65 rubles to 105 rubles. Moscow Radio Broadcast, 3 April 1991.
July	Decree of the Uk. SSR Council of Ministers "On Additional Measures for Strengthening the Social Protection of the Population in Connection with the Reform of Retail Prices," No. 86, issued 11 July 1991.
	USSR-Republics joint action program on social protection. Moscow Central Television broadcast 16 July 1991. Ukraine was a participant; few details were released. Text otherwise unavailable.
	Decree of the Uk. SSR Council of Ministers "On Additional Compensation to Be Paid to Families With Children for Expenses Arising From the Need to Purchase School Uniforms or Other Clothing for the Children," No. 101, issued 20 July 1991.
August	Law of the Ukrainian SSR "On a Minimum Consumer Budget." A general document basically approving the existing consumption basket methodology. No poverty level figures were specified.
December	Decree of the President of Ukraine "On the Social Protection of the Population in Conditions of Price Liberalization," issued 27 December 1991. Followed by 1 January 1992 decree of Uk. SSR Council of Ministers "On Implementing Urgent Measures to Guarantee Social Protection for the Population in Conditions of Price Liberalization."

Box 5.5: Ukrainian Social Welfare Policy Options

Group or Transfer	Soviet Baseline (1956 to 1990)	Ukrainian Additions (1991 to mid-1992)	Options (1992 and following)
Elderly	No means-test for pensions. Majority received more than minimum. Early retirement ages (60 for men, 55 for women). Double-dipping allowed with no reduction in benefits. Benefits not taxed.	All baseline provisions retained. Above-minimum pensions were greatly increased. Only 37 percent of old-age pensioners receive minimum pension.	Flat-rate old-age pension. Eliminate or reduce early retirement. Prorate or eliminate benefits for double-dippers. Increase retirement age to 65 for both men and women.
Disability	State was guarantor for all disability, work-related or general.	Benefits increased but still apparently too low.	As private firms appear, consider shifting work-related disability to insurers.
Survivor	Universal and for extended family structure.	Benefits increased.	Although social security survivor payments are not means-tested in the US, they are low and private insurance is available. This is one option to pursue.
Low-income	Means-tested benefits.	Benefits increased and special one-time payments adopted.	Retain and review. Supplements may be too low.
General family allowances	Enacted at the very end of Soviet rule.	Enacted separately by Ukraine before Soviet law. Universal subsidies to all children under 16 regardless of need.	Review and retain for low-income families.
Students (undergraduate universal and graduate)	Approximately 75 percent of full-time students received stipends in addition to free tuition.	Approximately 90 percent of full-time students received stipends in addition to free tuition.	Stipends for poor and vulnerable groups only. State should review policy of free tuition.
Maternity leave	Job held open for 1 year with modest monthly maternity benefit.	Maternity leave extended to three years and benefit raised. Possible supplemental payments for child care until age six.	Maternity leave should be reduced and supplemental payments could be eliminated.
One-time birth pro-natal payment	Established in 1947.	Amounts raised.	State may wish to retain this pro-natal policy on symbolic grounds.
Burial benefit	Well below cost of funeral but universal.	Increased but probably still below the cost of funeral.	Eliminate in favor of low-income (means-tested) cemeteries.
Price compensation	--	Wages, transfers, and savings deposits increased and system of indexation implemented.	Indexation should be limited to cash transfers. Somehow the message that price increases should not be the responsibility of the state should be conveyed to the general public.

RETIREMENT, DISABILITY, AND SURVIVORS' BENEFITS

1.   The growing evidence of the failure of the Soviet economy helped generate demands for social assistance during the 1980s that resulted in legislation in 1990 expanding the number of benefits and beneficiaries.   The newly independent Ukrainian Parliament tried throughout 1992 to ensure that social assistance was superior to that offered under the Soviet system, and that pensions and allowances were no less than Russia's.   The result throughout much of 1992 was a "benefits race" with acutely damaging fiscal implications.

2.   The introduction of coupons in 1992 freed Ukraine from limits on monetary emission, easing the administrative problem of paying cash benefits.   The resulting inflation, however, undermined the real value of nominal pensions and allowances.   By March 1993, government authorities knew, and Parliament leaders were beginning to recognize, that macroeconomic stability would only be feasible if government obligations for social assistance could be reduced to a sustainable level not much greater than what prevailed, as a share of GDP, in the 1980s.

3.   Since public social spending had risen from under 20 percent of GDP at the start of the Gorbachev years, to 25 percent of GDP at the end of the 1980s, and to a programmed 44 percent of in 1992, the new government in office as 1993 began, faced a major adjustment challenge.   This chapter and the next, which cover allowances and related benefits, break down the aggregate spending package for 1992 into some of its component parts with the intention of finding areas for spending cuts that will be least painful.   Further, these chapters seek to identify those parts of a social safety net that are most certainly essential to protect vulnerable groups against the social costs of poverty and adjustment.

4.   As this report was being prepared, government authorities were already beginning to take some steps to adjust spending to the severe limits of reduced revenues occasioned by the collapse of output.   Some suggestions and recommendations discussed below are already under review by the government. Implementation of reforms, particularly the sequencing of changes in social policy, must be fully integrated with overall economic policy. For example, pension and family-allowance policies must be developed in conjunction with employment, monetary, and fiscal policy.   When the government hardens the budget constraints on state enterprises, there will be substantial implications that could include reduced payments to the Pension Fund and related deficits; layoffs among the elderly who have continued to work; job loss in two-earner families that will probably fall most heavily on women; and high rates of unemployment and further collapse in demand in specific single-industry towns that face mass layoffs.   Social policy must be prepared to confront   such   possibilities;   the   financial soundness of the several social funds will be a critical aspect of the capacity of social policy to respond to this challenge.

PENSIONERS AND BENEFITS

5.   In January 1992, 13 million people received benefits from the Pension Fund, and the Ministry of Defense provided pensions for an additional 362,000 people in the security sector.   Thus, almost a quarter of Ukrainians receive a pension allowance (see Table 6.1). Retirees who have not yet reached pensionable age account for about 7.6 percent of total retirees.[24]   Tables A.73 to A.79 in the Statistical Annex of this report describe the benefits to which each group was entitled as of July 1, 1992.

Table 6.1: Pensioners and Their Benefits, January 1, 1992

Pensioners	Number (000)	Percent of Total	Avg. Amount as a Percent of Minimum Pension[1]
Pension Fund Supported	12,997	97	122
Retirees	10,318	77	125
Disabled	1,224	9	123
Dependents	693	5	96
Other[2]	500	4	75
Military	262	2	144
Military Paid from Ministry of Defense	362	3	522
Total	13,359	100	133

Notes: 1. Figures do not reflect July and October 1992 increases.

        2. People who never worked including those disabled from childhood and hobos.

Source: Ministry of Social Welfare

6.   Most benefits exceed the minimum pension.   Average pensions funded by the Pension Fund were about 22 percent above the minimum in June, 1992.   Average military pensions issued by the Pension Fund exceeded the minimum by 144 percent, while pensions issued by the Ministry of Defense averaged 522 percent of the minimum.   Pension benefits were greatly increased for farm workers[25] in 1992.

7.   The relationship of most people's benefits to the minimum pension underwent an upward revision in July, 1992 and again in October, 1992.   The legislature approved a new law that raised pensions for those who began receiving benefits before January 1992.[26]   The Pension Fund projected in July that by November virtually all pensioners would receive the maximum benefit of three times the minimum pension.   The Ministry of Finance projected that the average pension for Pension Fund beneficiaries would be 2.4 times the minimum.   With inflation at over 20 percent per month and no timetable for currency stabilization, it is virtually impossible to calculate the changing real value of nominal pensions or to predict the timing and amount of pension adjustments.

8.   Pensioners who continue to work after age 60 (55 for women) and disability pensioners who work and earn do so without reducing their benefits.   As of January, 1992, a quarter of recipients in both groups were earning a salary and receiving a pension benefit payment.   The proportion of double-dippers will decline over the next year as these groups are among those most likely to be laid off.

9.   Most disabled people who reach retirement age can choose between continuing to receive a disability pension or receiving a retirement pension.   Military retirees and Chernobyl victims can receive both disability and retirement pensions.

SOURCES OF FUNDS

10.   In 1992, budgeted funding for pensions accounted for 23 percent of total government revenues.[27]   The Pension Fund accounts for about 90 percent of total pension resources; state and local general revenues earmarked for security personnel, 7 percent; and the Chernobyl Fund earmarked for pension supplements for Chernobyl victims, 3 percent.[28]

11.   The employer social insurance payroll tax is the Pension Fund's primary source of funding, and accounts for 97 percent of Pension Fund resources.[29]   Additional revenue sources include a 1 percent tax on wages received by employees; a 10 percent payroll contribution from self-employed persons who do not have employer payroll contributions but nevertheless wish to be eligible for a disability or retirement pension; returns from Pension Fund investments; and grants from enterprises, charities and other sources (see Table 6.2).

USES OF FUNDS

12.   Pensions in 1992 accounted for the largest share of social sector spending: 32 percent of total spending and 14 percent of GDP.   Benefits to retirees and the military account for 75 percent of total pension spending; work disabled, 8 percent; those disabled from

childhood, dependents and other benefits, 8 percent; additional benefits for Chernobyl workers and victims, 3 percent; delivery and administrative expenses, 3 percent; expenses accrued by the Pension Fund in 1991 but not paid in that year, 3 percent (Table 6.3). Pension Fund estimates made in July, 1992 indicated that pension spending would reach R403.9 billion in 1992 while estimates by the Ministry of Finance placed total spending at R354.9 billion. The discrepancy between the two is primarily accounted for by the uncertainty over the effects of the July increase in pensions. Both projections were overtaken by the unexpected acceleration of inflation in the second half of 1992.

PENSION FUND SURPLUSES AND DEFICITS

13.   Pension Fund estimates indicate that pension spending would exceed revenues by 5.5 percent of total government and state fund revenues and 3 percent of GDP. According to Ministry of Finance calculations, pension spending would accrue a small surplus. The discrepancy between the two estimates was attributable to different assumptions regarding future employment and the effects of the July

and October pension increases. Data closing the books on the Pension Fund in 1992 were not available for this report.

Administration

14.   Payroll tax revenues for the Pension Fund are collected by district-level administration offices, consolidated and forwarded to the head office of the Pension Fund. Central Departments of the Ministry of Social Welfare (MSW)[30] on the district level collect pension-related documents from applicants and calculate individuals' benefits. This information is passed on to district payment centers of the MSW that instruct the head office of the Pension Fund regarding its total obligation each month and send the Ministry of Communication a list of beneficiaries, their addresses and the payment owed to each. The Pension Fund sends its total obligation to the Ministry of Communication which distributes the pensions to district post offices. Beneficiaries claim their pensions at the post office. If a beneficiary is disabled, the post office may deliver the funds. The Ministry of Communication charges the Pension Fund 4.2 percent of pension volume for its services.

Box 6.1: The Pension System

The pension system is based on benefits indexed to the cost of a minimum consumer budget for pensioners. To be eligible for full retirement benefits recipients must have worked for 25 years (20 for women). Pensions are calculated as a percentage of previous salaries. After 25 years of service (20 for women), workers receive a pension of 55 percent of their salary. For each additional year beyond the minimum that they work the replacement rate of their ultimate pension is increased by one percentage point. The maximum pension cannot exceed 300 percent of the minimum benefit.

Early retirement takes place before age 60 (55 for women), but after at least 25 (20 for women) years of service. Years of service include time spent in higher education; serving in the armed services; unemployed but seeking a job; and taking care of children under age 3 and disabled persons. Benefits are proportional to years worked but are below those received by retirees who have reached age 60 (55). Benefits cannot be below one-half the minimum pension.

Disability pensions are determined based on previous salary and severity of disability. The replacement rate varies from 40 to 70 percent depending on severity of disability. The local administrative office of the Ministry of Social Welfare can also make adjustments for individual cases. The minimum disability pension is 50 percent of the minimum wage, the maximum is 400 percent.

Minor children of workers who die receive a pension based on the income of their deceased parent and the length of time the parent worked. This pension cannot be below 50 percent of the minimum pension.

People who did not work but reached retirement age can receive a "social pension" set below the retirement pension. People disabled from childhood are also eligible for these pensions regardless of their age. This pension ranges from 30 to 50 percent of the minimum pension for people who did not work; and from 50 to 200 percent for people disabled from birth or childhood, depending on the severity of the disability.

15. The MSW's central departments are overburdened, and there is frequently a delay of one to nine months between the time a person retires and the first payments of pension benefits. This problem is expected to worsen as the departments must calculate new pension benefits for virtually all of the system's 13 million clients.

RECOMMENDATIONS

16. The estimates in Tables S.1 and 5.1 suggest that pension payments rose from around 5 percent of GDP in the Brezhnev years, to 7 percent of GDP in 1992. This level of spending is unsustainable, but reductions will not be easy. Both the number of pensioners and average payments have risen dramatically. the number of recipients rose by one-third and average pensions increased by a factor of 20 (before adjusting for inflation). Some eligible beneficiaries returned to Ukraine from other parts of the Soviet Union after its dissolution. Retirement benefits were extended to some additional collective-farm workers.

17. Changes in the real value of pensions are difficult to calculate; Table 6.4 offers one way to make an estimate. The combined effects of a 25 percent decline in GDP, a 100 percent increase in the pension share in GDP, and a 35 percent increase in the number of pensioners was a 10 percent increase in average pensions between 1990 and 1992. These crude estimates, if confined by more detailed studies, show that pensioners were more than protected; other sectors of the economy must have borne the brunt of the massive collapse of output. In 1993, and until the economy recovers its previous level of output, it may be essential that pension beneficiaries reduce their share of GDP, perhaps by a mix of three types of change: (1) reducing the number of beneficiaries, (2) reducing average pensions, but (3) increasing the pension floor to ensure protection against poverty and reducing the pension ceiling to promote social justice. The paragraphs that

Table 6.2: Projected Sources of Funds for Pensions

Source	1992 FY (million rubles)	Percent of Total	Percent of Government Revenue[1]
Total Pension Fund	322,137	90.3	20.7
Employer Payroll Tax	321,794	90.2	
Employee Payroll Tax	9,788	2.7	
Other[2]	175	0.0	
Non-Pension Commitments	(9,620)		
State General Revenues[3]	23,647	6.6	1.5
State Chernobyl Fund[4]	10,918	3.1	0.7
Total	356,702	100	22.9

Notes: Figures are averages of Pension Fund and Ministry of Finance forecasts.

  1. Includes state and local general revenues and revenues from the Pension, Social Insurance, Employment and Chernobyl Funds.
  2. Other includes self employed income tax of 10 percent, investments and grants.
  3. Earmarked for military pensions.
  4. Earmarked for additional benefits to Chernobyl workers.

Sources: Pension Fund Draft Budget for 1992 (Ministry of Finance and Pension Fund June 1992 versions), 1992 Draft Consolidated State Budget for Ukraine (June 1992 version), Draft of 1992 Chernobyl Fund Budget (June, 1992 version).

follow offer some suggestions for implementing such changes.

18. One suggestion is to introduce a unitary pension rate for the duration of the crisis and to adjust it periodically to ensure that all recipients are fully protected against inflation. This system would significantly ease the pension administrative burden. It would also be possible to ensure that the benefit is fully reflective of the social protection objective. Many pensioners now receiving several multiples of the minimum would lose support as a result of such a unitary benefit system. An option would be a dual level of benefits, thus simplifying administration but leaving some difference between poverty-related and higher benefits. In either case, high monthly inflation will require frequent adjustment of pension payments.

NORMAL RETIREMENT AGE

19. Normal retirement age for both men and women could be increased gradually over 10

years to age 62 or age 65 for actuarial and demographic reasons. Life expectancy is growing, the birth rate is already low, and the burden of the pensioner population on the working-age group, an inevitable feature of a pay-as-you go system of retirement benefits, will soon be too great for the economy to bear. The proposed increase amounts to an additional two years of work for men and seven working years for women. Men have a life expectancy of 72.4 at age 60; women's life expectancy is 79.5 at the same age. By the end of the 10-year adjustment period, total pension spending would be 20 percent lower than it would have been if the age limit had not been increased--a savings equivalent to about 3.5 percent of GDP.[31] Note, however, that these spending reductions lie mostly in the future and can have virtually no effect on current budget difficulties of the government. These considerations suggest that it may be unwise for the government to spend its scarce political capital to achieve this change during the period of crisis, no matter how essential such a change may be in the longer run.

Personal Security Accounts

20. A more attractive option being considered in the Ministry of Social Welfare is to institute a system of personal security accounts that would permit a more flexible approach to designation of the retirement age. With such a system, it would be both feasible and desirable to eliminate the provision of a mandatory retirement age. Able-bodied workers could then continue to be employed as long as they wish, with related provisions for many means to transfer pension rights to third parties or to use them for such purposes as financing private annuities or other expenses that do not interfere with the income security provisions of pension law.

Table 6.3: Uses of Pension Funds

Use	1992 FY (million rubles)	Share of 1992 FY Vol.	Percent of GDP
Total Pension Fund	344,828	90.9	12.6
Cash Benefits[1]	319,576	84.2	
Retired	252,600	66.6	
Disabled	29,884	7.9	
Dependent	16,394	4.3	
Never Worked[2]	11,551	3.0	
Military	6,547	1.7	
Additional Benefits	2,600	0.7	
Delivery Costs	7,425	2.0	
Repayment of 1991 Loan	4,246	1.1	
Add. Benefits Owed[3]	11,582	3.1	
Partial Administration Costs[4]	2,000	0.5	
Chernobyl Victims Add. Benefits	10,918	2.9	0.4
Min. of Defense	23,647	6.2	0.9
Total Pensions	379,393	100.0	13.9
Surplus (Deficit)	(22,691)	-6.0	-0.8

Notes: Figures are averages of Pension Fund and Ministry of Finance forecasts

1. Estimates for the breakdown of cash benefits between types of beneficiary were made based on the number of beneficiaries in each group and the average pension received.
2. People who never worked including those disabled in childhood and hobos.
3. Benefits accrued but not paid in 1991.
4. Includes only Pension Fund administration costs.

Sources: Pension Fund Draft Budget for 1992 (Ministry of Finance and Pension Fund June 1992 versions), 1992 Draft Consolidated State Budget for Ukraine (June 1992 version) and mission estimates.

Pension Benefits for Working People

21. About 25 percent of old-age and disabled pensioners continue to work (Mikhavlichenko, 1992). Given that the purpose of pensions is to support people who are too old or disabled to work, people who continue to earn income from their labor should receive a reduced benefit. Savings from this policy modification could reach 10 percent of total pension spending (about 2.2 percent of GDP) assuming that employment rates among retirees and the disabled do not decline over the period.[32] Virtually all savings from this policy

Table 6.4: Changes in Pension Spending, 1990-1992

Factor	1990	1992
1. GDP, 1990 = 100	100	75
2. Pensions, % of GDP	7	14
3. (line 1 x line 2)/100	7	10.5
4. Pensioners, millions	10	13.5
5. line 3/line4	0.70	0.77

Source: Estimated on the basis of official data

modification would be derived from reducing benefits for working retirees as the total number of working disabled is very small.

Early Retirement

22.   The option of early retirement for people who have worked more than 25 years (20 for women) but have not yet reached the normal retirement age of 60 years (55 for women) should be discontinued. Less than 5.6 percent of pension spending goes to early retirees so savings will be small.

Administration and Management

23.   The Pension Fund should separate its funding and administration of allowances and pension. An old-age, survivors' and disability insurance fund should not pay for or administer benefits that are not insurable risks. Social assistance, a responsibility of the state, should be funded from general revenues.

24.   The central offices of the Pension Fund and Ministry of Communication, and four separate district level administration networks, undertake pension-related activities. The process of collecting payroll tax revenues and calculating and distributing benefits should be simplified and rationalized.

25.   The Fund did not pay indexing benefits on April payments in 1992 because management knew that the minimum pension was to be increased in May. Indexing is also paid one to two months after the month in which the obligation is accrued without adjusting for the payment's loss in value. In the first quarter of 1992, the Pension Fund accrued a large surplus because the social insurance tax during that period was 61 percent. With some of this surplus, the Fund made unplanned payments of R2.6 billion. These ad hoc expenditures were equivalent to about 10 percent of the Fund's total planned payments for the period. The Pension Fund should systematize its payment of indexing and other benefits, and retain surpluses, not spend them unnecessarily.

26.   The Pension Fund could benefit from technical assistance in investment management. Investments are an insignificant share of total Pension Fund revenues currently but could become increasingly important over time. Macroeconomic instability poses enormous risks; training in risk management could yield substantial benefits.

Aggregate Pension Spending

27.   This discussion suggests a number of options open to the government for essential reduction in pension spending. Even in 1993 it would be possible to introduce a unitary benefit and set it at a level consistent with the financial capacity of the Pension Fund. For the next 12 to 36 months if it may be necessary to adopt a single, or two-tier, pension scheme to keep expenditures down while protecting the most vulnerable. It might also be possible to cut the benefits of those who continue to earn a salary (see Table 6.5). Given the predominance of regular retiree benefits, and payments to military retirees through the Ministry of Defense, these categories cannot escape reductions in any effort to bring pension spending back to the sustainable levels observed in the 1980s. Beyond 1993, changes in retirement age and introduction of personal security accounts could lead to somewhat lower pension spending.

Table 6.5: Current, Suggested, and Sustainable Policy for Pensions

Spending Category	Percent of Gross Domestic Product			Policy Actions Required
	1992 Budget	Suggested Program for 1993	Sustainable Program Beyond 1993	
Non-Working Retirees	6.6	5.1	2.5	In 1993, begin raising retirement age and eliminate early retirement option. Raise age by 1 year per year until age is 62 for men and women.[1] Alternatively, introduce individual security accounts.
Retirees Who Continue to Work	2.7	1.7	0.7	In 1993 reduce benefits by 50 percent for people who continue to work.[2]
Disabled	1.1	0.9	0.9	In 1993 reduce benefits by 50 percent for people who continue to work.
All Other Beneficiaries (Including Military)	2.6	2.6	2.6	
Administration and Other Costs	1.0	1.0	1.0	
Total[3]	14.0	11.3	7.7	

Notes: 1.   Eventual Savings from raising the retirement age could reach about 3.4 percent of GDP by 2003.
2.   Upper bound estimates of savings since many pensioners might decide to stop working.
3.   Does not sum exactly owing to rounding.

ALLOWANCES AND BENEFITS

1.   Family allowances and special cash allowances grew over the past decade parallel with, and for reasons similar to, the growth in pension spending. Events at Chernobyl, and the response to them, had a special role in expanding the demand for government assistance, especially when independence left the Government of Ukraine with a large responsibility that had previously been shared across a population five times that of independent Ukraine. Chapters 1 and 5 describe some features of these allowances; this chapter emphasizes the fact that costs rose dramatically to 8.7 percent of GDP in 1992, posing a serious fiscal problem. Early in 1993, government authorities began taking steps to reduce spending in this area yet concentrate resources of those groups most at risk of bearing the social costs of adjustment. The options suggested here must balance great need against limited resources.

2.   In 1992, Ukraine offered a large number of cash allowances and assistance programs to its citizens. Some transfers were directed to low-income and vulnerable groups; others went to the general population and non-vulnerable groups; and still others went to Chernobyl victims. In 1993, the authorities were moving to reduce the number of allowance recipients by as much as 90 percent; from 20 million to 2 million, concentrating more limited spending on poverty groups.

SOURCES OF FUNDS

3.   Allowances accounted for 20 percent of social sector spending in 1992 and about 8.8 percent of projected GDP. About 47 percent of total allowance funding derived from general government revenues, 38 percent from the Chernobyl payroll tax, 11 percent from the Social Insurance Fund and 4 percent from the Pension Fund (Table 7.1).

USES OF FUNDS

4.   In 1992, benefits targeted to Chernobyl victims accounted for 39 percent of social assistance spending; aid to vulnerable groups, 37 percent[33]; allowances available to the population as a whole and specific, non-vulnerable groups, 23 percent; and partial administration costs, 1 percent (Table 7.2).[34]

5.   The food subsidy program is part of a more general program of consumer subsidies. In 1992, consumer subsidies reached 5.1 percent of GDP. Subsidies for utilities and residential services accounted for about one-half of this spending. Food subsidies reached 1.9 percent of GDP. In July, 1992, the government eliminated all food subsidies except support for bread prices. Thus, the food subsidy budget for 1992 primarily reflected spending before that time. In July, the subsidy was replaced by a monthly cash allowance equal to 30-40 percent of the minimum wage for each child under 18, or pension-age adult if family income is below two minimum wages per person. These subsidies were again subjected to review early in 1993.

Chernobyl-Related Benefits

6.   Benefits to Chernobyl victims include wage bonuses and other benefits to workers in areas of radiation contamination. These benefits increase with radiation levels in the work site, and monetary bonuses range up to 100 percent of the worker's base wage. Housing and relocation benefits account for about 9 percent of Chernobyl-related allowance spending; disability and death compensation, 9 percent; supplemental family allowances, 4 percent; food provision, 4 percent; and other allowances, 6 percent. These outlays are financed from the Chernobyl Fund, which also funds medical care.

Benefits to Low-Income and Vulnerable Groups

7.   Assistance to low-income and vulnerable groups accounted for 37 percent of 1992 welfare spending, half of it through an allowance to low-income families for the purchase of food products. This benefit was introduced as a means of protecting the poor from the consequences of partial deregulation of food prices. The allowance is paid monthly for each child under 18 and pension-age adult, and ranges from 30-40 percent of the minimum wage. Annual allowances to compensate low-income families for increases in children's clothing and products prices account for 24 percent of vulnerable groups' allowances, and were also introduced to protect families from price decontrol; non-cash benefits to the infirm elderly account for 10 percent of funding; stipends to low-income families with children from age three to age six, six percent;[35] additional allowances to low-income families and single mothers, eight percent; and maintenance of orphanages, four percent. Assistance to low-income and vulnerable groups is funded from state and local general revenues.

Benefits for the General Population and Non-Vulnerable Groups

8.   Assistance to the general population and specific non-vulnerable groups accounts for 24 percent of social welfare spending. Stipends to all families with children under age three (under age two if the mother did not work prior to childbirth) account for 41 percent of non-vulnerable group welfare spending; sick leave and short-term disability pay, 27 percent; benefits for the disabled, 11 percent; recreation benefits, 8 percent; maternity benefits, 6 percent; and other benefits, 7 percent. The Social Insurance Fund pays for 42.5 percent of non-targeted benefits; state and local general revenues, 40 percent; and the Pension Fund, 17.5 percent.

Proliferation of Benefits

9.   The system that prevailed in the middle of 1992 offered over 60 allowances and benefits, many of which did not differ substantively from one another. For example, there were 12 cash allowances that low-income or vulnerable families could qualify for. These include separate stipends for children's food, children's clothing, children's products, and general child maintenance. Under the category of general child maintenance, families may qualify for different allowances, and different stipend levels within an allowance, depending on the number of children and age of children, whether the mother worked before childbirth, the age of the mother, whether the children are eligible for other allowances, whether the family is headed by a single parent, whether the absent parent pays alimony, and whether the single parent was raised in an orphanage. The annex tables include a list of allowances and benefits, the requirements for qualifying for each, and the size of the award or the nature of the benefit as of July, 1992. The list is being modified significantly in 1993.

Administration and Funding

10.   Administrative and funding

Table 7.1: Projected Sources of Funds for Allowances and Benefits, 1992

	Total (million rubles)	Percent of Total	Percent of GDP
General State Revenues	112,446	46.9	4.1
Payroll Taxes	127,099	53.1	4.7
Chernobyl Payroll Tax[1]	92,023	38.4	3.4
Social Insurance Payroll Tax	25,295	10.6	0.9
Pension Payroll Tax	9,781	4.1	0.4
TOTAL[2]	239,546	100.0	8.8

Notes: 1.   In practice incorporated into the state budget, but listed separately in this report. Chernobyl Fund documents were ambiguous. Actual figure is from 31 to 92 billion rubles.

2.   Does not sum exactly owing to rounding.

Sources: Ukraine Consolidated State and Local June 1992 Draft Budget for 1992, June 1992 Drafts of 1992 Budgets for the Pension Fund, Social Insurance Fund, and Chernobyl Fund.

Table 7.2: Projected Uses of Funds for Allowances and Benefits, 1992

Expenditure Item	Total (million rubles)	Percent of Total	Percent of GDP
Chernobyl Related	93,073	38.9	3.4
Employment	63,470	26.5	
Housing and Relocation	8,292	3.5	
Disability	7,901	3.3	
Family Allowance	4,110	1.7	
Food	4,038	1.7	
Other	5,262	2.2	
Low-Income and Vulnerable[1]	87,659	36.6	3.2
Food Allowance	42,288	17.7	
Children's Clothes/Products Allowances	21,003	8.8	
Benefits for Elderly Infirm[2]	8,568	3.6	
Low-Income/Single-Parent Allowances[3]	6,904	2.9	
Allowances for Children Ages 3-6[4]	5,219	2.2	
Orphanages[5]	3,677	1.5	
Not Income Targeted	55,872	23.3	2.1
Children Under Age 3[4]	22,633	9.4	
Sick Leave/Short-Term Disability	15,274	6.4	
Benefits for Disabled	6,297	2.6	
Recreation	4,556	1.9	
Maternity Leave	3,174	1.3	
Allowance for Families of Servicemen	2,700	1.1	
Compensation to Exonerated Citizens	800	0.3	
Support for Coal Miners' Union	299	0.1	
Other[6]	140	0.1	
Partial Administration Cost[7]	2,941	1.2	0.1
TOTAL	239,546	100.0	8.8

Notes:
1. Targeted to families earning less than two minimum wages per person and/or vulnerable groups. According to the 1990 census, approximately 42.5 percent of the population has an income of 2 minimum wages or less.
2. Includes day care and assistance with household chores. Listed under the line item "other local" in the national budget.
3. Includes a variety of allowances for low income families and single mothers. In Ukraine, most families headed by single women are low-income.
4. Allowances for all children below age 6 are grouped together in the national budget. Spending on allowances for children under age 3 (which are not means tested) and for children ages 3 to 6 (which are means tested) were separated based on the number of children in each category and the size of the benefit each is entitled to.
5. Assumed to be 33 percent of combined nursing home and orphanage expenses. Nursing home expenses are captured in the health sector.
6. Includes telephone installation for veterans and funeral allowances. Funeral allowance spending includes only funeral allowances for the employed, which are funded by the Social Insurance Fund. Funeral allowances for retired people are funded by the Pension Fund and for unemployed people by state general revenues. Neither the Pension Fund nor the state government explicitly budgets for this expenditure.
7. Includes only administration of the Social Insurance Fund and some state purchases of equipment and supplies for social welfare offices.

Sources: Ukraine Consolidated State and Local June 1992 Draft Budget for 1992, June 1992 Drafts of 1992 Budgets for the Pension Fund, Social Insurance Fund, and Chernobyl Fund.

responsibilities for benefits are set out in law, but vary by allowance (and often by status of beneficiary for the same allowance) and have little underlying logic. Many allowances are funded, administered and distributed by several agencies; others are funded by one agency, administered by a second, and distributed by a third. For example, all families are entitled to an allowance for each child under the age of three (two if the mother did not work or attend a higher education school and is over 18 prior to childbirth). The Pension Fund pays for these allowances out of its own resources for children under age 1.5. Stipends for children ages 1.5-3 (2) are funded by state general revenues given to the Pension Fund but earmarked for this purpose. If the mother worked or attended a higher education school prior to childbirth, and was still employed or was a student at the time the baby was delivered, the allowance is administered by the mother's enterprise or school. If the mother did not work or study prior to childbirth or was laid off before the birth, the allowance is administered by a district-level social welfare office.

RECOMMENDATIONS

11. The high share of family-assistance spending that prevailed in 1992 is probably unsustainable. Some principles must be adduced to govern the means by which the obligations of the state are trimmed back to a level that can be financed. The alternative is simply to allow inflation and the chance adjustments of benefit levels to provide social protection: experience in OECD countries indicates that the result will be greater suffering for the poor than would be necessary if a fully-articulated policy were to be adopted.

PROTECTING A POVERTY LINE

12. A principle that has guided analysis in other countries of Eastern Europe and the former Soviet Union is that those who are poor, or are likely to be made poor by the events associated with the collapse of output, must be *protected fully* against erosion of their levels of living. The means of protection is provision of adequate subsidies and social services. A first step in turning principle to practice is the establishment of a realistic poverty line, that is, a level of living below which no one should be permitted to fall. The first of these specific and calculated poverty lines was applied in the United States during the War on Poverty in the 1960s. It defined as poor those families that must devote more than one-third of their income to the purchase of food. Many countries have applied a similar standard but with a larger share of income allocable to food. In the poor countries of South Asia and Sub-Saharan Africa, for example, only households that allocate two-thirds or more of their expenditure to food are included among poverty groups. Such a measure is difficult to apply in Ukraine because the prices of commodities that would constitute a large share of food consumption are kept well below international prices. Before 1993, most households allocated a small share of income to food; by this measure, only a tiny percentage of the population live in poverty. But with higher real prices in 1993, the share is rising

13. There is an urgent need for development of the methodological and statistical basis for identifying those groups whose incomes the government must protect. The basket of goods currently used to measure movements in the aggregate level of prices is weighted too much toward commodities consumed among urban middle-income earners. A different basket of goods reflecting consumption by rural and urban lower-income earners is required. Development agencies are currently providing technical assistance to other republics of the former Soviet Union that aims to improve capacity to measure the impact on real incomes of variable price movements for farm and non-farm products. This assistance could usefully be extended to Ukraine. Early in 1993, the French statistical agency began a program for technical assistance in household and enterprise survey design and analysis for the benefit of Ukraine's Ministry of Statistics.

14. Pending development of an income-measurement tool, near-to-medium-term safety net policies could be built on the available knowledge about demographic characteristics, such as family size, structure, and composition, and including features of residence, disability, and dependency on friends or relatives outside

the household, as well as economic means that include the ability to work and to earn from past savings. Analysis of 1989 census data would reveal details about the numbers eligible for the food allowance provided to low-income families by oblast and subregion. Experience in the United States and the United Kingdom shows that one-third or more of all families and individuals eligible for various benefits do not collect them because of ignorance of their eligibility or the stigma that may attach to welfare dependence. The costs of social protection in Ukraine could be significantly affected by public attitude toward assistance programs.

15. The identification of those poor and vulnerable enough to require public assistance will change, perhaps dramatically, over time if unemployment strikes specific regions or single-industry towns, so government must have the capacity to monitor continuously and reshape its policies to address new needs. Once the groups and their needs are identified, the government must then establish benefit levels necessary to keep those at risk out of poverty. As prices continue to rise, benefits would, of course, have to be adjusted periodically to assure respect for the principle that those at risk be fully protected.

PREFERENTIAL TREATMENT FOR THE POOR

16. A second principle is that all benefits above the poverty line should be continued only to the extent that resources permit. The collapse in output, should it continue into 1993 and beyond, will severely limit the capacity of the state to make transfer payments to retirees, the disabled, and other pensioners, as well as to Chernobyl victims, workers on sick leave, families with minor children, and, most notably, the unemployed and displaced workers. Available resources may be driven down, for a time at least, to a level that would permit no payments, even those representing clear and certain obligations of government, beyond social protection for the poor and vulnerable. At that point, government must make hard choices that distinguish falling into poverty from maintenance of a reasonable standard of comfort. Inaction, or lack of a clear policy choice in favor of protecting those at greatest risk, would probably

result in acute misery for a significant share of the poorest, particularly the rural elderly living alone and children in single-parent households.

BEYOND THE CRISIS

17. In the longer run, the principles of risk sharing, social insurance, and earnings-related benefits should gradually be restored as the economy strengthens and public obligations no longer constitute a threat to macroeconomic stability. The treatment of these insurable risks varies widely from country to country, with some countries, such as the United States, giving preference to private markets, and others, especially among EC members, depending on the state, to finance and provide insurance (Barr, 1992). Whatever mechanism is chosen, these markets confront the dual problems of *moral hazard*, which is the risk that individuals will change their behavior because of the contractual relationship provided by insurance, and *adverse selection*, which is the tendency of asymmetric knowledge to lead to unsustainable outcomes. The best-known example and result of moral hazard is the savings-and-loan crisis in the USA, in which the government insured depositors against loss but allowed savings banks to make risky loans ending in their bankruptcy. An example of adverse selection is the unwillingness of private insurers to write contracts with individuals in demographic groups, by age, sex, and marital status, that have a high probability of contracting AIDS. Both phenomena lead to unacceptable outcomes for public and private approaches to insurance against social risk. Ukraine will want to consider its options carefully before committing to one approach of social insurance.

18. Unemployment insurance and workers' compensation are prepaid benefits with fee schedules that vary by industrial group according to risk in many OECD countries. They are financed from variable risk premiums by employers and thus have, over time, become integrated into labor costs in the several branches of trade and industry. Successful social insurance schemes protect members of many societies from income loss associated with illness and aging and against the risks of high costs for health care where private medicine

prevails. The government can create a regulatory framework that encourages savings so that individuals and families self-insure for their old age and other financial needs and risks that differ widely from person to person. All these steps require a broad legal framework that defines private-sector development and its responses to the demand for financial services that help reduce social risk. Experience among Eastern European countries in recent years indicates that false steps in these areas, particularly in the design of unemployment and health-insurance schemes, may prove to be costly and thus must be carefully conceived prior to implementation.

Vulnerable Groups

19.   Allowances (except sick pay, maternity leave, short-term disability and benefits for Chernobyl victims) should be offered only to families in specific vulnerable groups. The government's current policy of providing some benefits to all families and others targeted to low-income groups is flawed in two respects. The provision of general subsidies is inappropriate because allowances should be made available only to families who cannot obtain a basic level of subsistence without government aid. The assignment of benefits to recipients because of low income creates a disincentive for the poor to work. If they work more, they are likely to raise their income and disqualify themselves for benefits. Also, eligibility based on demographic characteristics is easier to monitor than eligibility based on income. Therefore, benefits should be assigned on the basis of demographic characteristics.

20.   Savings from this program modification would be at least 25 percent of total allowance spending and 40 percent of non-Chernobyl-related allowance spending in the first year it was implemented.[36]

Unnecessary Benefits

21.   Special benefits for servicemen's families, cars (or the cash equivalent) for some disabled persons, telephone service for veterans, and free access to vacation camps could be eliminated. Given the critical state of the economy, the state should provide only those allowances required for families to meet basic subsistence needs.

22.   Savings from the elimination of the above-specified benefits would be about 5.5 percent of the total allowance budget and 9 percent of non-Chernobyl expenditures in the first year.

Enterprise Administration of Allowances

23.   Enterprises should be insulated from the administration and distribution of allowances. These activities take resources away from enterprises' real mission--the production and sale of goods and services. Furthermore, requiring firms to undertake allowance administration places an unfair burden on small firms that do not have a system in place for performing this function.

24.   Eliminating enterprises' responsibilities in this area will transfer a burden onto the district social welfare offices. The state should devise a strategy to prepare these offices to accommodate their increased work load. The end of employer responsibility for allowance administration should be deferred until state offices are adequately prepared.

Chernobyl Allowances

25.   More than two-thirds of the volume of Chernobyl allowances and over one-quarter of the volume of total allowances are accounted for by salary bonuses to people working in the region affected by the Chernobyl accident, or working with contaminated materials. Rather than providing state-funded allowances to workers who are mandatory or voluntary transferees to the region, the enterprises in this area should attract workers via higher salaries and additional benefits if necessary. The state government's only role should be to ensure that candidates for this work have full information concerning the nature and degree of the risk they are undertaking.

26.   Most work in the area involves state-funded clean-up operations and social services. Thus, to the extent that workers' current salaries

and state subsidies represent a market-clearing wage, this policy modification will not result in a net savings to the government. It will, however, provide a more flexible and efficient means of determining appropriate compensation for this work.

Aggregate Spending

27.   Spending on allowances could be cut from 8.8 percent of GDP in 1992 and to a much smaller share of GDP in 1993 and the years thereafter (see Table 7.3, in which the numbers are indicative, not prescriptive, of the options facing the authorities). The main strategy is to target benefits on vulnerable groups. Costs for Chernobyl-related allowances are assumed eventually to decline as problems are solved. Administrative costs included in programs should also decline with consolidation.

Table 7.3: Current, Suggested, and Sustainable Policy for Allowances

Spending Category	Percent of Gross Domestic Product			Policy Actions Required
	1992 Budget	Suggested Program for 1993	Sustainable Program Beyond 1993	
Income Targeted	3.2	1.9	1.9	Target benefits to vulnerable groups
Not Income Targeted	2.0	0.9	0.9	Target benefits to vulnerable groups; eliminate unnecessary benefits
Chernobyl-Related[1]	3.4	3.4	0.6	Replace allowance for Chernobyl workers with higher salaries; eliminate housing and food subsidies as they become unnecessary
Administration	0.1	0.1	0.1	
Total	8.7	6.3	3.5	

Note: 1.   Forecasts of 1992 Chernobyl spending on the social sector that were made in July varied between 1.1 percent and 3.4 percent of GDP. Final data were not available for this report.

8
EDUCATION AND TRAINING

1.   This chapter offers a brief description of Ukraine's education and training system; identifies some of its distortions and weaknesses in the light of the new challenges facing the nation; and suggests some changes and recommends external technical and financial assistance which the Ukrainian authorities should consider to complement their own efforts. The analysis and description are far less thorough in this chapter than the subject merits. The reason is that education is in better condition than some other areas of public social spending so that reforms can be deferred. Moreover, basic change in education must occur with full regard for protection of the effective parts of the system. Vocational and technical training receive the fullest discussion because reform there must complement the shift of labor to a market economy.

2.   The education system's coverage is extensive from preschool through secondary, and enrollment rates at post-secondary level compare favorably with the rest of Europe. The dropout rate is negligible and the repetition rate is very low. Teacher qualifications are high, with most teachers in urban areas having several years of post-secondary education. The performance of the Soviet Union's secondary students in mathematics and the sciences has ranked high in international surveys and contests. More recently, Ukraine has scored very well in competitions among the Soviet republics.

3.   As part of the Soviet Union, Ukraine was well served by an education system that produced well-trained, specialized graduates to meet the needs of a command economy. The success of Ukraine's education system contributed significantly to the Soviet Union's emergence as a world leader in aerospace technology. But now that Ukraine has achieved nationhood, its aspirations and objectives are different from those of the former Soviet Union.

Ukraine aims to move toward a democratic political system with a market economy that will be integrated into the world economy. The government recognizes that its education system will have to play a crucial role in promoting these objectives, and that it will have to undergo major changes and adjustments in its organization, structure, content, and pedagogy. Moreover, these reforms will have to be made under austere and restrictive public expenditure policies as the government strives to promote macroeconomic stability as a condition for economic recovery and the transition toward a market economy.

4.   The urgency of education reform was highlighted by the recent report, "Ukraine of the 21st Century: National Program of Educational Renaissance," presented in December 1992 to the All-Ukrainian Congress of Educationists.

THE EDUCATION SYSTEM: DIMENSIONS AND STRUCTURE

5.   With a population of 52 million, Ukraine has 10.9 million full-time students enrolled in 47,500 establishments. Of these, 2.4 million children are preschoolers in 24,500 schools. The Ministry of Education oversees 32,000 establishments with 9.3 million students and preschoolers. These institutions employ 1,830,000 people, of whom 1,130,000 are teachers, making for an overall student/staff ratio of a little over 5:1. There are also hundreds of thousands of part-time students at vocational and post-secondary institutions. In addition, the larger enterprises also do a considerable amount of education and training. The overall student-teacher ratio in Ukraine is 8.2 compared with 15.3 in developed countries and 24.3 in developing countries (see Table 8.1). Ukrainian education authorities, who argue that more teachers are needed, dispute the comparability of the figures and

ratios shown in Table 8.1. Further study of the staffing issue is essential.

6.   In the 1980s, the number of teachers' college graduates nearly doubled, while

Table 8.1: Student/Teacher Ratios in Ukraine and Other Countries, 1989

	Ukraine	Developed Countries	Developing
Total Enrollment (millions)	9.3	231.2	720.3
Number of Teachers (millions)	1.13	15.1	29.7
Student / Teacher Ratio	8.2	15.3	24.3

Source: Ministry of Education and UNESCO Statistical Yearbook 1991. Data for developed and developing countries are for 1989. Ukraine data exclude part-time students.

education graduates at high-level institutions increased by 60 percent. The delivery of services was growing inefficient as the education sector absorbed the aspirations of many to join the intelligentsia. This demand for upward mobility in turn contributed to serious current issues: (1) the large amount of funds dedicated to education, particularly the share (over 75 percent in 1992) that must be allocated to salaries; (2) the ongoing complaints from teaching staff that salaries are too low and the ill-conceived plan to raise them to the level of industrial wages without any performance incentives; (3) the pressure, under conditions of inflation experienced recently in Ukraine, for nominal salaries to rise; (4) the inadequacy of supplies and space, revealed by the fact that over 1 million children are in double-shift classes; and (5) the desire of political authorities to respond positively to the wage demands of the largest element of the public sector work force, which is the teachers, who, with the relaxation of centralized authority under the former Soviet Union, seek to better their condition by threatening strikes and other labor actions that democratically elected officials cannot easily

ignore. This combination of factors presents the Government of Ukraine with a serious challenge as it tries to combine fiscal responsibility with attention to the legitimate demands of some of its most important and numerous public servants. Moreover, teachers have become, as they are in most countries, a political force of considerable strength.

SECTOR ORGANIZATION

7.   The current Ministry of Education's responsibilities result from the merging of three separate ministries on April 1, 1992. Other ministries, notably Health, Agriculture, and Culture, administer much of the education and training in health, agriculture and the arts. Because of this recent merger, the Ministry of Education is still in the process of organizing itself. For example, it compiles data only on post-secondary education (inherited from the former Ministry of Higher Education) while the Ministry of Statistics is responsible for data on the rest of the education sector. The Ministry of Education manages about 60 percent of the country's post-secondary institutions, including most of its research institutes, all of its universities, all technical secondary schools, and about 20 percent of secondary vocational schools, and also oversees the curricula of oblast (district) and regional as well as private schools. Other ministries are responsible for most of the secondary vocational schools and about 40 percent of specialized post-secondary institutions. For example, the Ministry of Health funds and oversees the medical schools.

Preschool Education and Day Care

8.   Ukraine has one of the most extensive networks of preschool education and day care centers in the world. The 2.4 million children that attend these institutions comprise 47 percent of the country's preschool-age (under six) population (53 percent in urban areas and 34 percent in rural areas). A third are funded and administered by the Ministry of Education, and oblast and local governments, two-thirds by enterprises, and a few others are private (Figure 8.1). The demand for these preschool and day care programs is on the decline. Recent legislation gives mothers leave at full pay during

pregnancy and through the first six months of the child's life and half pay for the subsequent two and a half years. This incentive to increase maternal time with infants and toddlers reduces the demand for day care. Another reason for the decline is that primary schools are starting to accept children at the age of six rather than seven, which was common in the past. There is growing resistance in many state enterprises to financing and managing preschool programs for children of their employees and others in their communities. The gradual transfer of these responsibilities to local governments will be one of the principal education issues of 1993.

Primary and Lower Secondary Education

9.   Primary and secondary schools in Ukraine are treated in combination and described as general education schools. Enrollment in primary through lower secondary (ninth grade) is compulsory and almost universal, except for isolated rural areas. There are nearly 7 million students (of whom 180,000 attend evening or correspondence schools) enrolled in 20,900 general education schools. These include 700 boarding schools for children without parents, the mentally retarded and physically

handicapped, and 12 special schools for children and teenagers who are "socially dangerous." The student/teacher ratio was 12.8 in the 1991-92 academic year (see Table 8.2). Between the academic years 1990-91 and 1991-92, enrollment dropped by 16,000 while the number of teachers rose by 6,000.

Table 8.2: Enrollment and Teachers in Primary and Secondary Schools, 1991-92

Indicator	Value
Total Enrollment (thousands)	6,918
No. of Teachers (thousands)	538
Student/Teacher Ratio	12.8

Source: Ministry of Statistics, Ukraine.

10.   Municipal and regional governments operate and fund the overwhelming majority of the country's primary, general secondary, and night schools. Oblast governments operate and fund some secondary vocational and night schools and the country's specialized schools for orphans and handicapped children. Oblasts also subsidize education spending by poorer regions.

11.   The content and style of general

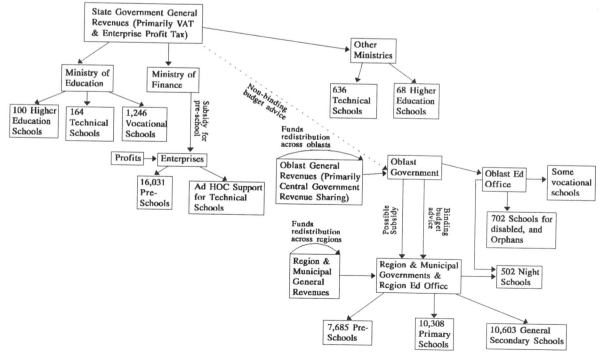

Figure 8.1: Diagram of Education Financing Flows and Organization of the School System

education has reflected the political and economic system and doctrines of the Soviet regime. It has been centrally controlled, with a uniform and rigid curriculum, a heavy emphasis on rote learning, and a pervasive ideological orientation in the teaching of the humanities and the social sciences. Nevertheless, the performance of secondary school students in mathematics and the sciences has measured up to the standards of middle and high-income countries.

12. A growing number of Ukrainian educators have become aware of the weaknesses in the above practices and have started to experiment with offering electives to secondary school students, adding new courses to the conventional curriculum and opening new schools for academically gifted children, but much more remains to be done.

13. General education appears to be of high quality, but there are not enough classrooms, infrastructure services, and satisfactory textbooks for multi-grade classes and other special needs. More than a third of the students in urban areas attend double-shift schools. About one-third of the rural schools have no water supply or central heating, and more than half have no indoor plumbing. Many of the rural schools, especially at the primary level, serve small catchment areas that have produced high costs per student and offer inferior education. Busing of students, that would enlarge the catchment areas and the size of the schools, is not widely practiced, allegedly because of the lack of, or poor quality of roads, and the shortage of buses, and currently of gasoline. These small rural schools undoubtedly contribute to the low student-teacher ratio in Ukraine's education system compared to those of other countries.

Streaming

14. Upon completion of ninth grade, students go on to one of three streams, depending mostly on their academic performance, and to a much lesser extent on their choices. Some 60-70 percent continue their general education for two more years and complete their secondary education; another 20-25 percent enter vocational schools; and around

10 percent go to technical schools. According to Ukrainian officials, the "most talented" students complete their general secondary education. Students in vocational and technical schools receive monthly government stipends, while general education students do not.

Vocational and Technical Schools

15. There are 1,246 vocational and technical schools with an enrollment of 650,000 students, excluding on-the-job training in enterprises, for which there are no centrally collected data. These schools produced an estimated 380,000 graduates who entered the labor market last year. Students generally attend vocational schools for three and a half years after completing ninth grade. They receive a certificate for the specialty they have studied and enter the labor market. Quite often, they are engaged by enterprises before graduating and work part-time for these enterprises while they are still in school.

16. The amount of schooling that students have when entering vocational schools varies widely. About 20 percent enter vocational schools after completing ninth grade, about half after the eleventh grade, and the rest are students with fewer than nine years of general education. All entering students take exams to determine which specialty they should study. There is little doubt that vocational education is the most diverse, diffused, and least structured part of the education system. It is in transition to a program that could better serve the nascent private sector.

17. The large number of narrow specialties is a legacy of the Soviet Union's command economy that required the education system to produce workers to fill specific jobs that were called for by the national economic plan. There are now 808 specialized crafts and occupations offered by vocational schools; this compares with 1,200 that were available in the Soviet era. There is a general awareness that there are too many specialties and that they are too narrow. The Ministry of Education is considering a proposal to reduce the number of specialties to around 300.

18.   The mission visited a representative vocational school in Kiev with 700-800 students, 74 teachers, of whom 45 teach practical subjects and are called "supervisors," and 71 administrative and maintenance personnel. The school offered three crafts: construction, auto mechanics, and painting and decorating. These crafts had formerly been offered in the form of nine more specialized ones. The construction and painting specialties were products of the school's history. The school was founded immediately after World War II and concentrated on training 12,000 construction workers to repair the war damage in Kiev. The director of the school told the mission that Kiev had eight vocational schools specializing in construction, too many in relation to current and future demand in the years ahead. The director recently visited a number of vocational schools in Germany and observed that vocational training in Ukraine was much more theoretical than in Germany and that the workshops in the German schools were much better equipped with state-of-the-art technology than those in Ukraine. Costs per student appear to be high, as is evidenced by a brief review of the school's budget for the first quarter of 1992, which showed that the projected annual cost per student amounted to the starting annual salary of a teacher.

19.   The vocational school system does have some capacity to retrain workers, but the size and content of this capacity has not been estimated. While the mission was in Ukraine, the government announced a program for retraining military personnel who have been stationed in East Germany. The retraining will be carried out by vocational schools, technicums, and polytechnics. Strengthening vocational and technical training is a major objective that would require significant external assistance. The Ministry of Education funds and manages all vocational schools.

Technicums

20.   The technicums are comparable to the *fachschule* of Germany. Most students enroll in them after completing their general secondary education (11 years), though about 20 percent enter after the ninth grade. Each technicum sets its own entrance exam and each applicant can apply to only one institution and propose three alternative programs of study or specialties. Admission is based on exam scores and academic performance in secondary schools. If an applicant is denied admission, he or she can reapply to the same institution or apply to some other technicum after waiting a year or sometimes less.

21.   A proposal is being considered by the Ministry of Education to modify the admission process to allow students to apply to three technicums and indicate an order of preference. The entrance exam would be the same for every technicum. This system would improve the chances for admission for the better applicants and improve the overall quality of the students in technicums, according to its proponents. It would also reduce the scope for using connections and bribes to gain admission for otherwise unqualified applicants. The proposed system is similar that in some Western European countries for selecting applicants to colleges and universities. The admission process for technicums has aroused controversy because competition for admission to certain programs has become very keen. For example, in Kiev, there have been three to four applicants for each place in the program of radio-electronics program and eight for each place in economics and management.

22.   Most students (those who enter after the eleventh grade), spend two years in a technicum before receiving diplomas as junior specialists; others who enter at an earlier stage, put in four years. Technicum graduates can enter the labor market or go on to university for another two or three years before receiving the equivalent of a bachelor's or first degree.

23.   The mission visited a technicum in Kiev that specialized in radio-electronics. It has 1,136 full-time students and 300 in evening courses, has 54 teachers, and 36 administrative and 52 maintenance personnel. The school's applicant/acceptance ratio was 10:1 in 1989, 5:1 in 1990 and 1991, and 2.3:1 in 1992. The director of the technicum explained the sharp drop in the number of applicants by saying that the word had gotten around about how difficult

it was to gain admission to his technicum. As in the lower levels of the education system, the curriculum for each specialty is fixed and there are no electives. The school has started to introduce "commercial" subjects such as market economics, finance, marketing and management. It does not use regular teachers, but relies on part-time teachers who are employed in enterprises. Since suitable textbooks are not available, the school is using notes prepared by the teachers of the various subjects. The current costs per student amount to five months of the starting salary for teachers.

24. The Ministry of Education funds and manages about 20 percent of technicum schools, virtually all of the rest are funded and managed by other ministries. A few are funded and managed by oblasts.

Higher Education

25. Ukraine has many institutions of higher learning. Table 8.3 shows a count of institutions by curricular categories. It is drawn from a recent statement by the Ministry of Education describing Ukraine's educational system.

Table 8.3: Types of Institutions of Higher Learning in Ukraine

Type of Institution	Number
Life Sciences, Humanities, and Economics/Law	104
Engineering/Technical	309
Transportation and Communication	55
Agriculture	123
Health Care	126
Physical Education and Sports	6
Pedagogical Studies	78
Art and Allied Fields	89

Table 8.3 includes almost entirely technicums and other post-secondary specialized institutions. The overall student/faculty ratio, counting only full-time students, is less than 5:1, which is below the ratio in most developed countries (see Table 8.4). Ukraine has 11 universities with a wide variety of faculties and departments (see Table 8.5).

26. The system of post-secondary education is extremely diffuse and complex; teacher training can be cited as an example: Pedagogical education is conducted by 29 pedagogical institutes with one affiliate, 51 pedagogical schools, 6 industrial-pedagogical colleges and technicums. Specialists for various types of educational establishments are trained in 19 major specialization areas in the pedagogical institutes, in 5 major professions in pedagogical schools, and 12 professions in industrial-pedagogical colleges and technicums.

27. The distinction between undergraduate and postgraduate education is blurred. The "Candidate of Science" degree is roughly equivalent to a Master's degree and the "Doctor of Sciences" degree to a doctorate. Ukrainian officials are aware of the need to clarify, consolidate, and streamline the post-secondary institutional setup. Given the plethora of institutions, it is not surprising that they are of uneven quality; the Ministry expects to introduce an accreditation system. There is also an effort under way to internationalize post-graduate education by having clearly defined bachelor's, master's and doctoral degrees similar to those in North America and some Western European countries.

28. Kiev State University was founded in 1836. Much of it was destroyed during World War II, but it has been fully restored. Its 17 faculties offer 42 specialized programs of study to a student body of 20,000, including 2,000 foreign students, mostly from Africa, Vietnam, and Afghanistan. As the most prestigious university in Ukraine, it draws 70 percent of its students from outside Kiev.

29. Its staff of 8,000 includes 2,000 faculty, 2,000 scientific researchers, 1,000 scientific administrators, 1,700 auxiliary personnel, and 1,300 administrative and maintenance personnel. The number of students given above is substantially greater than that in Table 8.5 because the former figure includes part-time students. The number of faculty shown in Table 8.5 includes a large number of researchers. The student/staff ratio of 2.5:1 appears extraordinarily low, even if the research personnel are subtracted. It is also surprising to

find almost half of the staff devoted to research, since most research is done in specialized institutes.

30. The Kiev Institute of National Economy, founded in 1908, offers a "National Education Certificate" in economics, banking, finance, and statistics to 12,000 students. The minimum educational requirement for admission is the successful completion of eleventh grade; some students enter after graduating from a technicum. The former take five years to receive a certificate and the latter three years.[37] The Institute staff of 1,760 includes 600 faculty and 160 auxiliary personnel. The curriculum of the Institute is changing as Ukraine moves towards a market economy. The rector attaches high priority to training his faculty in market economics and subjects appropriate to a market economy. He has started to make some foreign contacts for technical assistance. The Institute recently established a Business School that offers courses ranging from one month to a year. It has begun operating on a very limited scale and expects to expand rapidly. The Business School faces same problem as the rest of the Institute: how to train

its faculty to teach courses appropriate to a business school in a market economy. They have had a few visiting professors from abroad who have come for a few days or weeks, but much more needs to be done, especially in the production of suitable teaching materials.

Table 8.4: Enrollments and Faculty in Ukrainian Universities and in Equivalent Institutions in Selected Countries, 1991-92.

Country	Student Enrollment (000)	Number of Faculty (000)	Student/Faculty Ratio
France	1,124	46	24.4
Federal Republic of Germany	1,465	151	13.3
Italy	1,349	54	25.0
Korea	1,143	34	33.6
Spain	978	51	19.2
United States	7,716	494	15.6
Ukraine	67	14	4.8

Note: Data for Ukraine are not strictly comparable with those for other countries because they cover only the eleven universities in Ukraine and not "equivalent institutions." But this does not alter the fact that the student/faculty ratio is much lower than in the other countries. Data for the latter are for 1989 and 1992 for Ukraine

Source: For Ukraine: Ministry of Education; for other countries: UNESCO Statistical Yearbook 1991.

Table 8.5: Ukraine Universities, Students, Faculty, and Graduates, 1992

University	No. of Departments	No. of Full-Time Students	No. of Faculty	No. Holding Equivalent of Masters	No. Holding Equivalent of Doctorate
Dnepropetrovsk State University	12	8,835	1,277	559	83
Donetsk State University	11	5,593	1,062	524	64
Kiev State University	19	12,200	3,612	1,079	293
Lviv State University	13	7,230	1,911	529	96
Odessa State University	9	5,306	807	473	83
Simferopol State University	8	3,962	538	267	38
Ujgorof State University	10	4.340	916	329	75
Karkiv State University	12	6,845	1,857	875	129
Zapojie State University	10	3,893	553	193	25
Tchernovits State University	12	5,487	885	375	47
Karkiv Law Institute	4	3,188	371	184	40
Total		66,879	13,789	5,187	973

Source: Ministry of Education, Ukraine.

EDUCATION FINANCING AND THE USE OF RESOURCES

31.   Ukraine allocated 7.8 percent of GDP to education in the 1992 budget, one of the largest proportions in the world and the highest among countries at comparable levels of development (Table 8.6). This high percentage of GDP is partly due to the sharp decline in Ukraine's GDP since 1989.

32.   In the euphoria that accompanied Ukraine's political independence, the Law on Education was enacted, calling for a minimum expenditure on education amounting to 10 percent of GDP. This target would be extremely difficult to attain and sustain. It is also highly questionable whether the education sector should absorb such a large share of the nation's resources in view of the pressing needs in the rest of the economy.

33.   About 28 percent of total education spending is funded from general state revenues and managed by the Ministry of Education and other ministries. About 57 percent is managed by oblast regional and village governments and funded from their general revenues. Enterprises account for the remaining 15 percent of education expenditures.

34.   What accounts for the large amount of spending on education? The explanation has to be found in the large share of the budget that the Ministry of Education and local governments spend on wages and salaries, utilities and maintenance (Table 8.7). Wages are low, but there are so many personnel that the aggregate

Table 8.6: International Comparison of Spending on Public Education, 1990, and Ukraine, 1992

Country or Region	Percent of GNP Spent on Public Education
Ukraine, 1992	7.8
Europe, including former USSR	5.5
Developed Countries	5.8
Developing Countries	3.8
The World	5.5

Sources: UNESCO Statistical Yearbook, 1991, and Ukraine Ministry of Finance

wage bill is high. Another factor that has contributed to the recent growth of the education budget is the large increase in the cost of utilities.

Budgeting Process

35.   The budgetary process is evolving. From the mid-1970s to 1991, budgeting was done on a top-down basis. The Ukraine Ministry of Finance produced a budget for the Republic that had to be approved by the Ministry of Finance of the Soviet Union. Ukraine's Ministry of Finance then distributed funds to the districts which in turn channelled them to the schools. In 1992, the budgeting process was reversed from top-down to bottom-up, with individual schools preparing their own budgets in accordance with staffing and input norms based on enrollments. School budgets are consolidated for each region and have to be approved by regional governments.

36.   Budgeting in 1992 was fraught with uncertainty and instability. In presenting its first national budget to the legislature, the government had to submit four successive budgets before getting the approval of the Supreme Soviet of Ukraine. School principals have very little flexibility in spending their funds, nearly all of which are earmarked for salaries and wages, student stipends, utilities and food. Schools do not have bank accounts, but do receive a small amount of discretionary funds for materials and equipment that have to be bought in specially designated stores. They can also handle small emergencies such as repairing broken windows during winter. It could be useful to begin program budgeting in the Ministry of Education since it is in the process of reviewing education goals. Management by objective could help the ministry reallocate resources to priority spending areas; external assistance and expertise could be helpful in that process.

37.   Oblast finance and/or education offices help schools in the budgeting process by providing information about current education input costs and norms concerning staffing and equipment needs per student population at each grade level. These norms are uniform for urb

Table 8.7: Forecast 1992 Education Spending

Expenditure	1992 Budget (million rubles)	Percent Total Govt. Ed Budget	Percent Total Ed Expenditures	Percent of GDP
TOTAL STATE/LOCAL BUDGET	181,756	100.0	85.5	6.7
Total Personnel Costs	99,286	54.6	46.7	
Wages and Bonuses	72,648	40.0	34.2	
Payroll Tax (37 percent)	26,638	14.7	12.5	
Stipends	10,323	5.7	4.9	
Capital Repair	5,443	3.0	2.6	
Equipment Purchase	5,037	2.8	2.4	
Capital Investment	1,739	1.0	0.8	
Textbooks	980	0.5	0.5	
Computers	537	0.3	0.3	
Other (Inc. utilities and maintenance)	58,411	32.1	27.5	
Enterprises (16,031 Preschools)[1]	30,812	NA	14.5	1.1
TOTAL	212,567		100.0	7.8

Notes: Mission estimate based on spending per preschool by the state government.
1. Mission estimate based on day care spending by the state government.

Sources: June 1992 draft of the Ministry of Education's 1992 budget, the Ministry of Finance's June 1992 draft consolidated local education budget, mission estimates.

an and rural schools, and are suggestions rather than mandatory targets.

38.   In theory, regional and oblast finance offices carefully review and critique individual school budgets. In practice, these offices are not adequately staffed to undertake this function. The 1992 education budgets have been substantially modified almost every month since November 1991, owing to the unstable economic situation, and finance offices have time for little more than consolidation. The frequent revisions to the 1992 school budgets were time-consuming for all parties involved. While many schools have computers, they are used for teaching rather than administrative purposes. The chief of the finance office for Kiev oblast was not aware of any schools using computers for budgeting purposes.

39.   The Ministry of Finance (MOF) provides enrollment-based norms to Oblasts as recommendations, consolidates oblasts' education budgets, and advises them on their size and content. However, the MOF cannot require an oblast to modify its education spending. The state does not subsidize poorer oblasts' education spending directly, but Parliament, through the Council of Ministers and the Ministry of Finance, redistributes general revenues from richer to poorer oblasts.

40.   The Ministry of Education (MOE) derives its funds from central government general revenues, and the MOE's budget is subject to approval by the Ministry of Finance. According to Ukraine's Law on Education, the government is required by law to devote 10 percent of GDP to education. According to government forecasts, the state and local governments will devote approximately 6.7 percent of GDP to education in 1992.

Disbursements

41.   Schools undertake their own budget planning, but do not have their own bank accounts, and cannot purchase items on the open market. Each is awarded funds earmarked for teachers' and administrators' salaries, student stipends, utilities, and food based on the budget the school develops. In addition, the school receives an allowance of discretionary funds to spend on materials, equipment, etc. Schools are required to purchase these items in specialized education-materials stores. The size of these discretionary budgets is determined by school requests, resources available to the funding government body, and personal relationships between school and government administrators. Large discretionary items such as renovations must receive special approval and funding is determined on the basis of norms regarding size of area to be remodeled.

42.   Salaries for teachers and other education personnel were among the lowest in the economy. But, according to the recently enacted Law on Education, they were to be raised to the average wage level in manufacturing. They were more than doubled on May 1, 1992, though much of this increase only made up for the rapid inflation since the previous salary

increase. An anomalous situation of relative wages late in 1992 was that a school principal's salary exceeded that of a cabinet minister by 50 percent.

Non-Education Expenditures in Education

43.   In addition to tuition-free education at all levels, and free books and materials, the government provides free lunches to all students from preschool to university, and monthly stipends to all students in vocational schools and post-secondary institutions. The stipends amount to about 40 percent of the basic salary for teachers. The Ministry of Education also provides meals and clothing for students in vocational schools and housing and utilities for teachers in rural areas. These non-education outlays account for a significant share of the Ministry of Education budget.

External Assistance

44.   Ukraine's education sector is receiving remarkably little external assistance; examples encountered by the mission are few enough to be listed: seven foreign professors are due to teach economics at two universities in Kiev during the academic year 1992-93; Kiev State University has agreements with several foreign universities to exchange students and professors but there is no financing to implement them; the British Council is sponsoring a program to train 60 Ukrainian professors in accounting and auditing. The most substantial example of foreign technical assistance is a business school which is in the process of being established as a joint venture with the International Management Institute of Lausanne, Switzerland.

45.   This technical assistance is piecemeal, sporadic, and unorganized and falls woefully short of what is needed, perhaps because Ukraine developed few foreign contacts under the USSR government, especially outside the former Soviet bloc. There is strong and widespread interest in obtaining financial assistance for computer hardware and software; teaching aids such as audio and video cassettes for foreign language teaching; modern equipment for the workshops in vocational schools and technicums; communications

equipment; and paper for printing textbooks and other materials on new subjects such as market economics, finance, banking, and marketing. Technical assistance is needed to retrain professors and teachers, reform vocational education use of computers and other teaching aids, and reorganize post-secondary education.

46.   Education is absorbing too large a share of what is likely to be a shrinking national budget in the years ahead. The education budget is also too big in relation to the other high priority demands on the economy and compared with the relative size of education budgets of developed and middle-income countries. The following recommendations have financial implications that are intended to curtail and reduce public expenditures and to promote individual and family self-reliance. These recommendations provide for reductions in aggregate spending, but it should be possible to maintain quality through efficiency gains (see Table 8.8).

47.   The government should rescind the provision earmarking 10 percent of GDP for education as embodied in the Law on Education, and the 8 percent of GDP earmarked for culture; no country in the world approaches this level of spending. Earmarking portions of the national budget puts public authorities in a straitjacket that would impose a paralyzing rigidity on legislative and government action. It is a practice that is universally rejected by fiscal experts throughout the world.

48.   The government could aim to reduce education spending. Table 8.8 specifies several opportunities for reducing the size and scope of education spending that would cause little damage to education objectives. Student/teacher ratios could be significantly increased: if Ukraine adopted the developed countries' average, government personnel costs would have been 44 percent lower in 1992 and total education spending would have been 24 percent lower. Education spending would then have used 5.9 percent of GDP, which would be in line with countries throughout the world. Of course, a change of this magnitude could not be introduced in a single year.

49. Oblast and local governments now finance about one-quarter of the cost of preschool education programs, with the rest paid for by enterprises and parents. There is growing financial pressure on enterprises to reduce their share of this spending and the Ministry of Finance plans to subsidize these facilities. The government should resist filling this gap, leaving it instead to families to finance day care services. In fact, the Parliament recently took a backward step by enacting legislation that calls on the Ministry to provide free lunches for all

benefits could be reduced and targeted to students from needy families, as was done with student stipends before 1980. Targeting of benefits would promote equity, fiscal efficiency, and self-reliance.

51. The Ministry spends about 5 percent of its budget to finance the education and living costs of about 20,000 foreign students attending Ukrainian institutions. These students are mostly from Afghanistan, Angola, Mozambique, Ethiopia, and Vietnam. In view of the scarcity

Table 8.8: Current, Suggested, and Sustainable Spending on Education, 1993 and Beyond

Spending Category	Percent of GDP under Alternative Approaches			Policy Actions Required
	1992 Budget	Suggested Program for 1993	Sustainable Program Beyond 1993	
Personnel	3.6	3.4	2.8	Reduce staff by attrition
Stipends	0.4	0.3	0.2	Restrict to low-income families; reduce payments to foreign students
Buildings	0.3	0.3	0.2	
Equipment[1]	0.2	0.4	0.6	Increase purchases of essential software for training displaced workers.
Other[2]	2.2	2.0	1.8	Improve energy efficiency
Enterprises[3]	1.1	0.6	0.4	Shift costs to beneficiaries
Total	7.8	7.0	6.0	

Notes: 1. Includes computers, textbooks, and related teaching materials.
2. Includes utilities and maintenance.
3. Includes spending on day-care programs.

preschool children at an estimated cost of R4 billion a year, or more than 4 percent of the Ministry's 1992 budget. This legislation was reversed in 1993.

50. Ancillary costs unrelated to instruction have in recent years absorbed a growing share of the Ministry's budget. These costs include textbooks, student stipends, food, clothing for vocational school students, and housing and utilities for teachers in rural areas. Many of these outlays are legacies of the past. These

of resources, these expenditures should be cut. Early in 1993, the authorities decided to reduce to 2,000 the number of supported foreign students.

52. The government's goal of shifting from Russian to Ukrainian language instruction at all the levels of education should be pursued with the full recognition of the heavy costs of translating textbooks and retraining teachers. Until the current economic and financial crisis recedes, language conversion should proceed at

a prudent pace, influenced by the normal turnover of textbooks due to wear and tear.

53.   The country's 1,242 vocational schools, which far exceed the current and prospective needs, should consolidate, rationalize, streamline, and modernize their vocational education programs against a dated set of objectives.   A restructured program would assign a substantial role to enterprises and the private sector for conducting vocational education and training.   The Ministry should initiate an accelerated program for retraining teachers and producing materials to introduce new subjects such as market economics, finance, banking, and marketing, in post-secondary institutions.

54.   The budgeting process is norm based. The number of students forecast for each grade level largely determines staffing, facilities and equipment levels.   To enhance the system's ability to address specific educational objectives, and to enable administrators to better measure the costs of achieving these goals, increased attention should be given to program budgeting.

55.   The Ministry of Education, together with the larger post-secondary institutions, should establish contact with aid donors to obtain the benefits of the successful education and training experience of market economies.   These donors can provide the financial assistance for administrative and instructional staff at all levels of education in Ukraine to participate in external training, instructional conferences, and short visits by international experts to Ukraine.   The Ministry of Education should create a unit to provide a focal point for all technical assistance in the education sector.   This unit should not only become a repository of information on technical assistance, but also should develop the necessary expertise in the policies, practices, and procedures of donor agencies and organizations to assist Ukraine's educational institutions in obtaining technical assistance.

56.   As unemployment rises as a consequence of the reduction and elimination of government subsidies to enterprises, the Ministry of Labor and the enterprises themselves are expected to play a major role in retraining the unemployed for other jobs.   But the formal education system also has an important role to play in this effort, particularly vocational schools and post-secondary institutions.   The government should undertake a survey of the retraining capacity of the formal education system and define its national role in retraining.   Foreign technical assistance would be very helpful in carrying out this survey.

HEALTH SERVICES

1.   This chapter reviews the organization and management of health services, health finance, and current issues that need to be addressed to enhance sector efficiency and effectiveness. Between July, 1992 and March, 1993, the Government of Ukraine started to implement a number of the reforms suggested here.

HEALTH SYSTEM DEVELOPMENT

2.   Health system goals need to focus on reducing illness derived from preventible communicable diseases, chronic diseases, respiratory infections in children, tuberculosis in adults, alcoholism, smoking, and pollution. The challenge will be to redirect the present system so that it takes advantage of progress made internationally in the conceptualization of health and information on its determinants to meet new chronic-care needs of an aging population, and to contribute to the health and well-being of the whole population.

3.   Priority for protecting the health of adults and the elderly, as well as for the ongoing needs of children and vulnerable persons, will have to be maintained in the special context of added requirements to respond to the Chernobyl disaster and other ecological insults that undermine health status, and to the international interest such events have generated. It will be particularly important to separate real from imagined health effects of Chernobyl by relying on sound scientific principles and findings and limiting unnecessary institutionalization of separate programs to deal with them. Otherwise, the drain of Chernobyl-associated programs on the economy, and the attention and resources they divert from other area of real health needs, will leave parts of the population less well cared for than is necessary.

HEALTH SECTOR ORGANIZATION AND MANAGEMENT

Ministry of Health Structure

4.   The Minister of Health is part of the executive level of government and functions as the chief executive officer of the Ministry. The Ministry is organized around five functional lines of which four are headed by Deputy Ministers. The First Deputy Minister acts in the capacity of the Minister when he is away. The fifth line is headed by the Chief Financial Officer. Three key top level committees are the Executive Committee, the Academic Medical Council and the Pharmaceutical Committee. This senior level structure has direct responsibility for certain health care facilities, scientific research and teaching institutes, and general administrative and professional practice control over other health care institutions. The Ministry also has general administrative control over state distributing and manufacturing enterprises for pharmaceutical, general and medical supplies and medical technology. Sanitary epidemiological services, delivered through 780 centers and core public health services through 700 centers, are provided directly by the Ministry. Health programs, facilities and education are managed by the Ministry of Health, health offices reporting to oblast and regional governments, the Ministry of Education, and other ministries and enterprises (see Figure 9.1).

5.   The Ministry of Health (MOH) manages some specialized and teaching hospitals and clinics, research centers, and medical schools. In addition, the office has informal links with, and informal supervision of, oblast-level health offices. The Ministry of Education sponsors secondary-level health services training schools and schools for disabled children that combine education and health facilities. Some other ministries run their own clinics. The Ministry

of Social Welfare operates specialized programs and facilities for the elderly and disabled. Some enterprises operate sanitariums and clinics, and these are subsidized by the Social Insurance Fund. The Chernobyl Fund subsidizes Chernobyl victims' health care services provided by most of the above health care providers. Each oblast has its own health office reporting to the oblast presidential delegate. These offices run specialized hospitals and supervise and support regional-level health offices. Regional health offices report to regional governments and run the overwhelming majority of the nation's hospitals, polyclinics, sanitariums and public health projects.

Sources of Funds

6.   Health services are funded almost entirely by general government revenues and accounted for 7.4 percent of GDP in 1992 (see Table 9.1).[38] Resources raised through the Social Insurance payroll tax, 3.4 percent of health funding, subsidize workers' visits to sanitariums. The Chernobyl payroll tax accounted for about 2.3 percent of sector resources, and supported a variety of health care

for Chernobyl victims. Private individuals' expenditures finance only 3.3 percent of health services and are incurred primarily when public sector practitioners see patients in state-run facilities after official office hours. In addition, enterprises often provide clinics and sanitariums for workers and their families. Enterprise support for worker health care is shrinking rapidly as firms' profits decline.

Use of Funds

7.   Health care spending was budgeted at 17.5 percent of 1992 social sector spending, and 7.7 percent of GDP. Approximately 87 percent of health care spending is devoted to treatment facilities, and hospitals alone account for two-thirds of disbursements. Research and education account for about 3.3 percent of expenditures; public health, 2.7 percent;[39] pharmaceutical subsidies, 2.3 percent; and other expenditures, 4.7 percent. Each of the above-mentioned categories' share of total spending has been relatively constant over time (see Table 9.2). June 1992 forecasts called for wages to account for 27 percent of expenditures by the Ministry of Health and local health offices in 1992;

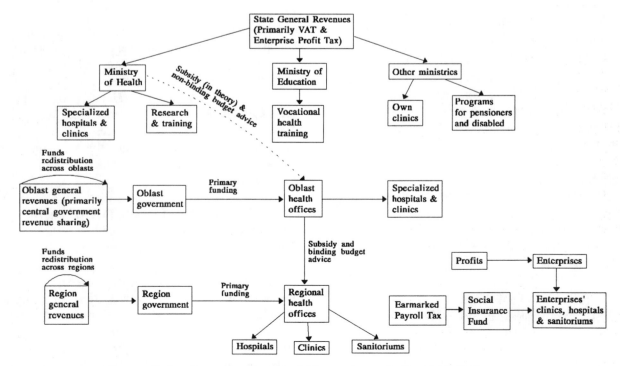

Figure 9.1: Organization and Financing of the Health System

equipment, 11 percent; drugs, 8 percent; and all other inputs (primarily maintenance of, and supplies for, facilities), 54 percent (Table 18).

8.   High and uneven inflation across health care inputs and increasingly restrictive budget constraints have precipitated large changes in the composition of spending over the last three years.   Since January, 1992 average health sector wages have been required by law to equal average industrial wages.   Despite this legislation and the resultant real wage growth in the health sector, wages will account for about 27 percent of total spending in 1992, down from 53 percent in 1989.   Maintenance of, and supplies for, facilities absorbed 25 percent of resources in 1991, up from only 13 percent the year before.   The Chief of Finance for the Ministry of Health predicts that these inputs'

share of total spending will continue to increase over time as their costs are rising much faster than general inflation.   Equipment spending increased from 3.9 percent of the health budget in 1989 to 11 percent in 1992.   Pharmaceuticals accounted for 10.6 percent of health care expenditures in 1989.   While pharmaceutical prices have risen faster than those of almost any other input, it has become extremely difficult to obtain drugs so that quantities available have fallen dramatically.   Construction outlays declined from 5.2 percent of total spending in 1989 to 0.1 percent in 1992, reflecting the fact that the state is focusing on immediate needs during the current budget crisis.

Budgeting Process

9.   In the past, budgeting was done on a top-down basis.   The Ministry of Health developed a budget for the entire Republic that had to be approved by the Ministry of Health for the USSR. This budget was funded from USSR general revenues.   Ukraine's Ministry of Health then distributed funds to each of the nation's oblasts and these funded regions which funded individual hospitals, clinics, and programs.   Budgeting was based on the number of hospital beds in service.   The state established how many hospital beds and clinic positions should be available per 10,000 people in a geographic area and, in turn, these requirements determined staffing and equipment levels and budgets.   No consideration was given to policy priorities, demographic characteristics of individual areas, or usage levels of individual facilities.

10.   In 1992, the budgeting process was reversed from top-down to bottom-up (Figure 9.1) so that individual hospitals and clinics prepared budgets that consolidated at the regional level into a health budget to be approved and funded by the regional government.   While funding for regional health facilities is derived

Table 9.1: Uses of Health Care Funds, 1992

	Total (million rubles)	Percent of Total	Percent GDP
Facilities	183,611	87.0	6.7
Hospitals	140,613	66.6	
Sanitariums	21,980	10.4	
Ambulatory Clinics	11,820	5.6	
Other Health Centers	5,171	2.5	
Ambulance Services	2,368	1.1	
Blood Transfusion Services	1,459	0.7	
Capital Construction	200	0.1	
Public Health[1]	5,778	2.7	0.2
Education	5,342	2.5	0.2
Subsidies for Pharmaceutical	4,835	2.3	0.2
Research	1,608	0.8	0.1
Other[2]	9,860	4.7	0.4
Total[3]	211,032	100.0	7.7

Notes: 1.   Additional public health expenditures are included in the budgets for specific facilities.
        2.   Additional treatment for Chernobyl victims and private payments for health services not included elsewhere.
        3.   Does not sum exactly due to rounding

Sources: June 1992 Drafts of the 1992 Budgets for the Ministry of Health, Social Insurance Fund, Chernobyl Fund, Pension Fund and Employment Fund.

from regional budgets, oblast governments can require regions to modify their health care spending, and sometimes provide subsidies to poorer regions. Also, oblasts redistribute revenues from richer to poorer regions, thereby reducing the disparity in social sector spending across regions. Since health care is funded primarily at the regional and oblast level, if a person receives treatment outside his home oblast, his city must compensate the facility for costs incurred.

11.   The MOH consolidates oblast budgets with budgets from national level facilities. The Ministry remains in a position to exercise control over methods and procedures in the delivery of treatment and care at the sub-national level, but it no longer has formal control over financial activities. In theory, the MOH can provide subsidies to poorer oblasts, but in practice the economic crisis has prevented it from doing so. The choice of budgeting procedures varies even within regions and is left largely to individual facilities. Budgeting is based either on the number of beds or people, or on the usage of specific services during the previous year. The Ministry of Health would like all budgeting to be done based on past usage of services. It cannot require this change in planning procedures, but has convinced many hospitals to make the switch voluntarily. Nevertheless, the Head of Finance of the Ministry of Health estimates that over one-half of Ukrainian hospitals used the norm-based budgeting system in July 1992.

12.   In previous years, budgeting was a once-a-year exercise. Due to the uncertainty of prices, wages, and government revenues, budget makers have revised their 1992 spending estimates every other month since November 1991. Revision is time consuming because the budgets are not computerized. In Kiev blast not even the oblast-level hospital uses a computer for this purpose. According to the Chief of Finance for the Health Office of Kiev oblast, most regional hospitals have computers, but they lack the software and training to use them for

Table 9.2: Percentage Distribution of Ministry of Health Spending on Local Health Inputs, 1989, 1991, and 1992

Inputs	Percent of Total		
	1989 Actual	1991 Actual	1992 Forecast
Wages	53.3	47.4	27.0
Maintenance and Supplies	13.4	25.4	NA
Pharmaceutical	10.6	6.3	8.0
Food	8.2	6.9	NA
Construct	5.2	2.1	0.1
Capital Repair	4.0	3.6	NA
Equipment	3.9	5.9	11.0
Other	1.4	2.4	NA
Total	100.0	100.0	100.0

Source: Ministry of Health

budgeting.

HEALTH SYSTEM RESOURCES

13.   The Ministry of Health oversaw 24,464 health facilities in 1991 which together employed 1,351,482 people, an increase in personnel of 2 percent from the previous year. The facilities include 48 scientific-research institutes (0.7 percent of total staff), 18 institutes of higher health education (1.7 percent of staff), 3,766 hospital facilities, 6,423 ambulatory centers as well as various other institutions such as ambulance centers and blood transfusion stations. The 3,766 hospital facilities had 671,096 beds (129.6 per 10,000 population). They are organized into a hierarchy of facilities at the district, central regional, city and oblast levels, as well as various specialty centers. There were 201,923 physicians employed (39.0 per 10,000) and 539,940 mid-level health personnel (104.2 per 10,000). The administrative complement was 61,219, or 5.7 percent of health care facility staff, which includes the 203 persons working for the Ministry and 15-30 staff for health administration at the oblast level. The Ministry staff is far too small to ensure both strategic management of the health system and responsiveness to questions and requests for information from the press, the public, and the legislature.

14.   There were 144 non-MOH hospital facilities in Ukraine and 501 ambulatory facilities with a total of 28,376 beds and 23,257 physicians in 1990, all run by other ministries and enterprises. The bed-and physician- supply ratios for Ukraine, with these facilities added, were 135.5 beds and 42.9 physicians per 10,000 in 1990, levels that are very high compared to the lowest OECD levels. For example, the low OECD bed supply rate is 21.0/10,000 and the low physician supply rate is 7.3/10,000, about one-sixth of the levels in Ukraine. The hospital admission rate in Ukraine in the Ministry of Health facilities is 24.3/100 population compared to the low OECD rate of 5.5/100; patient days per capita are 4.0 compared to the OECD low of 0.7; and length of stay is 16.5 days compared to the OECD low of 6.1 days.

15.   Even taking into account the poor status of facilities, equipment and their quality, there is a clear case for reducing the number of hospitals and staff. Closing some wards and whole facilities will permit re-deployment of resources to ensure their more effective use in health promotion, illness prevention, treatment, and rehabilitation. Removing expired and technologically inappropriate resources from the system would limit expectations that they will be replaced or modernized. Closing facilities will also make possible significant budget cuts to reduce the strain on the government budget.

CURRENT ISSUES

Shortages in Drugs, Supplies and Equipment

16.   The MOH needs a strategy for the pharmaceutical industry to secure inputs for production of basic drugs, supplies and equipment. The government should also encourage a major private sector role in the industry within an effective regulatory framework. In the past, Ukraine produced one-third of the 2,200 medical products produced in the former Soviet Union, but with many key inputs of raw materials coming from Russia, other former Soviet Union republics and the West. Only 8-10 percent of raw material inputs for production in Ukraine could be procured from within the country.

17.   Ministry officials report that in 1991, the equivalent of US$800 million of drugs and raw materials were imported to Ukraine principally from Soviet republics. In 1992, the value of imports dropped to zero because of the breakdown of exchange in the former Soviet Union and a hard currency shortage in Ukraine.

18.   The pharmaceutical and medical products industry is near collapse for lack of inputs. Barter among health care facilities was being used to obtain required drugs. Extensive substitution was common, often for drugs not considered an optimal choice for treatment. The most urgent needs identified by a visiting WHO team include the following items:

a)   drugs- insulin and oral anti-diabetics, hormones, including creams and ointments, anesthetics, bronchodilators, broad spectrum antibiotics and analgesics;

b)   supplies- glass and disposable syringes, needles, cold chain equipment, and renewable, basic, medical and surgical supplies; and

c)   equipment- insulin purification equipment/technology, clean room for aseptic production/technology, diagnostic, anaesthetic sterilization, and replacements for old, non-functioning and expired surgical equipment.

A way to clear the bottleneck needs to be found so that basic drugs and medical supplies can be obtained by importation or production, depending on the emerging comparative advantage of these potential industries in Ukraine.

19.   Ukraine needs technical assistance to help identify its areas of comparative advantage in pharmaceutical and medical equipment production. Donors could help finance imports of essential drugs and supplies for pharmaceutical production and technical assistance for short-term planning for procurement and distribution.

Blood Products

20.   There is no production of blood substitutes in Ukraine and the quality and

quantity of blood products available needs improvement. The Institute of Hematology and Transfusion, MOH, monitors the quality and safety of services provided by a network of some 630 blood transfusion centers. Three plasma fractionation facilities operate in Ukraine. The present system and facilities need to improve the safety of products and services, to increase the volume of production, and on a basis that supports priority needs of the health system, to increase the number of blood products available. Plasma production will need to be increased and a new plasma fractionation plant may be required. To achieve these ends will require a new central testing laboratory using Western reagents, the introduction of modern equipment and technology into the 27 blood centers to increase their production of plasma, and a computer-based management information system for monitoring and coordinating services. The starting point for such a program is a strategic plan for blood services, avoiding an expensive high-technology initiative that diverts attention from such seemingly prosaic, but critically important, health needs as programs for the elderly.

Training in Health

21.   Institutes for Higher Health Care Education train physicians in general practice, pediatrics, preventive medicine, dentistry, and pharmacy, with specialization in the final year. The system is being changed this year to improve quality. The MOH needs technical assistance in the form of training materials, curricula examinations, quality assurance, and total quality improvement methods and programs. From 1993, there will be a reduction in the intake of first-year students by 500 per year for a period of three years to achieve a norm of 34 physicians per 10,000 population. Some medical schools have been considered for closure, particularly in the western oblasts where there is an oversupply of physicians. Reducing intakes to medical training institutes is a sound beginning to medical human resources planning.

More needs to be done, including further review of the norm for physician supply, which is still higher than most OECD countries.

22.   Nurses are trained in 109 mid-level health education institutions reporting through oblast health administrations. These mid-level institutions train seven categories of health worker; about 30,000 nurses are trained per year. The roles of nurses and physicians are

Table 9.3: Sources of Funds for Health Care, 1992

Source	Total (million rubles)	Percent of Total	Percent of Govt Revenues[1]
State and Local General Revenues	191,987	91.0	12.3
Payroll Taxes	12,079	5.8	0.8
Social Insurance Fund	7,211	3.4	
Chernobyl Fund	4,868	2.3	
Individuals	6,967	3.3	NA
Total	211,032	100.0	13.5

Note: 1.   Includes state and local general revenues and resources of the Pension, Social Insurance, Employment and Chernobyl Funds.

Source: June 1992 Drafts of the 1992 Budgets for the Ministry of Health, Social Insurance Fund, Chernobyl Fund, Pension Fund and Employment Fund.

quite different from those in some OECD countries, with physicians providing much of the care nurses provide and nurses functioning like nursing auxiliaries. There are plans to decrease first year intakes and close some nursing schools. More consideration could be given to the future role of nursing in Ukraine in relation to international practice.

Legislative Reform

23.   A program of consolidation and reform of health legislation has been initiated as a result of moving legal responsibilities from Moscow to Kiev. This reform has produced several levels of draft legislation for eventual consideration by Parliament. Compared to Western health legislation, the present draft versions tend to include widely different types of functions in the same bill, ranging from general principles to budgetary matters such as the requirement to

spend no less than 10 percent of national income on health, to benefits relevant to an employment agreement. Advice from a team of health professionals with experience in developing health legislation that reflects contemporary health principles and system development directions would be valuable to Ukraine. The team would be likely to include a legal professional with significant experience in writing health legislation.

24. There is a need for all parties involved in developing legislation to become familiar with international directions before setting the basis for delivery of health services. These include the 1948 WHO Charter definition of health, the 1978 Alma Atta Declaration on Health for All and definition of primary care, the 1986 Ottawa Charter on Health Promotion, the 1988 Adelaide Consensus on Health Public Policy and the 1991 and 1992 Swedish and Brazilian agreements on a sustainable basis for health through reducing waste, avoiding overconsumption, and limiting environmental risks.

Perspectives on Value for Money Spent on the System

25. From the perspective of the recent past, Ukraine is likely to be getting reasonable value for the money spent on health care. Its health status indicators compare well with those of the former Soviet Union and a number of its former republics (with the exception of indicators such as with alcoholism, drug abuse, abortions, and congenital defects). Health status needs considerable improvement if it is to approach OECD levels. Yet health sector expenditures will have to shrink to reduce the pressures on the government budget. Several countries are able to do more with less;?; so can Ukraine.

Budget Cuts

26. Introducing greater efficiency into the health system is one important way of doing more with less. A valuable strategy is for the Ministry voluntarily to review the present budget and seek ways to reduce it but still maintain its services. Budget reduction must be done in a way that continues services provision to vulnerable groups. In particular, care must be

taken to maintain the *de facto* social service function carried out by clinics and feldsher stations in villages where there is a large elderly population, mainly female, that relies on local health facilities for support in daily living. The budget-cutting strategy should focus on measures that result in ongoing as well as one-time savings. Table 9.4 shows 1992 budget allocations for health, recommendations for 1993, and an estimated sustainable level of health spending beyond 1993. Ukraine historically used about 3 percent of GDP for health care, and government will have to cut back from the 7.7 percent of 1992. But reductions can offer a chance to improve efficiency and quality. By 1994, Ukraine could have a stronger and better system than it has today if the recommended changes are made.

Recommended Short-Term Action

27. The following steps are already under consideration in the MOH or, in selected cases, by early 1993, they had already been taken in whole or in part:

- **Outpatient Care.** Shift 30 percent of inpatient procedures and treatments to ambulatory care that can be done safely on an outpatient, ambulatory basis.

- **Personnel Norms.** Revise norms for bed and physician supply to make them closer to international comparator levels, and link staffing to the care needs of the patient not to the number of beds available.

- **Excess Capacity.** Withdraw unnecessary hospital beds from service, preferably by closing whole wards in order to gain full impact of staffing reductions; rationalize hospital service delivery by retaining only programs relevant to service area needs, especially in rural and oblast facilities, and closing nonviable, unnecessary hospitals.

- **Medical Education.** Decrease the intake of medical students (and possibly middle level health personnel; rationalize the number of medical school facilities and close those that are unnecessary.

These changes could reduce spending on hospitals considerably, with no loss in quality of service. The expenditure scenario in Table 9.4 provides for a 30 percent reduction from 1992 to 1993 in hospital spending. This cut may seem large, but the 1992 budgeted level was far above

year, and reviewing the feasibility of other closures. The decision to cut medical school enrollment is sound, since unemployment among physicians is already appearing. The MOH may close some schools for training middle-level health personnel and has shifted some treatments and procedures to an ambulatory setting. However difficult it may be, medical school closures must be addressed.

Table 9.4: Current, Suggested, and Sustainable Policy for Health Spending

Spending Category	Percent of GDP under Alternative Approaches			Policy Actions Required
	1992 Budget	Suggested Program for 1993	Sustainable Program Beyond 1993	
Hospitals	5.1	3.8	3.1	Shift a third of all treatments to out-patient care
Other Facilities	1.6	1.6	1.3	Strengthen basic care and community-based care but with fewer physicians
Public Health(1)	0.2	1.0	1.2	Invest in health promotion, anti-smoking campaign and a program to reduce injury, other prevention programs
Public Health Education	0.2	0.2	0.1	
Subsidies for Pharmaceutical	0.2	0.1	0.1	Prepare plan for imports from West; selected local production capacity expansion
Research	0.1	0.1	0.1	
Other(2)	0.4	0.2	0.1	
Total, Health(3)	7.7	7.0	6.0	

Notes:	(1)	Additional public health expenditures are included in the budgets for specific facilities.
	(2)	Additional treatment for Chernobyl victims and private payments for health services not included elsewhere.
	(3)	Does not sum exactly due to rounding.
Sources:		June 1992 Drafts of the 1992 Budgets for the Ministry of Health, Social Insurance Fund, Chernobyl Fund, Pension Fund and Employment Fund.

previous years' spending levels. The 1993 recommendations call for other categories of spending, except for Chernobyl-related health spending, which could be covered from other accounts, to remain the same.

28.   In 1993, the Ministry of Health was already taking a number of these recommended steps, including the closure of beds in the past

Restructuring for Long-Term Efficiency

29.   By acting now, the Ministry can lay the basis for long-term health system efficiency and effectiveness with the following four components in its strategic vision:

- Financing imports of essential drugs and supplies for pharmaceutical production, to include (*i*) short term planning for acquiring the required drugs and supplies and determining how, when, and where they will be distributed to ensure that priority needs are met, and (*ii*) developing a strategy for the pharmaceutical industry in Ukraine to secure supplies for the population, encouraging a major private sector role within an effective regulatory framework.

- Introducing reforms in health-system management to improve effectiveness, to include (*i*) planning a strategic health policy that focuses on primary care, health promotion, and healthy social and physical environments; (*ii*) rationalizing the structure and functions of the health system from the Ministry level down, reinforcing local participation, accountability, and responsibility; (*iii*) developing contemporary methods for financial planning and control based on program budgeting; (*iv*) rationalizing relationships between the MOH and the Ministries of Finance, Environment, Education, and Social Welfare to strengthen MOH control and accountability for its stewardship of the health system; (*v*) introducing modern health information system methods that bring together health status, clinical, financial and utilization data streams in an integrated way for managing the system at each level; and (*vi*) developing and enabling coordinated regulatory legislation; and (*vii*) improving the quality of services and their delivery by introducing quality assurance, and accreditation methods.

- Strengthening and modernizing primary care (basic) health services, including those targeted to women and children, family planning services, and the elderly, to include (*i*) introducing health promotion, and strengthening prevention programs; (*ii*) introducing family planning programs to enable women to have more control over their reproductive role; (*iii*) increasing access to contraceptives to lower the present high rate of abortions, including the possibility of developing a productive capacity for self-sufficiency in contraceptives; (*iv*) strengthening child health programs for women and children to lower present levels of morbidity and mortality; (*v*) assisting other vulnerable groups, particularly persons with long-term psychiatric illness; and (*vi*) developing a range of health and support programs, both institutional and home based, to meet the needs of the elderly.

- Developing health personnel, including assistance with restructuring the present approach to training medical and other health professionals, and initiating health management training, to include (*i*) restructuring the process of training health professionals, introducing new curricula, teaching, and examination methods; (*ii*) introducing the concept of "approved acts" as a basis for defining the role and scope of practice of a health profession to permit labor-substitution effects, strengthening the role and profession of nursing.

- Planning the financing of health service delivery through a national health insurance scheme, including (*i*) the principles for its delivery and their economic implications, (*ii*) the relationship of the scheme to other social safety net programs; (*iii*) alternative arrangements for organizational responsibility and accountability for its implementation and operations; (*iv*) associated reforms necessary for the viability and success of the scheme in the health sector financial administration and other areas, and their relative timing; (*v*) enabling legislation; and (*vi*) a strategy for implementation and a plan and timetable for organizing and proceeding with the scheme.

These steps, if introduced in 1993, can help lessen the demands on hospital care because they help prevent illness, as with abortion-related hospital costs that would be avoided with family planning services. Management improvements can both reduce costs and improve quality.

Health Insurance

30.   The introduction of health insurance has been characterized by some as a way to solve many of the financial problems of the health system. However, a health insurance scheme does not create new money in the economy for health care. Financing will have to come from existing resources. Health insurance introduces a new set of complex dynamics into the health system that can adversely affect service delivery. Premature introduction of health insurance can lead to financial problems, distortions in priority for service delivery, and distraction away from the need to deal with more fundamental problems in the health system. Several East European countries, especially the Czech and Slovak Republics and Hungary, are experiencing

serious difficulties because of the ill-timed introduction of a health insurance scheme. Once such distortions set in they are very difficult to overcome, a particularly dangerous situation since the distortions would add to the problems of the present ineffective system.

31.   Proceeding at this time with the introduction of health insurance is premature for a number of reasons: (*i*) the instabilities in the economy; (*ii*) the absence of management and financial administration tools; (*iii*) the lack of consensus among key stakeholders on values and principles of a new scheme; and (*iv*) the need to study the financial implications and implementation requirements. Nonetheless, planning assisted by experienced health-finance specialists from OECD countries should continue as a part of strategic management for the health sector.

CHAPTER NOTES

1. Active policies, including job-matching services, training, and skills assessment, help the unemployed worker get a new job. Passive policies, such as cash benefits or severance pay, compensate for lost income without contributing to finding work.

2. World Bank staff in Washington DC are currently preparing a major worldwide review of pension experience and will offer recommendations for substantial changes in pension systems. The results of this study can be provided to the Government of Ukraine when available.

3. These groups would include aged rural people living alone, orphans, the seriously disabled, families with three or more children, single parents and pensioners receiving less than 1.5 times the minimum pension. These groups constitute from 10 to 20 percent of the population.

4. In preparing this report, Bank staff did not attempt to review the many complex arrangements for consumer subsidies, because an IMF mission analyzed them in some detail (Chu and others, 1992). They are discussed briefly only as part of the aggregate program of public social spending.

5. In this section, various health indicators of Ukraine are compared with those of six countries: Belarus, Poland, Portugal, the United Kingdom, Sweden, and Canada. Belarus and Poland are not only neighbors but were also part of the former communist bloc. Portugal has a population distribution very close to that of Ukraine, and by some estimates a comparable GNP. It also has the feature of being on the regression line of per capita expenditure on health regressed against GDP per capita, arguably spending about the right amount on health for its economy. The United Kingdom has a population that is comparable in size to Ukraine and spends a share of GNP on health that is also comparable, although much more in per capita terms because of its high income. Sweden and Canada are included to offer comparisons with two countries that have well-respected and relatively mature health care systems.

6. *Lancet* editorial, 1992. Environmental pollution: it kills trees, but does it kill people? *Lancet 340*, 3 October 1992, 821-2.

7. Most disabled, on reaching retirement age, can choose between a disability or retirement pension. Military retirees and Chernobyl victims can receive both disability and retirement pensions.

8. Most of these allowances are available to families with incomes below two minimum wages per person. According to income distribution data from 1990, this is approximately 42.5 percent of the population.

9. In theory, the Chernobyl payroll tax is earmarked for social assistance, health care and environmental interventions relating to the Chernobyl disaster. In practice, the tax is incorporated into the general government budget, and Chernobyl-related expenses are disbursed from the budget.

10.   All children below age three (age two if the mother did not work prior to childbirth) receive an allowance from the state. The allowance for children between the ages of three (two) and six is reserved for low income families.

11.   These benefits exclude monthly stipends discussed in Chapter 6 of this report. The disabled could be considered a vulnerable group, but are not classified as such here. In Ukraine, even people with minor handicaps can be considered disabled. Furthermore, many of the benefits included here, such as provision of a car or the equivalent monetary compensation, do not appear to address basic needs.

12.   For example, there are 12 cash allowances that low-income or vulnerable families can qualify for. These include separate stipends for children's food, children's clothing, children's products, and general child maintenance. Under the category of general child maintenance, families may qualify for different allowances, or different stipends levels within an allowance, depending on the number of children they have, the age of their children, their income, whether the mother worked before childbirth, the age of the mother, whether the children are eligible for other allowances, whether the family is headed by a single parent, whether the absent parent pays alimony, and whether the single parent was raised in an orphanage.

13.   For example, all families are entitled to an allowance for each child under the age of 3 (2 if the mother did not work or attend a higher education school and is over 18 prior to childbirth). The Pension Fund pays for these allowances out of its own resources for children under age 1.5. Stipends for children ages 1.5 to 3 (2) are funded by state general revenues given to the Pension Fund but earmarked for this purpose. If the mother worked or attended a higher education school prior to childbirth and was still employed or a student at the time the baby was delivered, the allowance is administered by the mother's enterprise or school. If the mother did not work or study prior to childbirth or was laid-off before the birth, the allowance is administered by a district-level social welfare office.

14.   For an analysis of the reasons for labor hoarding in socialist economies, see Rutkowski (1990). For estimates of its magnitude for the Soviet Union, see Porket (1984).

15.   Explaining the reasons for different labor market reactions to demand and supply shocks is beyond the scope of the study. The important intermediate point in the explanation is that enterprises tend to regard the supply shock as **temporary** and continue to hoard labor, whereas they tend to regard the demand shock as **more permanent** and thus start laying off.

16.   Fretwell et.al.(1991, pp. 16-18) argue strongly in favor of active policies on the grounds of overall cost reduction.

17.   This option is similar to a solution recently adopted in Sweden, where the budget of the national training agency, AMU, was shifted to the Employment Service and used to procure training services on the open market. The AMU was forced to compete for funding. The AMU financed 80 percent of expenditures on training with the private sector providing the remainder.

18.   A subsequent visit with the Ministry of Education revealed as many as 800 specializations available in vocational schools, although there is discussion of reducing this number to 300. See the chapter on education services, especially the sections on vocational and technical education and training.

19.   This box is based on Ulrich Zachau's compilation from R. Layard, S. Nickell, and R. Jackman (1991); J. Ahmad, F. Corricelli, and A. Revenga (1992); F. Coricelli and A. Revenga (1992); T. Lane (1992); and M.A. Kiguel and N. Liviatan (1992).

20.   There is an extensive English language literature on the Soviet welfare state, including the definitive (but somewhat dated) study of McAuley (1979). A more recent but uneven collection of studies was edited by Lapidus and Swanson (1988). Additional sources and Russian language materials have been noted in the bibliography. See Braithwaite and Heleniak (1990).

21.   Before 1990, disaggregated employment statistics were released, but the current Nargos Uk. 1990 does not have a separate line item for miners. Military personnel were eligible for enhanced old-age pensions, disability benefits, and survivor benefits under the Soviet system. Ukraine passed its own version of a law regulating military pensions in 1991 and a supplementary law on non-cash benefits in January, 1992.

22.   The 1990 all-union pension law reaffirmed the right of certain individuals to higher, personal, pensions for special service to the state paid to artists, athletes, politicians, and others deemed to have served in some special fashion. The money amounts of these pensions are usually several orders of magnitude beyond the standard allowances, according to passing references in the press, but the number of personal pensioners is small.

23.   The exact ruble amounts are readily available in Svod zakonov SSSR (Code of Law of the USSR, Vol. 2, pp. 678-686; 712-718).

24.   People engaged in hard labor can retire with full benefits earlier than the general population. In addition, people in other jobs can retire after 25 years of service (20 for women) regardless of their age, although benefits for this group are lower than for those who work until full retirement age.

25.   In the past it was assumed that the collective farms where these individuals had worked would take care of them upon retirement. For this reason these retirees received only a small pension from the state. Currently, this group receives on average only slightly less than urban retirees.

26.   Pensions are calculated as a function of salary at the time of retirement. The adjusted pensions will be calculated by increasing the person's retirement-date income to 1992 levels. For example, a person who retired in 1974 would have his or her base income increased by 14.8 times, whereas the income of a person who retired in 1988 would be increased by 10.5 times. The replacement rate on this new income will continue to depend on length of service.

27.   Government revenues include state and local revenues and income from the Pension, Chernobyl, Employment and Social Insurance Funds.

28.   Ranges are given throughout this chapter to capture the fact that the Ministry of Finance and the Pension Fund differed in their July, 1992 forecasts for total 1992 Pension Fund revenues and expenditures. Final data for the year was not available for this report.

29.   The social insurance payroll tax rate for the first quarter 1992 was 61 percent, but was 37 percent thereafter. Eighty-four percent of this tax is earmarked for the Pension Fund.

30.   These are offices of the MSW located in each district of Ukraine that undertake a variety of tasks associated with pension and allowance administration.

31.   To arrive at these savings, the following simple assumptions were made: 1) the retiree population is spread evenly across ages and does not increase over time such that the same number of people retired or died in each of the next seven years. 2) Life expectancy for people age 60 does not change over the next seven years. Women currently retire at age 55 and, if they reach their 60th birthday, die on average at age 79.5. Thus, they experience 24.5 years of retirement on average. At the end of seven years, they will be retiring at age 62 so that their average years spent in retirement will decline to 17.5. Men currently retire at age 60 and, if they reach their 60th birthday, die on average at age 72.4. Thus men experience 12.4 years of retirement on average. At the end of two years, they will be retiring at age 62 so their average years spent in retirement will decline to 10.4. Thus, the total of men and women's client years in the system at a given point in time will decline from 36.9 to 27.9--a reduction of 24 percent. Thus, total spending on cash benefits would be reduced by an equal amount. It is assumed that the cash benefit share of total pension spending is equal to the share forecast for the second semester of 1992. Estimated savings as a share of total spending is not significantly influenced by the choice of the Pension Fund's or Ministry of Finance's estimated 1992 budget.

32.   Forecast pension spending over the July, 1992 to June, 1993 period is compared to forecast spending with benefits reduced by 50 percent for retired and disabled people who continue to work. Spending in the January to June, 1993 period is assumed to equal spending for the last six months of 1992 in current rubles.

33.   Most of these allowances are available to families with incomes below two minimum wages per person. According to income distribution data from 1990, this is approximately 42.5 percent of the population.

34.   Includes only administrative expenses for the Social Insurance Fund and some expenditures by social welfare offices. Additional administrative cost information was not available.

35.   All children below age three (age two if mother did not work prior to childbirth) receive an allowance from the state. The allowance for children between the ages of three (two) and six is reserved for low income families.

36.   To arrive at these figures, savings were estimated for each type of benefit based on the likely reduction in spending that would result from the above-specified demographic requirements. For example, estimated future benefits for the informed elderly were not reduced from their current level on the assumption that most beneficiaries in this category would be classified as disabled. The new estimate for the allowance for children under age three was 20 percent of its current level, on the assumption that not more than 20 percent of the general population would be included in the new target group. In each case, savings were conservatively estimated to arrive at the minimum amount the government could save by adopting this policy.

37.   The applicant/acceptance ratio was 5:1 in 1991 and dropped to 2.5:1 in 1992. The rector speculated that the sharp decline in the number of applicants was mostly due to the shrinking salary gap between people with and without higher education. This appears to be at variance with the reports to the mission that there is a strong demand for graduates in economics, finance, and related fields.

38.   Total state revenues include state and local general revenues and resources of the Pension, Social Insurance, Employment and Chernobyl Funds. The range in the health sector's share

of total government income reflects the fact that the Pension Fund and the Ministry of Finance differ significantly in their forecasts for Pension Fund revenues.

39.   In addition, some public health expenditures are included in the budgets for specific facilities.

BIBLIOGRAPHY

REPORTS PREPARED BY UKRAINIAN CONSULTANTS FOR THE STUDY

Assonov, George Fedorovych. 1992. On the Economic Situation and Employment in Ukraine.

Golovana, Yevgeniy and Nataliy Panina. 1992. Population's State of Health and Development of the Health Protection System.

Golovaty, Nikolai F. 1992. Social Problems of Ukraine and Some Possible Solutions.

Khodorovskiy, Georgiy. 1992. Family Planning and Health of Women in Ukraine.

Kryukov, Vitaliy. 1992. Legal Provisions for the Social Sphere in Ukraine: Current State, Problems and Prospects.

Lazaretnec, Boris. 1992. Use of Medical Technology to Reduce Health Care Costs in Ukraine.

Libanova, Alla. 1992. Ukraine's Labor Market: the Present and the Future.

Litoshenko, Alexandr. 1992. Lonely Elderly People in Ukraine Have Need of Help.

Lukovnykov, Fyodor Volodymyrovych, and I. Deikun. 1992. State-of-the-Art, Problems and Main Trends in the Development of Education in Ukraine. Kiev: Ministry of Education.

Mikhavlichenko. 1992. Social Security and Pension Benefits in the Course of Economic Reforms in Ukraine. Kiev.

Nemiria, Gregory M. 1992. Social Policy in the Donbass Region.

Pirozhkov, Serge and Natalija Lakiza-Sachuk. 1992. Demo-Social Consequences of Modern Family Planning in the Ukraine and their Influence on Demographic Development of the Republic. Kiev.

Pribytkova, Irina. 1992. Priority Lines for Financial and Technical aid Granted to Ukraine's Social Sphere: Groups Endangered, Their Social Protection Level, Emergency.

Prodanchuk, Mykola. 1992. Proposals of Health Service System Reconstruction Including Public Health and Medical Service Supplies.

Sinenko, Alla Ivanonva, Verkhovodova, Lidya Tarasovna and Pogrebinsky, Mikhail Borisovich. 1992. Social Mechanism of Ensuring Economic Reforms in Ukraine.

Solodchuk, Olexsandr. 1992. Social-Economic Situation in the Southern Region of Ukraine.

Yeremenko, Valentina and Zhebrovsky, Boris Mikhailovich. 1992. Priority Lines of Social Support for Public Education in Ukraine During the Transition to a Market Economy.

OTHER SOURCES

Ahmad, Junaid, Fabrizio Coricelli and Ana Revenga. 1992. Wage Policy during the Transition to a Market Economy: The Case of Poland in Wage Policy During the Transition to a Market Economy. World Bank Discussion Paper No. 158. Washington, DC: World Bank.

Atkinson, Anthony B. 1992. On Targeting Social Security: The Experience of Western Countries with Family Benefits. *Public Expenditures and the Poor: Incidence and Targeting, a World Bank Conference.* Washington, DC: World Bank.

Barr, Nicholas. 1991. Issues in the design of a system of income support. Wash DC: World Bank. p. 9. Also available in Russian translation.

Barr, Nicholas. 1992. Economic theory and the welfare state: A survey and interpretation. *Journal of Economic Literature* 30:2(741-803).

"Belorussian SSR Law On Indexation of the Income of the Population Taking Into Account Inflation." *Ekonomika i zhizn.* No. 8. February 1991. p. 20. Translated. JPRS-UEA-91-016. 2 April 1991. pp. 15-17.

Brada, Josef. (Arizona State University) and Arthur E. King (Lehigh University). 1991. *Sequencing Measures for the Transformation of Socialist Economies to Capitalism: Is There a J-Curve for Economic Reforms?* Research Series/Number 13. Department of Economics.

Braithwaite, Jeanine D. and Timothy E. Heleniak. 1990. Social Welfare in the USSR: The Income Recipient Distribution. Washington, DC: US Bureau of Census, Center for International Research.

Braithwaite, Jeanine. 1990. Income Distribution and Poverty in the Soviet Republics. *Journal of Soviet Nationalities 1*, 3, 158-73.

Center for International Health Information. 1992. Ukraine USAID Health Profile (Selected Data). Arlington, Va.: ISTI.

Chu, Ke-Young, Sanjaev Gupta, Emily Andrews, and Steven Wess. 1992. Ukraine: Budgetary implications of social safety net options. Washington, DC: IMF.

Coase, R. H. 1988. *The Firm, the Market and the Law.* Chicago: University of Chicago Press.

Coricelli, Fabrizio and Ana Revenga. 1992. Wages and Unemployment in Poland: Recent Developments and Policy Issues : The Case of Poland in Wage Policy During the Transition to a Market Economy, World Bank Discussion Paper No. 158. Washington, DC: World Bank.

Demokratichna Ukraina. 28, 31 December 1991.

Fan, Qimiao. and Mark E. Schaffer. 1991. *Enterprise Reforms in Chinese and Polish-Owned Industries.* Research Series/Number 11. London: London School of Economics.

Foster, Andrew and Mark Rosenzweig. 1993. Information Flows and Discrimination in Labor Markets in Rural Areas in Developing Countries. Proceedings of the World Bank Annual Conference on Development Economics, 173-215. Washington, DC: World Bank.

Freeman, Richard. 1993. Labor Market Institutions and Policies: Help or Hindrance to Economic Development? Proceedings of the World Bank Annual Conference on Development Economics 1992, 117-44. Washington, DC: World Bank.

Fretwell, David, 1992, *Developing Effective Employment Services*, Washington, DC: World Bank.

Fretwell, David; Malcolm Lovell and Robert W. Bednarzik. 1991. *Employment Dimensions of Economic Restructuring*. The World Bank, EMTPH, April 30.

Golovachev, V. 1991. What's in the Mysterious Market Basket... *Trud*. 9 May 1991. Translated. JPRS-UEA-91-027. 31 May 1991. pp. 66-71. [1991a]

Golovachev, V. 1991. Where Does the Poverty Line Lie? *Trud*. 19 March 1991. p. 2. Translated. JPRS-UEA-91-014. 26 March 1991. pp. 85-87.

Gomulka, Stanislaw. 1991. *The Causes of Recession Following Stabilization*. Research Series/Number 15. London: School of Economics.

Gomulka, Stanislaw. *Economic Reforms in Poland, 1989-91: Aims, Policies and Outcomes*. Research Series/Number 19. London: School of Economics. 1991.

Gomulka, Stanislaw. *The Puzzles of Fairly Fast Growth and Rapid Collapse Under Socialism*. Research Series/Number 18. London: School of Economics. 1991.

Hamermesh, Daniel, 1992, *Unemployment Insurance for Developing Countries*, Working Paper Series 897. Washington, DC: The World Bank.

Hansson, Carola and Karen Liden. 1983. *Moscow Women*. New York: Random House.

IMF. 1991. Reform of Ukraine's public finance: Immediate policy tasks. Washington, DC: IMF, Fiscal Affairs Department.

INTERFAX. "Business Today." 27 March 1991. Translated. FBIS-SOV-91-102. 28 May 1991. pp. 46-47.

INTERFAX. "Soviet Business Report." 29 October 1991. Translated. FBIS-SOV-91-210. 30 October 1991. p. 47.

INTERFAX. "Soviet Business Report." 5 November 1991. Translated. FBIS-SOV-91-215. 6 November 1991. pp. 31-33.

INTERFAX. 13 September 1991. Translated. JPRS-UEA-91-036. 17 September 1991. p. 11.

INTERFAX. 28 October 1991. Translated. FBIS-SOV-91-209. 29 October 1991. p. 64.

Izvestiya. "At the USSR State Committee for Prices and the USSR Ministry of Finance." 30 April 1991. pp. 1-2. Translated as "Finance Bodies on Estimated Effect of Prices." FBIS-SOV-91-091. 10 May 1991. pp. 26-27.

Izvestiya. "Foundations of Legislation of the USSR and the Republics on Income Indexation." 9 July 1991. p. 2. Translated. JPRS-UEA-91-031. pp. 1-4.

Izvestiya. "What the Compensation Payments Will Be." 21 March 1991. p. 2. Translated. JPRS-UEA-91-015. 29 March 1991. p. 62-64.

Izvestiya. 16 October 1991. p. 1.

Jackman, Richard. 1992. Wage Policy in the Transition to a Market Economy: The Polish Experience, The Case of Poland in Wage Policy During the Transition to a Market Economy, World Bank Discussion Paper No. 158, Washington, DC: World Bank.

Jarvis, Sarah J. and John Micklewright. 1992. The Targeting of Family Allowance in Hungary. *Public Expenditures and the Poor: Incidence and Targeting, a World Bank Conference.* Washington DC: World Bank.

Jenkins, Glenn P. 1992. Implications of Economic Transition and Demographics for Financing Pensions in the Former Socialist Economies. Harvard University.

Kazakhstanskaya pravda. 2 August 1991. p. 2. Translated as "Law on Income Indexation." FBIS-USR-91-046. 5 November 1991. pp. 34-37.

Keynes, John Maynard. 1936. *The General Theory of Employment, Interest, and Money.* Cambridge: Cambridge University Press.

Khudyakova, T. 1991. "Pension Fund 'On the Rocks.'" *Izvestiya.* p. 3. Translated. FBIS-SOV-91-087. 6 May 1991. p. 28.

Kincaid, Ward. 1991. Regional variations in Soviet mortality by cause of death: An analysis of years of potential life lost. Washington, DC: US Census Bureau.

Kormilkin, A.V. 1990. "About Poverty--Not for the Last Time." *Ekonomika I Organizatsiya Promyshlennogo Proizvodstva (EKO).* Translated. JPRS-UEA-90-040. pp. 75-80.

Kornai, Janos, 1980, *Economics of Shortage*, North-Holland, Amsterdam.

Kornai, Janos, 1990, *The Socialist System*, Princeton University Press, Princeton.

Kovalev, A. 1989. "Kto i pochemu za chertoy bednosti." *Ekonomicheskaya Gazeta.* No. 25. p. 11.

Lancet Editorial. 1992. Environmental pollution: It kills trees, but does it kill people? *Lancet 340*, 3 October 1992:821-22.

Lane, Timothy D. 1992. Wage Controls in Reforming Socialist Economies: Design, Coverage, and Enforcement: The Case of Poland in Wage Policy During the Transition to a Market Economy, World Bank Discussion Paper No. 158. Washington, DC: World Bank.

Lapidus, Gail W. and Guy E. Swanson. Eds. 1988. *State and Welfare: USA/USSR.* Research Series/Number 71. Berkeley: Institute of International Studies.

"Law on Social and Juridical Protection of Uniformed Military and Their Families." *Pravda Ukrainy.* 11 January 1992.

Layard, Richard, Stephen Nickell and Richard Jackman. 1991. Unemployment. Oxford University Press: Oxford.

McAuley, Alastair. 1979. *Economic Welfare in the Soviet Union.* Madison: University of Wisconsin Press.

Milanovic, Branko. 1992. Distributional impact of cash and in-kind transfers in Eastern Europe and Russia. Public expenditures and the poor: Incidence and targeting, a World Bank conference. Washington, DC: World Bank.

Moskvin, O. 1990. Analiz tendentsii zminy rivnya zhyttya naselennya URSR. *Economika Radyans' Koi Ukrainy*, 2: 13-21.

OECD. 1990. Health Care Systems in Transition - The Search for Efficiency. Paris.

Orlova, L. 1991. "The Order is to Survive." *Torgovaya gazeta*. p. 1. Translated. JPRS-UEA-91-010. p. 51.

Osipov, O. 1991. "One Must Pay, But the Coffers are Empty." *Trud*. p. 1. Translated. JPRS-UEA-91-031. pp. 65-66.

Oxenstierna, Susanne, 1990, *From Labour Shortage to Unemployment? The Soviet Labor Market in the 1980s*, Swedish Institute for Social Research, University of Stockholm.

Poland. Ministry of Public Education. 1990. Statistical Yearbook. Warszawa.

Porket, Josef L., 1984, *The Shortage Use and Reserves of Labour in the Soviet Union*, Osteuropa Wirtschaft, vol. 29, No.1, pp. 8-24, March.

POSTFACTUM. "Trade Unions Report Cost of Living Increase." Moscow. FBIS-SOV-92-015.

Pravda. "On Compensating the Population..." 25 March 1991. p. 1. Translated as "Ukase on Savings Compensation Published."

Pravda. "On the Reform of Retail Prices and the Social Protection of the Population." 21 March 1991. pp. 1-2. Translated as "Text of Cabinet Price Reform Published." FBIS-SOV-91-056. pp. 32-40.

Pravda. 1991. pp. 1,2. Translated as "Gorbachev Issues Decree on Retail Prices," "Agreement with Republics on Price Reform," and "Funding Arrangements Detailed." FBIS-SOV-91-054. 20 March 1991. pp. 14-23.

Pravda ukrainy. 2 Apr, 6 Aug 91, 11 Jan, 21 Mar 1992. Law on Minimum Consumer Budget; [English translation, 6 August 1991]; Decree on the Protection of the Population; [English translation, 2 April 1991].

Pronina, L. 1991. "How Much Has the Cost of Living Increased?" *Argumenty i Fakty*. No. 16. Translated. JPRS-UEA-91-024. 17 May 1991. pp. 75-78.

Rapawy, Stephen. 1992. Socio-Economic Indicators for Ukraine. Washington, DC: Center for International Research, US Bureau of the Census.

Robinson, E.A.G. 1931, rev ed., 1958. *The Structure of Competitive Industry*. Cambridge: Cambridge Univ Press.

Romanyuk, V. 1991. That Exorbitant Minimum Consumption Budget. *Izvestiya*. 26 July 1991. p. 1. Translated. FBIS-SOV-91-146. pp. 61-62. [1991a]

Romanyuk, V. 1991. USSR President's Decree on the Minimum Consumption Budget..." *Izvestiya*. 23 May 1991. Translated. FBIS-SOV-91-103. 29 May 1991. p. 52. [1991b]

Romanyuk, V. 1991. Whom Does Indexation of Income Protect? *Izvestiya*. 3 August 1991. p. 1. Translated. JPRS-UEA-91-034. 23 August 1991. pp. 29-30. [1991c]

Rose, Richard. 1992. Divisions and contradictions in economies in transition: Household portfolios in Russia, Bulgaria and Czechoslovakia. mimeo. Washington, DC: World Bank.

Rutkowski, Michal, 1990, *Labour Hoarding and Future Open Unemployment in Eastern Europe: The Case of Polish Industry*, London School of Economics, Centre for Economic Performance Discussion Paper No. 6. July.

Scherer, Peter, 1990, *A Review of National Labor Market Policies in OECD Countries*, Seminar on Economic Adjustment: Employment and Social Dimensions. Washington, DC: World Bank (processed)

Schulz, James H. 1992. Economic Support in Old Age: The Role of Social Insurance in Developing Countries. Brussels: International Social Security Association.

Schumpeter, Joseph A. 1942, 4th ed., 1952. Capitalism, socialism, and democracy. London: George Allen & Unwin.

Sen, Amartya. 1992. The Political Economy of Targeting. *Public Expenditures and the Poor: Incidence and Targeting, a World Bank Conference*. Washington, DC: World Bank.

Simon, D., and Ustenko, 1993. Labor in Kiev. *Financial Times*.

Sotsialisticheskiy trud. No. 3. 1987.

Svod zakonov SSSR. 1984. Vol. 2. Moscow: "Izvestiya."

Trud. 1991. p. 4. Translated. JPRS-UEA-91-035. 9 September 1991. p. 90.

Ukraine, Government of. 1993. Action plan for the Government of Ukraine to implement and develop "the basis of the national economic policy" for the year 1993. Kiev: Council of Ministers.

Ukraine, Law. 1993. On state assistance to families with children. Kiev: Council of Ministers.

Ukraine, Ministry of Health. 1992. File on Draft National Legislation: Bill on Principles for Legislation on Health Care; Bill on Medical Insurance; Bill on Transplantation of Organs and Tissues; Bill on Medical-Legal Expertise; Bill on Psychiatric Care. Mimeo. Kiev.

Ukraine, Ministry of Health. 1992. Indicators of Population Health and Activity of Health Care Facilities of Ukraine for 1990-1991. Vol. 1. Kiev. Indicators of Resources for Health Care for the Population and their Use in Ukraine. Networks and Personnel. Statistical Material for 1990-1991.

Ukraine, Ministry of Statistics. 1991. Narodne gospodarstvo ukrains'koi RSR u 1990 rotsi. Kiev: "Tekhnika."

Ukraine, Ministry of Statistics. 1991. "Socio-Economic Conditions in Ukraine for 9 Months in 1991." Kiev.

Ukraine, Ministry of Statistics. 1992. "Socio-Economic Conditions of Ukraine in 1991." Kiev.

Ukraine, Ministry of Statistics. 1992. "About Social and Economic Development of Ukraine: First Quarter 1992." Kiev.

UNDP. 1991. *Human Development Report*. New York: Oxford University Press.

U.S. Bureau of Census, Center for International Research. 1992. "Ukraine: Statistical Summary." Translation of Ukrainian materials. Washington, DC: Census Bureau.

U.S. Department of Labor, 1986, *Economic Adjustment and Worker Dislocation in a Competitive Society*, Report of the Secretary of Labor's Task Force on Economic Adjustment and Worker Dislocation. Washington, DC: Department of Labor.

USSR, Goskomstat. 1990. *SSSR v tsifrakh v 1990 godu*. Moscow: Finansy i statistika.

USSR, Goskomstat. 1991. *Narodnoye khozyaystvo SSSR v 1990 g*. Moscow.

USSR, Goskomstat. *Press-vypusk*. Issued irregularly.

"USSR Law on Pensions for USSR Citizens." *Trud*. 30 May 1990. Translated. FBIS-SOV-90-121. 22 June 1990. pp. 33-54.

Uryadovyy Kuryer. 1992. Social Protection Guaranteed by Government. English translation, January 1992.

Vestnik statistiki. 1988. No. 9.

WHO, 1992. World Health Statistics Annual. Geneva.

WHO, EURO. 1992. HFA Statistical Indicator Database. Copenhagen.

WHO, EURO. 1992. Highlights on Ukraine. Draft. Copenhagen.

WHO, EURO. 1992. Ukraine, Population by Country, Age Group and Sex.

World Bank. 1987. Poland: Reform, Adjustment and Growth. *Report No. 6736-POL*. Washington, DC: World Bank.

World Bank. 1989. Poland Subsidies and Income Distribution. *Report No. 776-POL*. Washington, DC: World Bank.

World Bank. 1991. Hungary Reform and Decentralization of the Public sector. Volume I. *Report No. 10061-HU*. Washington, DC: World Bank.

World Bank. 1991. Poland Income Support and the Social Safety Net: Policies for the Transition. *Report No. 9661-POL*. Washington, DC: World Bank.

World Bank. 1991. Wage and Employment Policies in Czechoslovakia. Luis A. Riveros. *Working Paper 730*. Washington, DC: World Bank.

World Bank. 1991. *World Development Report*. New York: Oxford University Press.

World Bank. 1992. Options for Pension Reform in Tunisia. Dimitri Vittas. Financial Policy and Systems Division, Country Economics Department, World Bank.

World Bank. 1992. Poland Health System Reform: Meeting the Challenge. *Report No. 9182-POL*. Washington, DC: World Bank.

World Bank. 1992. Poland Social Sectors Expenditures Review. *Report No. 10158-POL*. Washington, DC: World Bank.

World Bank. 1992. Unemployment Insurance for Developing Countries. *Report No. 897*. Washington, DC: World Bank.

Yakovlev, Ye. 1991. "Interview with Ye. Katulskiy, Deputy Minister Goskomtrud USSR." *Pravitelstvennyy Vestnik*. No. 2. p. 5. Translated. JPRS-UEA-91-035. p. 65.

STATISTICAL APPENDIX

CONTENTS

FIGURES

Table A.1 UKRAINE: Population by Age Groups and Oblasts

(1989 Data; In Thousand People)

	up to 14	14	15	16	17	18	19	20-24	25-29	30-34	35-39	40-44	45-49	50-54	55-59	60-64	65-69	70+	Total a
Total:	10,374	720	727	755	733	694	640	3,352	3,958	3,900	3,741	2,706	3,220	3,705	2,953	3,232	2,020	4,002	51,439
Male	5,279	362	372	386	378	350	321	1,684	1,969	1,924	1,826	1,295	1,504	1,727	1,314	1,275	663	1,100	23,863
Female	5,094	357	354	369	355	344	319	1,667	1,989	1,976	1,915	1,411	1,716	1,978	1,639	1,958	1,357	2,901	27,576
Crimea R.	513.5	35.5	34.0	35.2	32.4	30.6	30.4	154.0	191.7	200.1	199.1	137.7	159.6	174.3	134.8	143.4	77.8	142.4	2,430
Vinnytsia	356.9	27.3	27.6	28.7	26.5	24.2	22.5	113.6	127.6	122.1	124.9	96.7	129.0	141.1	121.5	139.5	99.3	191.9	1,921
Volyn	241.9	17.0	17.1	16.9	15.8	14.1	13.0	67.9	82.0	79.4	67.4	51.6	55.0	65.9	74.0	64.8	41.6	73.1	1,058
Dnipropetrovsk	769.8	52.0	52.6	56.1	56.0	54.2	49.5	260.4	308.2	294.3	286.8	197.3	257.4	305.5	209.4	247.9	129.0	285.3	3,870
Donetsk	1033.0	69.7	68.5	73.0	71.1	68.1	60.7	322.8	414.0	423.4	411.4	269.3	338.8	421.4	344.3	359.3	176.2	386.6	5,312
Zhytomyr	312.3	23.4	23.1	23.2	20.8	20.0	19.0	94.4	106.8	107.1	99.9	77.4	96.4	110.0	95.3	104.3	72.4	131.8	1,538
Zakarpattia	307.2	21.6	21.7	21.7	21.0	18.6	18.6	92.2	103.2	98.4	88.8	71.5	65.4	70.2	67.9	59.5	43.9	54.1	1,246
Zaporizhzhia	417.0	28.4	28.4	30.0	29.0	27.1	25.2	136.2	162.7	162.2	162.5	105.0	139.2	154.1	110.7	135.0	68.8	152.3	2,074
Ivano-Frankivsk	320.1	21.8	21.3	21.5	20.5	19.3	18.8	100.0	115.4	107.8	92.5	74.3	75.9	88.7	92.2	75.2	56.9	91.1	1,413
Kiev Region	389.0	27.3	27.6	28.2	26.5	24.6	22.8	125.3	148.9	141.7	133.7	97.0	125.9	142.4	95.7	122.4	86.1	169.5	1,934
Kirovohrad	237.1	17.1	17.1	17.4	15.9	14.9	13.6	73.5	84.7	82.8	84.8	65.4	83.6	91.0	62.5	89.1	56.3	121.1	1,228
Luhansk	564.9	37.1	37.3	39.3	38.6	36.8	32.6	173.9	228.3	227.4	212.8	138.5	180.9	233.5	178.5	187.8	91.7	217.2	2,857
Lviv	574.8	39.2	41.9	43.9	45.7	45.2	41.5	206.4	229.3	210.6	173.3	151.9	149.3	169.7	169.3	142.1	107.2	186.1	2,727
Mykolaiv	284.3	19.4	19.8	20.5	18.0	16.2	15.0	85.2	105.8	103.5	101.1	72.0	88.2	89.7	68.6	79.2	46.0	96.0	1,328
Odessa	526.5	37.5	37.4	39.1	37.9	36.9	34.3	184.0	203.6	201.4	202.8	145.6	174.5	184.9	139.7	151.7	100.1	186.0	2,624
Poltava	320.2	23.4	23.6	24.7	23.5	21.2	19.7	106.6	121.4	116.5	120.2	88.0	116.4	133.4	93.2	123.5	88.3	184.4	1,749
Rivne	275.1	18.8	18.6	18.6	17.4	16.4	15.8	79.7	92.9	89.6	74.1	58.3	63.5	72.1	72.9	60.5	43.6	76.4	1,164
Sumy	267.5	19.2	19.4	20.0	19.4	17.3	15.4	82.6	100.4	102.1	101.3	68.4	87.6	104.3	79.6	105.0	70.2	145.8	1,427
Ternopil	241.4	16.9	16.7	16.5	15.6	14.7	14.4	73.3	86.4	82.4	72.7	59.5	66.2	76.8	83.3	70.9	56.4	99.9	1,164
Kharkiv	597.1	41.2	40.9	44.2	47.7	47.3	42.5	223.1	250.1	243.5	244.1	170.5	188.5	232.6	160.7	204.4	122.3	273.7	3,175
Kherson	271.0	18.9	18.9	19.4	17.5	16.2	15.3	81.6	96.8	98.1	94.5	64.1	82.7	88.6	64.6	71.1	39.2	78.3	1,237
Khmelnytsky	294.4	22.0	21.9	22.4	20.4	19.0	18.2	91.8	108.6	107.6	100.0	79.1	95.8	100.0	101.1	103.5	76.7	143.2	1,522
Cherkasy	286.3	21.6	22.1	22.5	20.8	18.1	15.7	85.4	103.8	101.4	105.4	79.0	101.9	119.6	78.3	112.7	75.7	155.6	1,527
Chernivtsi	205.6	14.2	15.1	16.0	16.1	14.5	13.0	65.3	72.0	68.7	64.6	46.5	54.3	57.5	57.6	52.7	42.5	64.7	941
Chernihiv	252.3	18.5	17.8	18.5	16.5	15.3	14.3	75.5	90.7	96.6	94.1	67.7	86.4	104.5	95.4	114.9	78.8	155.1	1,413
Kiev (City)	514.3	30.8	36.1	37.8	42.3	43.1	38.2	196.9	222.6	231.0	228.3	174.0	157.6	173.5	101.8	112.2	72.8	140.2	2,559

Source: Council for Exploration of Productive Resources of Ukraine.

a/ Including non-Ukrainians

Table: A.2 UKRAINE: SOUTHEAST: Population by Age Groups, Sex and Oblast
(1989 Data; In Thousand People)

	up to 14	14	15	16	17	18	19	20-24	25-29	30-34	35-39	40-44	45-49	50-54	55-59	60-64	65-69	70+	Total a
SOUTHEAST																			
Crimea R.	514	35	34	35	32	31	30	154	192	200	199	138	160	174	135	143	78	142	2,430
Male	262	18	18	18	17	16	16	78	94	97	95	64	75	81	59	57	26	39	1,131
Female	251	17	16	17	15	15	14	76	98	103	104	73	85	94	75	86	52	104	1,299
Dnipropetrovsk	770	52	53	56	56	54	49	260	308	294	287	197	257	305	209	248	129	285	3,870
Male	392	26	27	28	28	26	24	129	153	144	139	92	119	145	96	102	42	78	1,788
Female	378	26	26	28	28	28	26	132	156	150	148	105	138	160	114	146	87	208	2,082
Donetsk	1,033	70	69	73	71	68	61	323	414	423	411	269	339	421	344	359	176	387	5,312
Male	526	36	35	37	36	34	31	160	207	212	202	128	154	194	159	146	57	104	2,458
Female	507	34	34	36	35	34	30	163	207	211	209	141	184	227	186	214	119	282	2,853
Kharkiv	597	41	41	44	48	47	43	223	250	243	244	171	189	233	161	204	122	274	3,175
Male	305	21	21	22	25	23	20	113	123	118	118	82	88	108	71	81	38	72	1,449
Female	292	20	20	22	23	24	22	110	127	126	126	89	100	124	90	123	84	201	1,726
Kherson	271	19	19	19	18	16	15	82	97	98	94	64	83	89	65	71	39	78	1,237
Male	138	10	10	10	9	8	7	40	48	49	47	31	39	42	29	28	13	20	577
Female	133	9	9	10	9	8	8	41	49	50	48	33	43	46	36	43	27	58	660
Luhansk	565	37	37	39	39	37	33	174	228	227	213	139	181	234	178	188	92	217	2,857
Male	288	19	19	20	20	18	16	86	115	114	105	66	82	108	84	76	29	56	1,321
Female	277	18	18	19	19	18	16	87	113	113	108	72	99	125	95	112	63	161	1,536
Mykolaiv	284	19	20	20	18	16	15	85	106	104	101	72	88	90	69	79	46	96	1,328
Male	144	10	10	10	9	8	7	41	52	51	49	35	42	43	31	31	15	26	616
Female	140	10	10	10	9	8	8	44	53	53	52	37	46	47	38	48	31	70	712
Odessa	527	38	37	39	38	37	34	184	204	201	203	146	175	185	140	152	100	186	2,624
Male	267	19	19	20	20	19	17	93	102	98	98	69	82	87	62	59	35	56	1,221
Female	259	19	18	19	18	18	17	91	102	103	105	77	92	98	78	93	65	131	1,403
Zaporizhzhia	417	28	28	30	29	27	25	136	163	162	162	105	139	154	111	135	69	152	2,074
Male	212	14	14	15	15	13	12	66	80	79	79	49	65	73	50	55	22	41	955
Female	205	14	14	15	14	14	13	70	83	83	84	56	74	81	61	80	47	111	1,119

Source: Council for Exploration of Productive Resources of Ukraine.

Note: Totals may not add up due to rounding.

a/ Non-Ukrainians

127

	up to 14	14	15	16	17	18	19	20-24	25-29	30-34	35-39	40-44	45-49	50-54	55-59	60-64	65-69	70+	Total
CENTER																			
Cherkasy	286	22	22	23	21	18	16	85	104	101	105	79	102	120	78	113	76	156	1,527
Male	146	11	11	11	10	9	8	42	51	50	51	38	48	56	34	44	24	38	682
Female	141	11	11	11	10	9	8	44	52	52	54	41	54	63	45	69	52	118	845
Chernihiv	252	18	18	18	17	15	14	75	91	97	94	68	86	104	95	115	79	155	1,413
Male	128	9	9	9	9	8	8	38	45	48	47	33	40	48	42	44	24	37	626
Female	124	9	9	9	8	7	7	38	45	48	47	35	46	56	54	71	55	118	786
Khmelnytsky	294	22	22	22	20	19	18	92	109	108	100	79	96	100	101	103	77	143	1,522
Male	150	11	11	12	11	10	10	47	53	53	49	38	45	46	42	39	25	37	691
Female	145	11	11	11	9	9	8	44	55	55	51	41	51	54	59	64	51	106	830
Kiev Region	389	27	28	28	27	25	23	125	149	142	134	97	126	142	96	122	86	169	1,934
Male	198	14	14	14	14	12	11	62	74	71	67	48	59	67	41	47	27	43	883
Female	191	13	14	14	13	12	11	64	75	71	67	49	67	75	54	75	59	127	1,051
Kiev (City)	514	31	36	38	42	43	38	197	223	231	228	174	158	174	102	112	73	140	2,559
Male	263	13	19	19	22	21	18	100	107	108	106	82	76	83	47	46	24	43	1,203
Female	251	18	17	18	21	22	20	97	116	123	122	92	82	91	54	66	49	97	1,356
Kirovohrad	237	17	17	17	16	15	14	73	85	83	85	65	84	91	63	89	56	121	1,228
Male	121	9	9	9	8	8	7	37	42	41	41	31	40	43	28	34	18	32	558
Female	116	8	8	8	8	7	7	37	43	42	43	34	43	48	35	55	38	89	670
Poltava	320	23	24	25	23	21	20	107	121	117	120	88	116	133	93	123	88	184	1,749
Male	163	12	12	13	12	10	9	53	61	57	59	42	56	64	41	48	28	45	785
Female	158	12	12	12	11	11	10	53	61	59	62	46	61	69	52	76	61	139	963
Sumy	267	19	19	20	19	17	15	83	100	102	101	68	88	104	80	105	70	146	1,427
Male	136	10	10	10	10	8	8	41	50	51	51	34	41	49	33	40	22	37	643
Female	132	9	10	10	10	9	9	42	50	51	51	35	46	55	46	65	48	109	784
Vinnytsia	357	27	28	29	26	24	22	114	128	122	125	97	129	141	122	139	99	192	1,921
Male	181	14	14	15	14	13	12	57	63	61	61	46	59	65	51	52	31	49	857
Female	176	13	13	14	13	11	11	56	64	62	64	50	70	76	71	88	69	143	1,064
Zhytomyr	312	23	23	23	21	20	19	94	107	107	100	77	96	110	95	104	72	132	1,538
Male	158	12	12	12	11	11	10	49	54	54	50	38	45	51	41	40	24	36	831
Female	154	12	11	11	10	9	9	46	53	53	50	40	51	59	54	64	49	96	706

Source: Council for Exploration of Productive Resources of Ukraine.

Note: Totals may not add up due to rounding.

a/ Non-Ukrainians

Table A.4   UKRAINE: WEST: Population by Age Groups, Sex and Oblast
(1989 Data;   In Thousand of People)

	up to 14	14	15	16	17	18	19	20-24	25-29	30-34	35-39	40-44	45-49	50-54	55-59	60-64	65-69	70+	Tota
WEST																			
Chernivtsi	206	14	15	16	16	15	13	65	72	69	65	47	54	58	58	53	43	65	9.
Male	104	7	8	8	8	7	7	32	35	33	31	22	25	26	25	21	16	22	4:
Female	101	7	7	8	8	8	7	33	37	35	33	25	30	31	32	32	27	43	5(
Ivano-Frankivsk	320	22	21	22	21	19	19	100	115	108	92	74	76	89	92	75	57	91	1,4:
Male	163	11	11	12	11	10	10	51	58	54	46	36	35	40	41	30	19	29	66
Female	157	11	10	10	10	10	9	49	57	54	47	39	41	49	51	46	37	62	74
Lviv	575	39	42	44	46	45	42	206	229	211	173	152	149	170	169	142	107	186	2,72
Male	292	20	22	23	24	24	22	108	117	106	85	74	71	78	76	55	37	61	1,29
Female	282	19	20	21	22	21	20	98	112	105	88	78	79	91	94	87	70	125	1,43
Rivne	275	19	19	19	17	16	16	80	93	90	74	58	63	72	73	60	44	76	1,16
Male	139	9	10	10	9	9	8	41	47	46	37	28	30	33	33	23	15	24	55
Female	136	9	9	9	8	8	7	39	46	44	37	30	34	39	40	37	29	52	61
Ternopil	241	17	17	16	16	15	14	73	86	82	73	60	66	77	83	71	56	100	1,16
Male	123	9	9	8	8	8	7	38	44	41	35	29	31	35	37	27	19	30	53
Female	119	8	8	8	8	7	7	35	43	41	37	31	36	42	47	44	37	70	62
Volyn	242	17	17	17	16	14	13	68	82	79	67	52	55	66	74	65	42	73	1,05
Male	123	9	9	9	8	7	7	35	42	40	34	26	26	29	32	25	15	24	49
Female	119	8	8	8	7	7	6	33	40	39	34	26	29	36	42	40	27	49	55
Zakarpattia	307	22	22	22	21	19	19	92	103	98	89	72	65	70	68	60	44	54	1,24
Male	156	11	11	11	11	9	10	46	51	49	44	35	31	32	30	25	18	20	60:
Female	151	11	11	10	10	9	9	46	52	50	45	36	35	38	38	35	26	34	64.

Source: Council for Exploration of Productive Resources of Ukraine.

Note: Totals may not add up due to rounding.

a/ Non-Ukrainians

129

Table A.5 UKRAINE: Population by Working Age, Urban Residence, and Oblasts
(In Percent Shares of Ukraine's Total)

	Percent of Population Total	Below Working Age	Of Which Living In Towns	Working Age	Of Which Living In Towns	Over Working Age	Of Which Living In Towns
Ukraine Total	100.0	22.9	68.0	55.8	70.8	21.2	56.0
Crimea R.	4.8	23.8	65.9	57.9	70.2	18.2	70.1
Vinnytsia	3.7	21.4	50.6	52.6	50.1	26.0	28.2
Volyn	2.1	26.0	51.4	52.8	54.7	21.2	34.4
Dnipropetrovsk	7.5	22.5	84.0	57.3	85.6	20.2	76.7
Donetsk	10.3	22.0	90.2	56.9	91.3	21.2	87.5
Zhytomyr	3.0	23.3	58.1	53.1	58.8	23.6	37.7
Zakarpattia	2.4	27.9	40.0	56.1	43.1	16.0	35.7
Zaporizhzhia	4.0	22.8	76.3	57.1	78.8	20.1	67.5
Ivano-Frankivsk	2.8	25.7	42.6	54.7	46.1	19.7	30.6
Kiev Region	3.8	22.9	59.4	54.9	58.7	22.2	36.9
Kirovohrad	2.4	22.1	64.1	53.6	64.3	24.3	46.6
Luhansk	5.5	22.3	86.8	56.7	87.9	20.9	81.9
Lviv	5.3	24.0	59.0	56.3	64.1	19.7	47.1
Mykolaiv	2.6	24.3	65.8	56.2	68.5	19.5	58.6
Odessa	5.1	22.8	63.4	57.5	69.4	19.7	58.4
Poltava	3.4	21.0	60.4	53.6	61.7	25.4	41.4
Rivne	2.3	26.8	46.9	53.9	51.1	19.2	30.5
Sumy	2.8	21.4	68.5	53.1	67.8	25.5	45.4
Ternopil	2.3	23.7	45.2	52.6	47.0	23.7	24.8
Kharkiv	6.2	21.3	79.7	56.9	81.4	21.8	70.2
Kherson	2.4	24.8	59.2	57.0	63.4	18.2	57.6
Khmelnytsky	2.9	22.2	56.4	52.7	54.0	25.0	27.9
Cherkasy	3.0	21.6	59.3	53.2	58.2	25.2	37.0
Chernivtsi	1.8	24.8	41.2	54.6	49.4	20.6	33.1
Chernihiv	2.7	20.4	62.6	51.1	60.5	28.4	35.1
Kiev (City)	5.0	22.8	100.0	62.3	100.0	14.9	100.0

Source: Statistical Yearbook, 1990, pp. 29 and 30, and staff
   calculations.

130

Table A.6 UKRAINE: Population by Working Age, Urban Residence, and Oblasts
(In Percent)

	Population Total	Below Working Age	Of Which Living In Towns	Working Age	Of Which Living In Towns	Over Working Age	Of Which Living In Towns
Ukraine Total	100.0	100.0	100.0	100.0	100.0	100.0	100.0
Crimea R.	4.8	5.0	4.8	5.0	4.9	4.1	5.2
Vinnytsia	3.7	3.5	2.6	3.5	2.5	4.5	2.3
Volyn	2.1	2.3	1.8	1.9	1.5	2.1	1.3
Dnipropetrovsk	7.5	7.4	9.1	7.7	9.3	7.2	9.8
Donetsk	10.3	9.9	13.1	10.5	13.5	10.3	16.1
Zhytomyr	3.0	3.0	2.6	2.8	2.3	3.3	2.2
Zakarpattia	2.4	3.0	1.7	2.4	1.5	1.8	1.2
Zaporizhzhia	4.0	4.0	4.5	4.1	4.6	3.8	4.6
Ivano-Frankivsk	2.8	3.1	1.9	2.7	1.8	2.6	1.4
Kiev Region	3.8	3.8	3.3	3.7	3.1	3.9	2.6
Kirovohrad	2.4	2.3	2.2	2.3	2.1	2.7	2.3
Luhansk	5.5	5.4	6.9	5.6	7.0	5.5	8.0
Lviv	5.3	5.6	4.8	5.3	4.8	4.9	4.1
Mykolaiv	2.6	2.7	2.6	2.6	2.5	2.4	2.5
Odessa	5.1	5.1	4.7	5.2	5.1	4.7	4.9
Poltava	3.4	3.1	2.8	3.3	2.8	4.1	3.0
Rivne	2.3	2.7	1.8	2.2	1.6	2.1	1.1
Sumy	2.8	2.6	2.6	2.6	2.5	3.3	2.7
Ternopil	2.3	2.3	1.6	2.1	1.4	2.5	1.1
Kharkiv	6.2	5.7	6.7	6.3	7.2	6.3	7.9
Kherson	2.4	2.6	2.3	2.5	2.2	2.1	2.1
Khmelnytsky	2.9	2.9	2.4	2.8	2.1	3.5	1.7
Cherkasy	3.0	2.8	2.4	2.8	2.3	3.5	2.3
Chernivtsi	1.8	2.0	1.2	1.8	1.2	1.8	1.0
Chernihiv	2.7	2.4	2.2	2.5	2.1	3.7	2.3
Kiev (City)	5.0	5.0	7.4	5.6	7.9	3.5	6.3

Source: Statistical Yearbook, 1990, pp. 29 and 30, and staff
  estimates.

Table A.7 UKRAINE: Population by Age Groups, Sex and Employment
(1989 Data; In Thousand People)

	Total	Male	Female	Employed Total	Male	Female	State Enterprises Total	Male	Female	Kolhoz Total	Male	Female
up to 14	10,374	5,279	5,094	0	0	0	0	0	0	0	0	0
14	720	362	357	1	1	0	1	1	0	0	0	0
15	727	372	354	12	7	5	9	5	4	3	2	1
16	755	386	369	40	24	16	30	17	13	9	6	3
17	733	378	355	151	74	76	124	56	69	25	18	7
18	694	350	344	334	182	152	282	142	140	50	39	12
19	640	321	319	413	212	201	355	170	185	56	42	15
20-24	3,352	1,684	1,667	2,648	1,344	1,304	2,333	1,139	1,194	296	192	104
25-29	3,958	1,969	1,989	3,668	1,893	1,775	3,261	1,637	1,623	378	236	143
30-34	3,900	1,924	1,976	3,712	1,880	1,832	3,305	1,631	1,674	379	229	149
35-39	3,741	1,826	1,915	3,594	1,785	1,810	3,190	1,549	1,642	380	219	161
40-44	2,706	1,295	1,411	2,592	1,259	1,333	2,252	1,080	1,173	323	168	155
45-49	3,220	1,504	1,716	3,017	1,435	1,581	2,449	1,162	1,287	553	265	288
50-54	3,705	1,727	1,978	3,214	1,548	1,666	2,548	1,220	1,327	653	320	333
55-59	2,953	1,314	1,639	1,489	1,023	466	1,153	750	404	327	269	58
60-64	3,232	1,275	1,958	686	404	281	590	333	257	88	68	21
65-69	2,020	663	1,357	229	124	105	199	103	96	27	19	7
70+	4,002	1,100	2,901	113	63	50	96	53	43	13	8	5
Total a/	51,439	23,863	27,576	25,916	13,260	12,656	22,181	11,049	11,132	3,562	2,100	1,462

Source: Council for Exploration of Productive Resources of Ukraine.

a/ Including non-Ukrainians

132

Table A.8

Population Growth
Ukraine 1981-1992[1,2]
(in 1000's)

	1981	1982	1983	1984	1985	1986	1987	1988	1989	1990	1991	1992
Total	50,169.8	50,357.5	n/a	n/a	50,914.1	51,076.5	51,237.6	51,376.9	51,514.8	51,636.8	51, 745.8	51, 801.9
Male	22,954.3	23,070.0	n/a	n/a	23,402.9	23,501.4	23,602.2	23,697.4	23,795.5	23,884.1	n/a	n/a
Female	27,215.5	27,287.5	n/a	n/a	27,511.1	27,575.1	27,635.4	27,679.6	27,719.3	27,752.7	n/a	n/a

Source: 1. Years 1980-1990 WHO/EURO-ESR Unit May 19, 1992 Mid Year Estimates
2. Years 1991-1992, MOH. Ukraine 1992 is as of 1st January

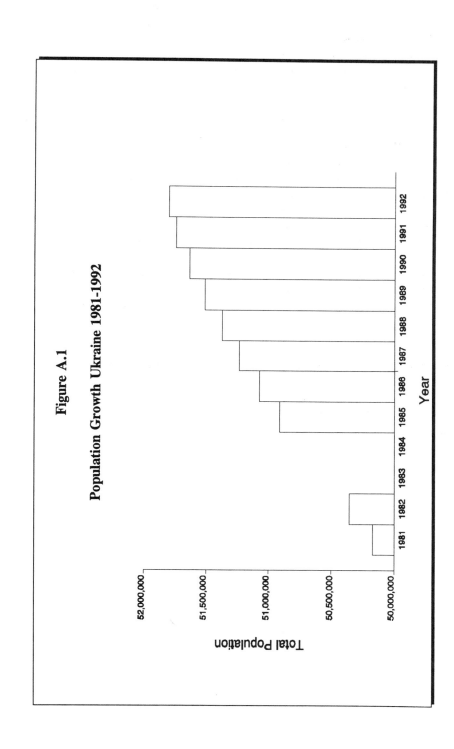

Figure A.1

Population Growth Ukraine 1981-1992

Table A.9

Population Structure All Ukraine

All Ukraine	Age Group						
	0-14	15-49	50-59	60-64	65-69	70+	Total
Total Population (thousands)	11093.1	24425.1	6658.1	3232.5	2020.0	4001.9	51430.7
Age Category as % of Total	21.6	47.5	12.9	6.3	3.9	7.8	100.0
Male	5641.4	12009.2	3041.3	1275	663	1100	23730.5
Female	5451.7	12415.9	3616.8	1958	1357	2901	27700.2
Males as % of Age Category	50.9	49.2	45.7	39.4	32.8	27.5	46.1
Cumulative % Males	23.8	74.4	87.2	92.6	95.4	100.0	
Females as % of Age Category	49.1	50.8	54.3	60.6	67.2	72.5	53.9
Cumulative % Females	19.7	64.5	77.6	84.6	89.5	100.0	

Source: Council for Exploration of Productive Resources of Ukraine, Kiev, 1989 data

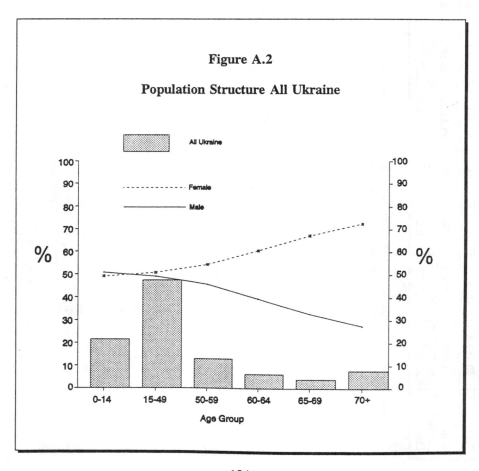

Figure A.2

Population Structure All Ukraine

Table A.10

Population Characteristics Of Oblasts
Ukraine

Oblast	Population	% of All Ukraine	% Population 60 and Greater	% of Females 60 and Greater	% of Males 60 and Greater
All Ukraine	51430.7	100.0	19.0	22.4	12.8
Vinnytsia	1920.8	3.7	22.4	28.2	15.3
Volyn	1058.4	2.1	17.0	20.6	12.9
Dnipropetrovsk	3871.9	7.5	17.1	21.2	12.4
Donetsk	5311.8	10.3	17.4	21.6	12.5
Zhytomyr	1537.6	3.0	20.1	25.1	14.1
Zakarpattia	1245.6	2.4	12.6	14.6	10.6
Zaporizhzhia	2073.9	4.0	17.2	21.3	12.4
Ivano-Frankivsk	1413.2	2.7	15.8	19.4	11.8
Kiev Region	1934.3	3.8	19.5	24.8	13.2
Kirovohrad	1228.0	2.4	21.7	27.2	15.2
Luhansk	2857.0	5.6	17.4	21.9	12.2
Lviv	2727.4	5.3	16.0	19.7	11.8
Mykolaiv	1328.3	2.6	16.6	20.8	11.8
Odessa	2624.1	5.1	16.7	20.6	12.2
Poltava	1748.0	3.4	22.7	28.6	15.4
Rivne	1164.2	2.3	15.5	19.3	11.3
Sumy	1425.4	2.8	22.5	28.3	15.5
Ternopil	1164.0	2.3	19.5	24.0	14.2
Kharkiv	3174.7	6.2	18.9	23.7	13.2
Kherson	1236.9	2.4	15.2	19.3	10.6
Khmelnytsky	1525.6	3.0	21.2	26.5	14.7
Cherkasy	1525.9	3.0	22.5	28.3	15.5
Chernivtsi	940.8	1.8	17.0	20.2	13.3
Chernihiv	1412.8	2.7	24.7	31.0	16.8
Kiev City	2553.4	5.0	12.7	15.6	9.5
Crimea	2426.6	4.7	15.0	18.7	10.7

Source: Council for Exploration of Productive Resource of Ukraine, Kiev, 1989 data

Table A.11

Percent Distribution of Population by Broad Categories
Ukraine and Selected Countries

Category	Ukraine	Belarus	Poland	Portugal	United Kingdom	Sweden	Canada	Europe
0-14	21.4	23.1	25.2	21.2	19.0	17.3	20.9	22.6
15-64	66.4	66.3	64.9	65.9	65.6	64.6	67.7	65.9
65+	12.1	10.6	10.0	12.9	15.4	18.1	11.4	11.5

Source: 1991 World Health Statistics Annual, WHO Geneva 1992

Table A.12

Population Structure Vinnytsia Oblast

Vinnytsia Oblast	Age Group						
	0-14	15-49	50-59	60-64	65-69	70+	Total
Total Population (thousands)	384.2	843.4	262.6	139.5	99.3	191.9	1920.9
Age Category as % of Total	20.0	43.9	13.7	7.3	5.2	10.0	100.0
Male	194.5	415.2	116.1	51.6	30.6	48.7	856.8
Female	189.7	428.1	146.5	87.8	68.7	143.2	1064.0
Males as % of Age Category	50.6	59.2	44.2	37.0	30.8	25.4	44.6
Cumulative % Males	22.7	71.2	84.7	90.7	94.3	100.0	
Females as % of Age Category	49.4	50.8	55.8	63.0	69.2	74.6	55.4
Cumulative % Females	17.8	58.1	71.8	80.1	86.5	100.0	

Source: Council for Exploration of Productive Resources of Ukraine, Kiev, 1989 data.

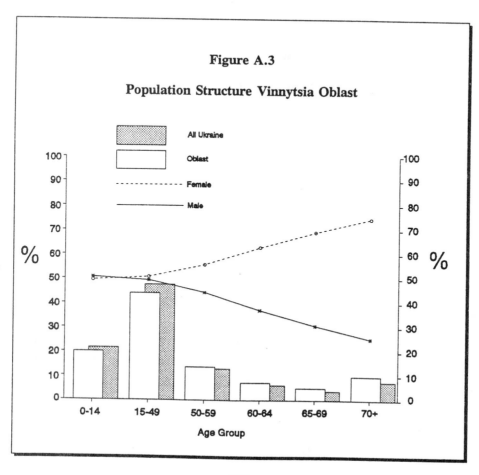

Figure A.3

Population Structure Vinnytsia Oblast

Table A.13

Population Structure Volyn Oblast

Volyn Oblast	Age Group						Total
	0-14	15-49	50-59	60-64	65-69	70+	
Total Population (thousands)	258.9	480.2	139.9	64.8	41.6	73.1	1058.4
Age Category as % of Total	24.5	45.4	13.2	6.1	3.9	6.9	100.0
Male	131.6	241.9	61.6	25.0	15.1	24.1	499.3
Female	127.3	238.3	78.2	39.9	26.5	49.0	559.2
Males as % of Age Category	50.8	50.4	44.1	38.5	36.3	33.0	47.2
Cumulative % Males	26.4	74.8	87.1	92.1	95.2	100.0	
Females as % of Age Category	49.2	49.6	55.9	61.5	63.7	67.0	52.8
Cumulative % Females	22.8	65.4	79.4	86.5	91.2	100.0	

Source: Council for Exploration of Productive Resources of Ukraine, Kiev, 1989 data.

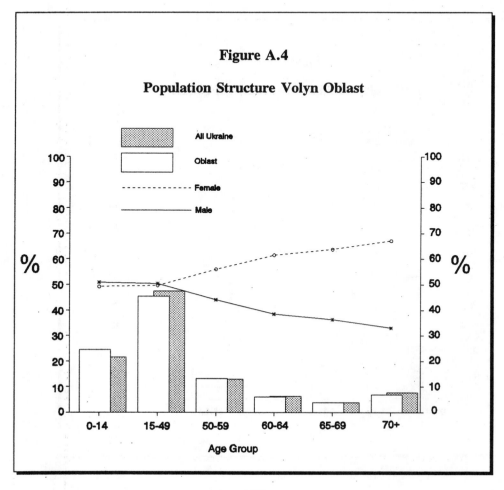

Figure A.4

Population Structure Volyn Oblast

Table A.14

Population Structure Dnipropetrovsk Oblast

Dnipropetrovsk Oblast	Age Group						
	0-14	15-49	50-59	60-64	65-69	70+	Total
Total Population (thousands)	821.8	1872.9	514.9	247.9	129.0	285.3	3871.9
Age Category as % of Total	21.2	48.4	13.3	6.4	3.3	7.4	100.0
Male	418.2	908.4	241.3	101.9	42.3	77.6	1789.8
Female	403.6	964.4	273.7	146.0	86.7	207.8	2082.1
Males as % of Age Category	50.9	48.5	46.9	41.1	32.8	27.2	46.2
Cumulative % Males	23.4	74.1	87.6	93.3	95.7	100.0	
Females as % of Age Category	49.1	51.5	53.1	58.9	67.2	72.8	53.8
Cumulative % Females	19.4	65.7	78.8	85.9	90.0	100.0	

Source: Council for Exploration of Productive Resources of Ukraine, Kiev, 1989 data

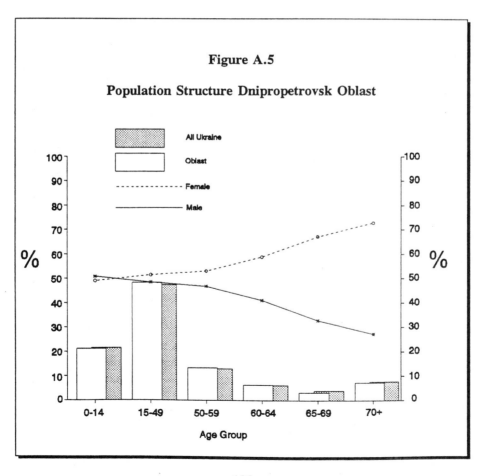

Figure A.5

Population Structure Dnipropetrovsk Oblast

Table A.15

Population Structure Donetsk Oblast

Donetsk Oblast	Age Group						
	0-14	15-49	50-59	60-64	65-69	70+	Total
Total Population	1102.8	2521.2	765.7	359.3	176.2	386.6	5311.8
Age Category as % of Total	20.8	47.5	14.4	6.8	3.3	7.3	100.0
Male	562.0	1236.7	352.6	145.8	57.1	104.3	2458.4
Female	540.8	1284.5	413.1	213.5	119.2	282.3	2853.4
Males as % of Age Category	51.0	49.1	46.1	40.6	32.4	27.0	46.3
Cumulative % Males	22.9	73.2	87.5	93.4	95.8	100.0	
Females as % of Age Category	49.0	50.9	53.9	59.4	67.6	73.0	53.7
Cumulative % Females	19.0	64.0	78.4	85.9	90.1	100.0	

Source: Council for Exploration of Productive Resources of Ukraine, Kiev, 1989 data

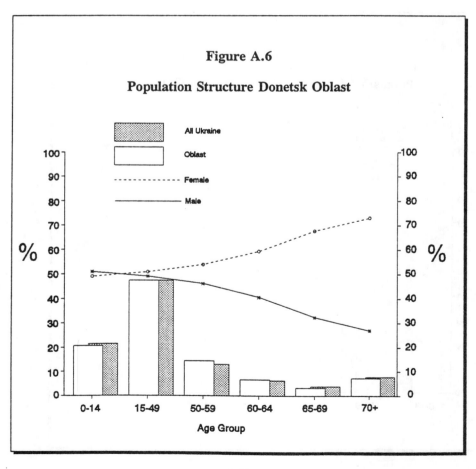

Figure A.6

Population Structure Donetsk Oblast

Table A.16

Population Structure Zhytomyr Oblast

Zhytomyr Oblast	Age Group						
	0-14	15-49	50-59	60-64	65-69	70+	Total
Total Population (thousands)	335.7	688.0	205.4	104.3	72.4	131.8	1537.6
Age Category as % of Total	21.8	44.7	13.4	6.8	4.7	8.6	100.0
Male	169.7	345.4	91.7	40.1	23.7	35.7	706.4
Female	165.9	342.6	113.7	64.2	48.7	96.2	831.2
Males as % of Age Category	50.6	50.2	44.7	38.5	32.8	27.1	45.9
Cumulative % Males	24.0	72.9	85.9	91.6	95.0	100.0	
Females as % of Age Category	49.4	49.8	55.3	61.5	67.2	72.9	54.1
Cumulative % Females	20.0	61.2	74.9	82.6	88.4	100.0	

Source: Council for Exploration of Productive Resources of Ukraine, Kiev, 1989 data

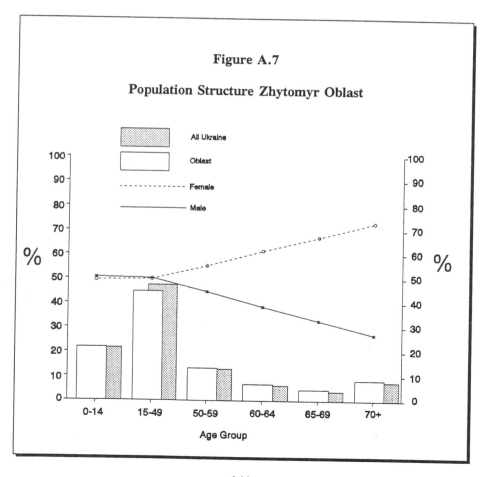

Figure A.7

Population Structure Zhytomyr Oblast

Table A.17

Population Structure Zakarpattia Oblast

Zakarpattia Oblast	Age Group						
	0-14	15-49	50-59	60-64	65-69	70+	Total
Total Population (thousands)	328.7	621.2	138.2	59.5	43.9	54.1	1245.6
Age Category as % of Total	26.4	49.9	11.1	4.8	3.5	4.3	100.0
Male	167.3	309.0	61.8	25.0	18.1	20.4	601.6
Female	161.4	312.3	76.4	34.5	25.9	33.6	644.1
Males as % of Age Category	50.9	49.7	44.7	42.0	41.1	37.8	48.3
Cumulative % Males	27.8	79.2	89.4	93.6	96.6	100.0	
Females as % of Age Category	49.1	50.3	55.3	58.0	58.9	62.2	51.7
Cumulative % Females	25.1	73.5	85.4	90.8	94.8	100.0	

Source: Council for Exploration of Productive Resources of Ukraine, Kiev, 1989 data

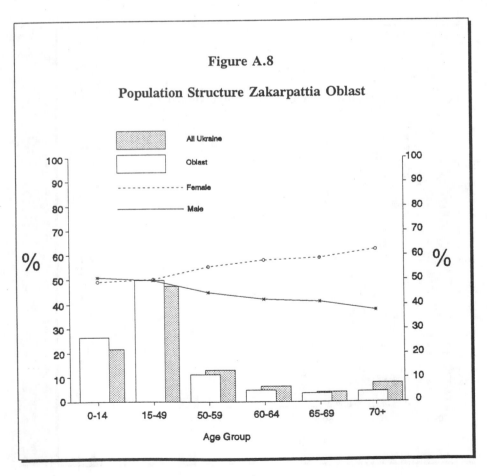

Figure A.8

Population Structure Zakarpattia Oblast

Table A.18

Population Structure Zaporizhzhia Oblast

Zaporizhzhia Oblast	Age Group						
	0-14	15-49	50-59	60-64	65-69	70+	Total
Total Population (thousands)	445.4	1007.5	264.8	135.0	68.8	152.3	2073.9
Age Category as % of Total	21.5	48.6	12.8	6.5	3.3	7.3	100.0
Male	226.7	487.1	123.1	54.7	22.2	41.4	955.3
Female	218.6	520.4	141.7	80.3	46.6	110.9	1118.6
Males as % of Age Category	50.9	48.3	46.5	40.5	32.3	27.2	46.1
Cumulative % Males	23.7	74.7	87.6	93.3	95.7	100.0	
Females as % of Age Category	49.1	51.7	53.5	59.5	67.7	72.8	53.9
Cumulative % Females	19.5	66.1	78.7	85.9	90.1	100.0	

Source: Council for Exploration of Productive Resources of Ukraine, Kiev, 1989 data

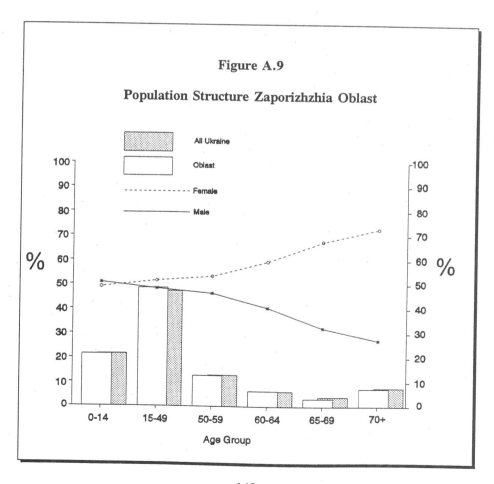

Figure A.9

Population Structure Zaporizhzhia Oblast

Population Structure Ivano-Frankivsk Oblast

Ivano-Frankivsk Oblast	Age Group						Total
	0-14	15-49	50-59	60-64	65-69	70+	
Total Population (thousands)	341.9	667.2	180.9	75.2	56.9	91.1	1413.2
Age Category as % of Total	24.2	47.2	12.8	5.3	4.0	6.4	100.0
Male	174.3	332.2	80.5	29.6	19.4	29.3	665.3
Female	167.6	335.1	100.4	45.6	37.5	61.8	747.9
Males as % of Age Category	51.0	49.8	44.5	39.3	34.2	32.2	47.1
Cumulative % Males	26.2	76.1	88.2	92.7	95.6	100.0	
Females as % of Age Category	49.0	50.2	55.5	60.7	65.8	67.8	52.9
Cumulative % Females	22.4	67.2	80.6	86.7	91.7	100.0	

Source: Council for Exploration of Productive Resources of Ukraine, Kiev, 1989 data

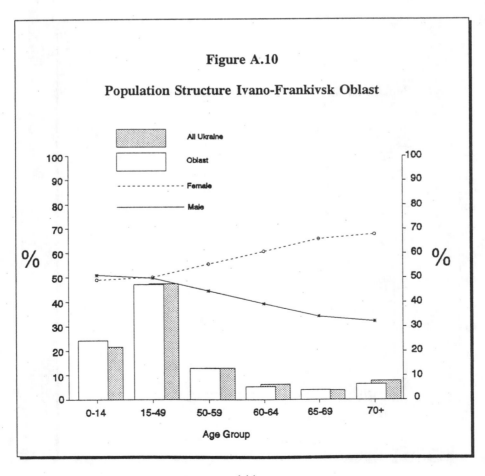

Figure A.10

Population Structure Ivano-Frankivsk Oblast

Population Structure Kiev Region

Kiev Region	Age Group						Total
	0-14	15-49	50-59	60-64	65-59	70+	
Total Population (thousands)	416.2	902.1	238.1	122.4	86.1	169.5	1934.3
Age Category as % of Total	21.5	46.6	12.3	6.3	4.5	8.8	100.0
Male	212.0	446.2	108.4	47.0	27.3	42.5	883.5
Female	204.2	455.8	129.8	75.4	58.8	126.9	1050.9
Males as % of Age Category	50.9	49.5	45.5	38.4	31.7	25.1	45.7
Cumulative % Males	24.0	74.5	86.8	92.1	95.2	100.0	
Females as % of Age Category	49.1	50.5	54.5	61.6	68.3	74.9	54.3
Cumulative % Females	19.4	62.8	75.2	82.3	87.9	100.0	

Source: Council for Exploration of Productive Resources of Ukraine, Kiev, 1989 data

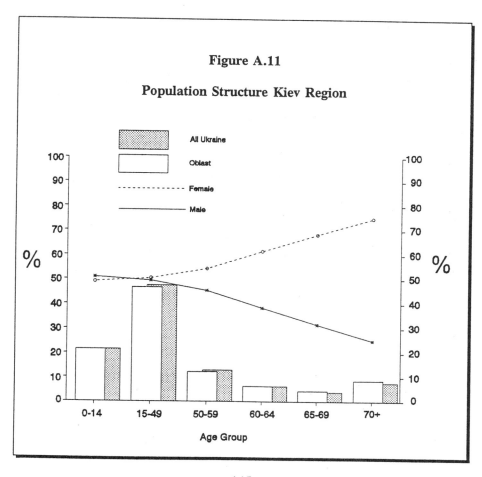

Figure A.11

Population Structure Kiev Region

All Ukraine
Oblast
Female
Male

145

Table A.21

Population Structure Kirovohrad Oblast

Kirovohrad Oblast	Age Group						Total
	0-14	15-49	50-59	60-64	65-59	70+	
Total Population (thousands)	254.2	553.8	153.5	89.1	56.3	121.1	1228.0
Age Category as % of Total	20.7	45.1	12.5	7.3	4.6	9.9	100.0
Male	129.4	273.2	71.0	34.0	18.4	32.2	558.2
Female	124.8	280.6	82.5	55.1	37.9	89.0	669.8
Males as % of Age Category	50.9	49.3	46.3	38.2	32.7	26.5	45.5
Cumulative % Males	23.2	72.1	84.8	90.9	94.2	100.0	
Females as % of Age Category	49.1	50.7	53.7	61.8	67.3	73.5	54.5
Cumulative % Females	18.6	60.5	72.8	81.1	86.7	100.0	

Source: Council for Exploration of Productive Resources of Ukraine, Kiev, 1989 data

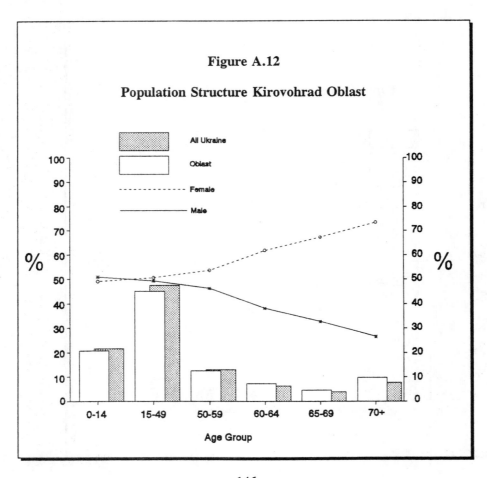

Figure A.12

Population Structure Kirovohrad Oblast

Table A.22

Population Structure Luhansk Oblast

Luhansk Oblast	Age Group						
	0-14	15-49	50-59	60-64	65-69	70+	Total
Total Population	602.0	1346.3	412.0	187.8	91.7	217.2	2857.0
Age Category as % of Total	21.1	47.1	14.4	6.6	3.2	7.6	100.0
Male	306.9	661.9	191.8	76.2	28.7	55.9	1321.4
Female	295.1	684.4	220.2	111.6	63.0	161.3	1535.7
Males as % of Age Category	51.0	49.2	46.6	40.6	31.3	25.7	46.2
Cumulative % Males	23.2	73.3	87.8	93.6	95.8	100.0	
Females as % of Age Category	49.0	50.8	53.4	59.4	68.7	74.3	53.8
Cumulative % Females	19.2	63.8	78.1	85.4	89.5	100.0	

Source: Council for Exploration of Productive Resources of Ukraine, Kiev, 1989 data

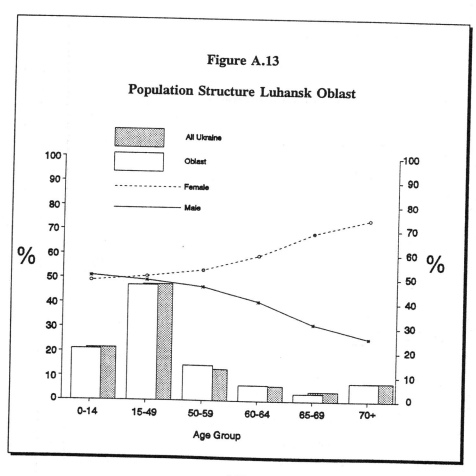

Figure A.13

Population Structure Luhansk Oblast

147

Table A.23

Population Structure Lviv Oblast

Lviv Oblast	Age Group						
	0-14	15-49	50-59	60-64	65-69	70+	Total
Total Population (thousands)	614.0	1339.0	339.0	142.1	107.2	186.1	2727.4
Age Category as % of Total	22.5	49.1	12.4	5.2	3.9	6.8	100.0
Male	312.2	674.2	154.1	55.5	37.0	60.9	1293.8
Female	301.8	664.8	184.9	86.6	70.3	125.3	1433.6
Males as % of Age Category	50.9	50.4	45.5	39.0	34.5	32.7	47.4
Cumulative % Males	24.1	76.2	88.2	92.4	95.3	100.0	
Females as % of Age Category	49.1	49.6	54.5	61.0	65.5	67.3	52.6
Cumulative % Females	21.0	67.4	80.3	86.4	91.3	100.0	

Source: Council for Exploration of Productive Resources of Ukraine, Kiev, 1989 data

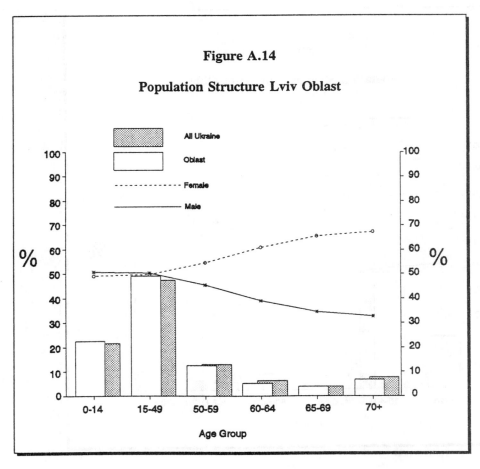

Figure A.14

Population Structure Lviv Oblast

Table A.24

Population Structure Mykolaiv Oblast

Mykolaiv Oblast	Age Group						
	0-14	15-49	50-59	60-64	65-59	70+	Total
Total Population (thousands)	303.7	645.1	158.3	79.2	46.0	96.0	1328.3
Age Category as % of Total	22.9	48.6	11.9	6.0	3.5	7.2	100.0
Male	154.3	315.2	73.6	31.3	15.2	26.5	616.1
Female	149.4	330.0	84.7	47.9	30.8	69.5	712.2
Males as % of Age Category	50.8	48.9	46.5	39.5	33.0	27.6	46.4
Cumulative % Males	25.0	76.2	88.2	93.2	95.7	100.0	
Females as % of Age Category	49.2	51.1	53.5	60.5	67.0	72.4	53.6
Cumulative % Females	21.0	67.3	79.2	85.9	90.2	100.0	

Source: Council for Exploration of Productive Resources of Ukraine, Kiev, 1989 data

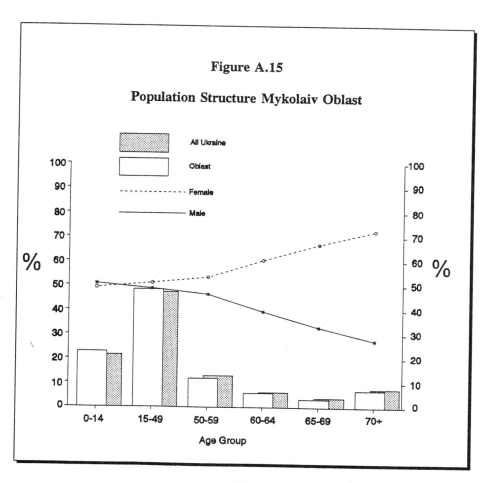

Figure A.15

Population Structure Mykolaiv Oblast

Table A.25

Population Structure Odessa Oblast

Odessa Oblast	Age Group						Total
	0-14	15-49	50-59	60-64	65-69	70+	
Total Population (thousands)	564.0	1297.6	324.6	151.7	100.1	186.0	2624.1
Age Category as % of Total	21.5	49.5	12.4	5.8	3.8	7.1	100.0
Male	286.4	636.8	148.8	59.0	34.8	55.5	1221.3
Female	277.6	660.8	175.8	92.7	65.3	130.5	1402.8
Males as % of Age Category	50.8	49.1	45.8	38.9	34.7	29.8	46.5
Cumulative % Males	23.5	75.6	87.8	92.6	95.5	100.0	
Females as % of Age Category	49.2	50.9	54.2	61.1	65.3	70.2	53.5
Cumulative % Females	19.8	66.9	79.4	86.0	90.7	100.0	

Source: Council for Exploration of Productive Resources of Ukraine, Kiev, 1989 data

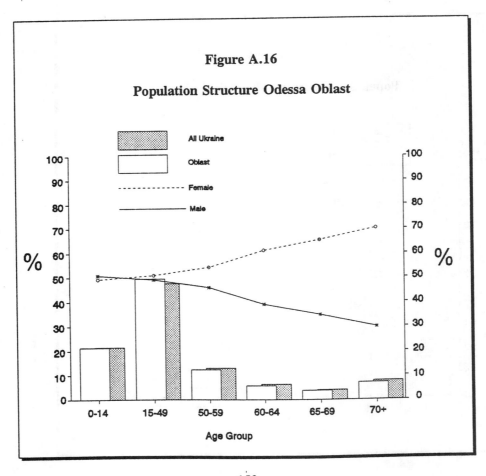

Figure A.16

Population Structure Odessa Oblast

Table A.26

Population Structure Poltava Oblast

Poltava Oblast	Age Group						
	0-14	15-49	50-59	60-64	65-69	70+	Total
Total Population (thousands)	343.7	781.7	226.5	123.5	88.3	184.4	1748.0
Age Category as % of Total	19.7	44.7	13.0	7.1	5.1	10.5	100.0
Male	174.6	384.1	105.3	47.9	27.6	45.4	785.1
Female	169.0	397.5	121.2	75.5	60.7	139.0	963.0
Males as % of Age Category	50.8	49.1	46.5	38.8	31.2	24.6	44.9
Cumulative % Males	22.2	71.2	84.6	90.7	94.2	100.0	
Females as % of Age Category	49.2	50.9	53.5	61.2	68.8	75.4	55.1
Cumulative % Females	17.6	58.8	71.4	79.3	85.6	100.0	

Source: Council for Exploration of Productive Resources of Ukraine, Kiev, 1989 data

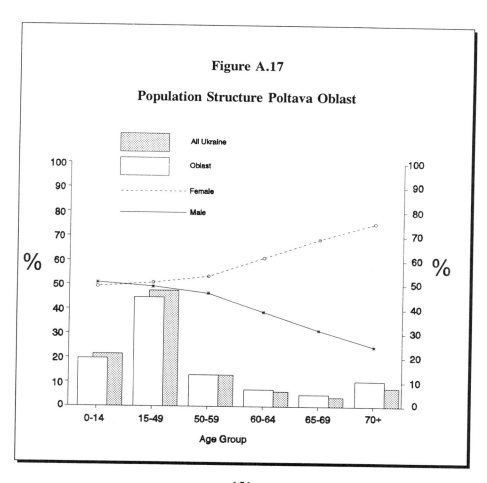

Figure A.17

Population Structure Poltava Oblast

Population Structure Rivne Oblast

Rivne Oblast	Age Group						Total
	0-14	15-49	50-59	60-64	65-69	70+	
Total Population (thousands)	293.8	544.9	145.0	60.5	43.6	76.4	1164.2
Age Category as % of Total	25.2	46.8	12.5	5.2	3.7	6.6	100.0
Male	148.9	274.9	65.3	23.1	14.9	24.5	551.6
Female	145.0	270.0	79.7	37.4	28.7	51.9	612.7
Males as % of Age Category	50.7	50.5	45.1	38.2	34.1	32.0	47.4
Cumulative % Males	27.0	76.8	88.7	92.9	95.6	100.0	
Females as % of Age Category	49.3	49.5	54.9	61.8	65.9	68.0	52.6
Cumulative % Females	23.7	67.7	80.7	86.8	91.5	100.0	

Source: Council for Exploration of Productive Resources of Ukraine, Kiev, 1989 data

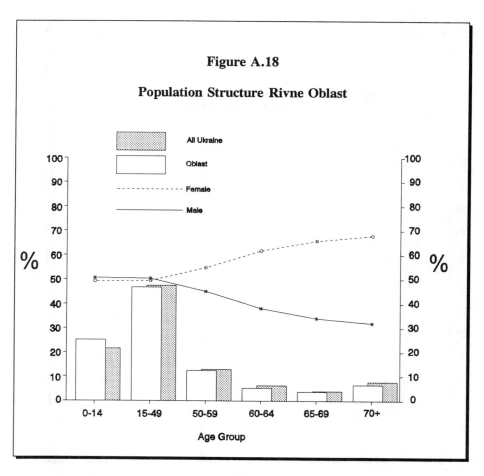

Figure A.18

Population Structure Rivne Oblast

152

Population Structure Sumy Oblast

Sumy Oblast	Age Group						
	0-14	15-49	50-59	60-64	65-69	70+	Total
Total Population (thousands)	286.7	633.9	183.9	105.0	70.2	145.8	1425.4
Age Category as % of Total	20.1	44.5	12.9	7.4	4.9	10.2	100.0
Male	145.6	313.8	82.7	40.5	21.9	37.0	641.5
Female	141.0	320.1	101.2	64.5	48.2	108.8	784.0
Males as % of Age Category	50.8	49.5	45.0	38.6	31.2	25.3	45.0
Cumulative % Males	22.7	71.6	84.5	90.8	94.2	100.0	
Females as % of Age Category	49.2	50.5	55.0	61.4	68.8	74.7	55.0
Cumulative % Females	18.0	58.8	71.7	80.0	86.1	100.0	

Source: Council for Exploration of Productive Resources of Ukraine, Kiev, 1989 data

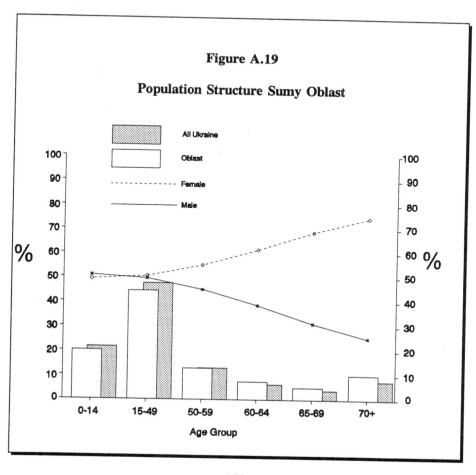

Figure A.19

Population Structure Sumy Oblast

Table A.29

Population Structure Ternopil Oblast

Ternopil Oblast	Age Group						
	0-14	15-49	50-59	60-64	65-69	70+	Total
Total Population (thousands)	258.3	518.4	160.1	70.9	56.4	99.9	1164.0
Age Category as % of Total	22.2	44.5	13.8	6.1	4.8	8.6	100.0
Male	131.1	257.1	71.6	26.6	19.3	30.4	536.1
Female	127.2	261.2	88.5	44.3	37.0	69.5	627.8
Males as % of Age Category	50.8	49.6	44.7	37.5	34.3	30.4	46.1
Cumulative % Males	24.5	72.4	85.8	90.7	94.3	100.0	
Females as % of Age Category	49.2	50.4	55.3	62.5	65.7	69.6	53.9
Cumulative % Females	20.3	61.9	76.0	83.0	88.9	100.0	

Source: Council for Exploration of Productive Resources of Ukraine, Kiev, 1989 data

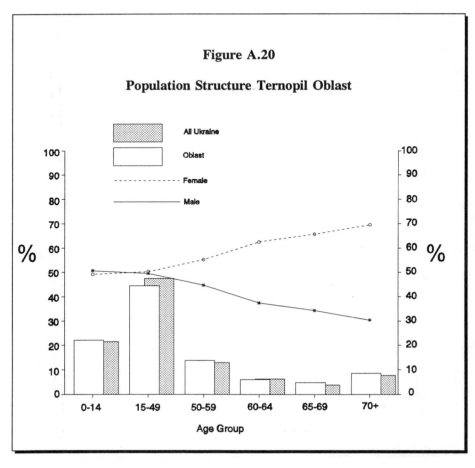

Figure A.20

Population Structure Ternopil Oblast

Table A.30

Population Structure Kharkiv Oblast

Kharkiv Oblast	Age Group						
	0-14	15-49	50-59	60-64	65-69	70+	Total
Total Population (thousands)	638.3	1542.6	393.3	204.4	122.3	273.7	3174.7
Age Category as % of Total	20.1	48.6	12.4	6.4	3.9	8.6	100.0
Male	325.5	752.4	179.0	81.1	38.4	72.4	1448.8
Female	312.8	790.2	214.4	123.3	83.9	201.3	1725.9
Males as % of Age Category	51.0	48.8	45.5	39.7	31.4	26.5	45.6
Cumulative % Males	22.5	74.4	86.8	92.4	95.0	100.0	
Females as % of Age Category	49.0	51.2	54.5	60.3	68.6	73.5	54.4
Cumulative % Females	18.1	63.9	76.3	83.5	88.3	100.0	

Source: Council for Exploration of Productive Resources of Ukraine, Kiev, 1989 data

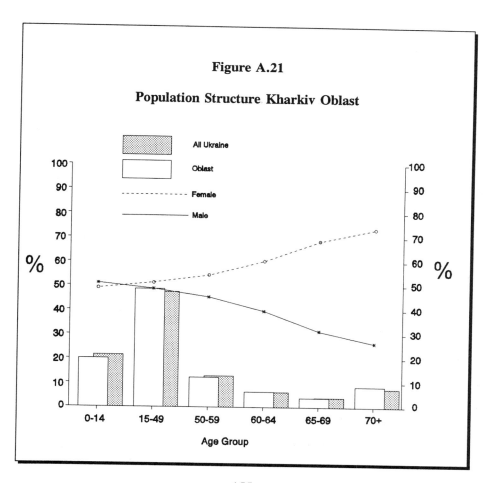

Figure A.21

Population Structure Kharkiv Oblast

Table A.31

Population Structure Kherson Oblast

Kherson Oblast	Age Group						
	0-14	15-49	50-59	60-64	65-69	70+	Total
Total Population (thousands)	289.9	605.2	153.2	71.1	39.2	78.3	1236.9
Age Category as % of Total	23.4	48.9	12.4	5.7	3.2	6.3	100.0
Male	147.4	297.6	71.3	28.0	12.6	20.3	577.3
Female	142.5	307.5	81.9	43.0	26.5	58.0	659.6
Males as % of Age Category	50.8	49.2	46.5	39.4	32.3	25.9	46.7
Cumulative % Males	25.5	77.1	89.4	94.3	96.5	100.0	
Females as % of Age Category	49.2	50.8	53.5	60.6	67.7	74.1	53.3
Cumulative % Females	21.6	68.2	80.7	87.2	91.2	100.0	

Source: Council for Exploration of Productive Resources of Ukraine, Kiev, 1989 data

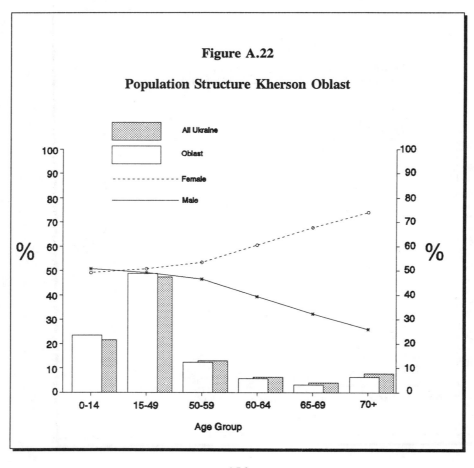

Figure A.22

Population Structure Kherson Oblast

Population Structure Khmelnytsky Oblast

Khmelnytsky Oblast	Age Group						
	0-14	15-49	50-59	60-64	65-69	70+	Total
Total Population (thousands)	316.4	684.8	201.0	103.5	76.7	143.2	1525.6
Age Category as % of Total	20.7	44.9	13.2	6.8	5.0	9.4	100.0
Male	160.8	340.1	88.4	39.4	25.2	37.2	691.2
Female	155.6	344.7	112.6	64.0	51.4	106.0	834.4
Males as % of Age Category	50.8	49.7	44.0	38.1	32.9	26.0	45.3
Cumulative % Males	23.3	72.5	85.3	91.0	94.6	100.0	
Females as % of Age Category	49.2	50.3	56.0	61.9	67.1	74.0	54.7
Cumulative % Females	18.7	60.0	73.5	81.1	87.3	100.0	

Source: Council for Exploration of Productive Resources of Ukraine, Kiev, 1989 data

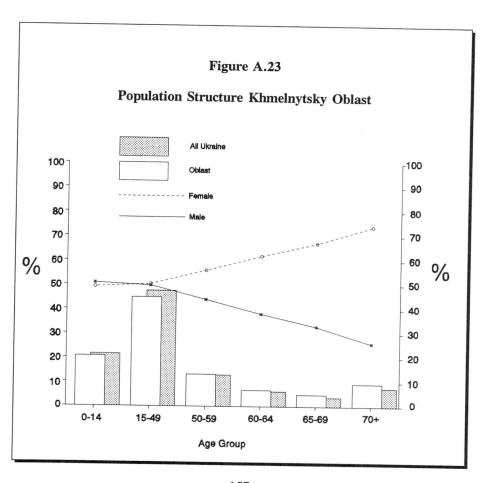

Figure A.23

Population Structure Khmelnytsky Oblast

Table A.33

Population Structure Cherkasy Oblast

Cherkasy Oblast	Age Group						
	0-14	15-49	50-59	60-64	65-69	70+	Total
Total Population (thousands)	307.9	676.1	197.9	112.7	75.7	155.6	1525.9
Age Category as % of Total	20.2	44.3	13.0	7.4	5.0	10.2	100.0
Male	156.6	329.4	90.2	43.5	23.9	38.0	681.6
Female	151.3	346.7	107.7	69.1	51.9	117.6	844.3
Males as % of Age Category	50.9	48.7	45.6	38.6	31.5	24.4	44.7
Cumulative % Males	23.0	71.3	84.5	90.9	94.4	100.0	
Females as % of Age Category	49.1	51.3	54.4	61.4	68.5	75.6	55.3
Cumulative % Females	17.9	59.0	71.7	79.9	86.1	100.0	

Source: Council for Exploration of Productive Resources of Ukraine, Kiev, 1989 data

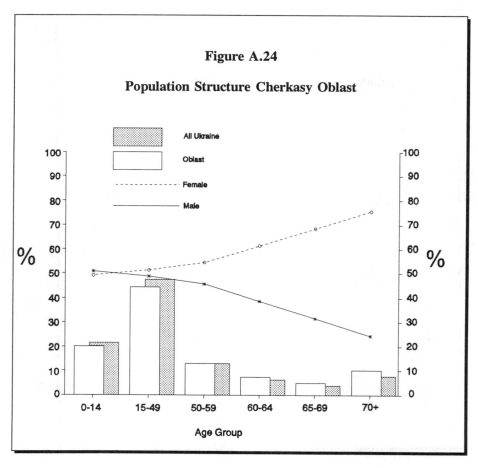

Figure A.24

Population Structure Cherkasy Oblast

Table A.34

Population Structure Chernivtsi Oblast

Chernivtsi Oblast	Age Group						Total
	0-14	15-49	50-59	60-64	65-69	70+	
Total Population (thousands)	219.8	446.0	115.1	52.7	42.5	64.7	940.8
Age Category as % of Total	23.4	47.4	12.2	5.6	4.5	6.9	100.0
Male	111.5	216.6	51.2	20.6	15.7	21.8	437.4
Female	108.2	229.4	63.9	32.2	26.8	42.9	503.4
Males as % of Age Category	50.7	48.6	44.5	39.0	36.9	33.7	46.5
Cumulative % Males	25.5	75.0	86.7	91.4	95.0	100.0	
Females as % of Age Category	49.3	51.4	55.5	61.0	63.1	66.3	53.5
Cumulative % Females	21.5	67.1	79.8	86.1	91.5	100.0	

Source: Council for Exploration of Productive Resources of Ukraine, Kiev, 1989 data

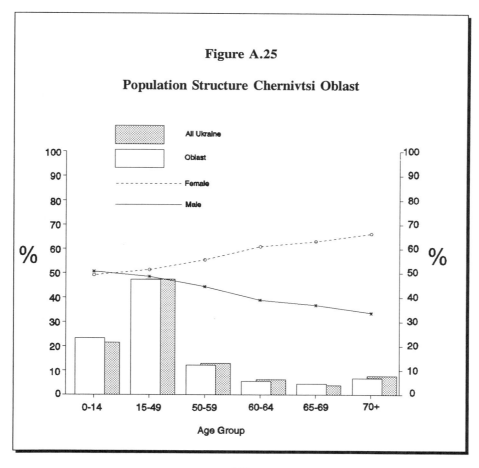

Figure A.25

Population Structure Chernivtsi Oblast

159

Table A.35

Population Structure Chernihiv Oblast

Chernihiv Oblast	Age Group						Total
	0-14	15-49	50-59	60-64	65-69	70+	
Total Population (thousands)	270.7	593.4	199.9	114.9	78.8	155.1	1412.8
Age Category as % of Total	19.2	42.0	14.1	8.1	5.6	11.0	100.0
Male	137.4	293.8	90.0	43.9	24.1	37.1	626.4
Female	133.3	299.6	109.9	71.0	54.6	118.0	786.4
Males as % of Age Category	50.8	49.5	45.0	38.2	30.6	23.9	44.3
Cumulative % Males	21.9	68.8	83.2	90.2	94.1	100.0	
Females as % of Age Category	49.2	50.5	55.0	61.8	69.4	76.1	55.7
Cumulative % Females	17.0	55.0	69.0	78.0	85.0	100.0	

Source: Council for Exploration of Productive Resources of Ukraine, Kiev, 1989 data

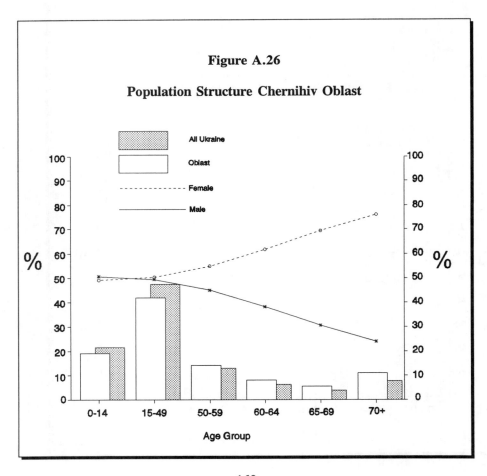

Figure A.26

Population Structure Chernihiv Oblast

Table A.36

Population Structure Kiev City

Kiev City	Age Group						
	0-14	15-49	50-59	60-64	65-69	70+	Total
Total Population (thousands)	545.1	1407.9	275.3	112.2	72.8	140.2	2553.4
Age Category as % of Total	21.3	55.1	10.8	4.4	2.9	5.5	100.0
Male	276.2	678.1	130.0	46.3	24.2	42.8	1197.5
Female	268.9	729.8	145.3	65.9	48.6	97.4	1355.9
Males as % of Age Category	50.7	48.2	47.2	41.3	33.3	30.5	46.9
Cumulative % Males	23.1	79.7	90.5	94.4	96.4	100.0	
Females as % of Age Category	49.3	51.8	52.8	58.7	66.7	69.5	53.1
Cumulative % Females	19.8	73.7	84.4	89.2	92.8	100.0	

Source: Council for Exploration of Productive Resources of Ukraine, Kiev, 1989 data

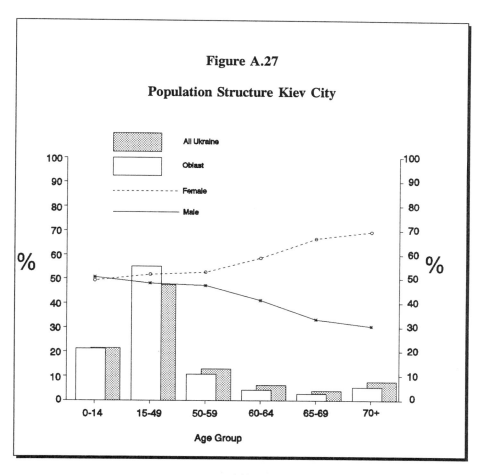

Figure A.27

Population Structure Kiev City

161

Table A.37

Population Structure Crimea

Crimea	Age Group						
	0-14	15-49	50-59	60-64	65-69	70+	Total
Total Population (thousands)	549.0	1204.8	309.1	143.4	77.8	142.4	2426.6
Age Category as % of Total	22.6	49.7	12.7	5.9	3.2	5.9	100.0
Male	280.2	587.6	140.0	57.1	25.5	38.7	1129.2
Female	268.8	617.2	169.1	86.3	52.3	103.8	1297.4
Males as % of Age Category	51.0	48.8	45.3	39.8	32.8	27.1	46.5
Cumulative % Males	24.8	76.9	89.3	94.3	96.6	100.0	
Females as % of Age Category	49.0	51.2	54.7	60.2	67.2	72.9	53.5
Cumulative % Females	20.7	68.3	81.3	88.0	92.0	100.0	

Source: Council for Exploration of Productive Resources of Ukraine, Kiev, 1989 data

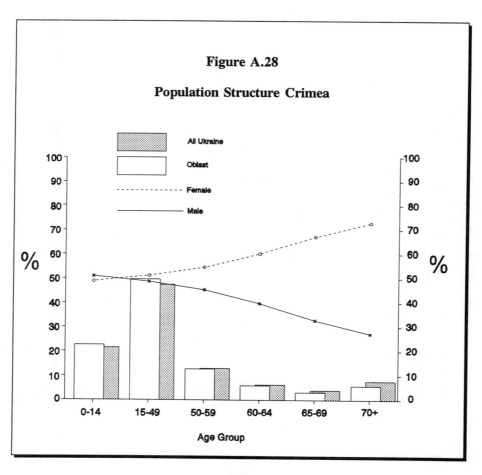

Figure A.28

Population Structure Crimea

162

Table A.38

**Life Expectancy and Survival by Gender
Ukraine and Selected Countries**

		Ukraine 1990		Belarus 1990		Poland 1990		Portugal 1990		United Kingdom 1990		Sweden 1988		Canada 1989	
		Life Expectancy to Age X	% Survivors to Age X	Life Expectancy to Age X	% Survivors to Age X	Life Expectancy to Age X	% Survivors to Age X	Life Expectancy to Age X	% Survivors to Age X	Life Expectancy to Age X	% Survivors to Age X	Life Expectancy to Age X	% Survivors to Age X	Life Expectancy to Age X	% Survivors to Age X
Males	Age														
	0	65.6	100.0	66.2	100.0	66.5	100.0	70.1	100.0	73.0	100.0	74.2	100.0	73.7	100.0
	1	65.6	98.5	66.1	98.6	66.7	98.2	70.0	98.8	72.6	99.1	73.7	99.3	73.3	99.2
	15	52.2	97.6	52.6	97.8	53.1	97.6	56.5	98.0	58.9	98.7	59.9	99.0	59.6	98.8
	45	25.8	87.9	26.2	88.4	26.1	89.7	29.3	91.5	30.4	95.3	31.5	95.2	31.5	94.5
	65	12.5	59.7	12.9	60.7	12.5	61.8	13.8	72.4	14.2	78.2	15.0	80.3	15.3	78.4
Females	Age														
	0	74.9	100.0	75.8	100.0	75.6	100.0	77.3	100.0	78.7	100.0	80.1	100.0	80.6	100.0
	1	74.8	98.9	75.5	99.0	75.6	98.6	77.0	99.0	78.2	99.3	79.5	99.5	80.1	99.4
	15	61.2	98.3	62.0	98.5	61.9	98.2	63.4	98.5	64.4	99.0	65.7	99.3	66.3	99.1
	45	32.6	95.2	33.2	95.6	33.1	95.6	34.6	96.0	35.3	97.2	36.6	97.3	37.3	97.1
	65	15.8	81.7	16.5	82.8	16.2	82.8	17.0	86.6	18.1	86.3	18.8	88.9	19.8	87.9

Source: 1991 World Health Statistics Annual, WHO Geneva 1992

163

Table A.39

Vital Events Rates Per 100,000
Ukraine and Selected Countries 1990[1]

	Ukraine	Belarus	Poland	Portugal	United Kingdom	Sweden	Canada
Birth Rate	12.7	13.9	16.4	13.5	13.6	12.9	14.1
Death Rate	12.2	10.7	9.9	10.1	11.8	12.1	7.5
Natural Increase	0.5	3.2	6.5	3.4	1.8	0.8	6.6

Source: 1991 World Health Statistics Annual, WHO Geneva 1992
Note: 1.   Canada 1985-90

Table A.40

**Vital Events Rates Per 100,000
Ukraine**

Year	Live Births	Deaths	Natural Increase
1980	14.8	11.3	3.5
1981	14.6	11.3	3.3
1982	14.8	11.3	3.5
1983	16.0	11.5	4.5
1984	15.6	12.0	3.6
1985	15.0	12.1	2.9
1986	15.5	11.1	4.4
1987	14.8	11.4	3.4
1988	14.4	11.6	2.8
1989	13.3	11.6	1.7
1990	12.7	12.1	0.6
1991	12.4	13.5	-1.1
1992[1]	11.5	14.6	-3.1

Source: MOH as cited in Khodorovsky, George;
            Family Planning and Health of Women in Ukraine, July 1992.
Note: 1.   First Quarter 1992

165

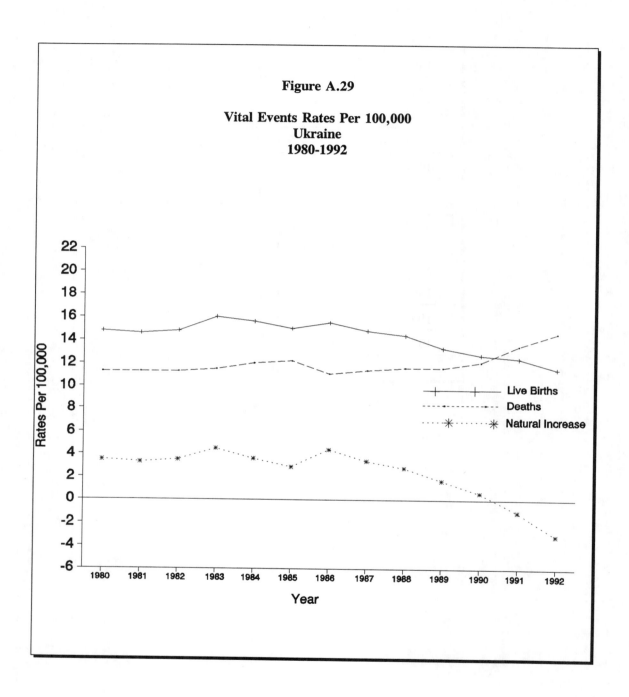

Figure A.29

Vital Events Rates Per 100,000
Ukraine
1980-1992

Table A.41

Main Causes of Death
Crude Death Rate Per 100,000 and Percent of Deaths
Ukraine
1990

Cause (ICD-9 Basic Tabulation List)	Male		Female	
	Crude Death Rate	% Deaths	Crude Death Rate	% Deaths
Diseases of the Circulatory System (25-30) of which	559	44.9	718	60.0
• Acute Myocardial Infarction (270)	30	2.4	17	1.4
• Other Ischemic Heart Diseases (279)	294	23.6	352	29.4
• Cerebrovascular Disease (29)	163	13.1	251	21.0
• Atherosclerosis, Embolism and Other Diseases of Arteries Etc. (300-302)	40	3.2	70	5.9
Malignant Neoplasms (08-14) of which	238	19.1	161	13.5
• Stomach (091)	37	3.0	23	1.9
• Trachea Bronchus and Lung (101)	78	6.3	14	1.2
• Breast	-.-	-.-	24	2.0
Accidents and Adverse Effects, suicide, Homicide, and Other Violence (E47-E56) of which	179	14.4	46	3.8
• Accidents and Adverse Effects (E47-53)	121	9.7	30	2.5
• Suicide (E54)	35	2.8	9	0.8
Diseases of the Respiratory System (31-32) of which	95	7.6	53	4.4
• Bronchitis, Chronic and Unspecified Emphysema and Asthma (323)	69	5.5	39	3.3
Four Listed Causes	1,071	86.0	978	81.7
All Causes	1,246	100.0	1,196	100.0

Source: 1991 World Health Statistics Annual, WHO Geneva, 1992

Table A.42

Age Standardized[1] Death Rates Per 100,000 for All Ages and Both Genders By Selected Causes, Ukraine and Selected Countries

Cause of Death (ICD-9 Basic Tabulation List)	Country and Year						
	Ukraine 1990	Belarus 1990	Poland 1990	Portugal 1990	United Kingdom 1990	Sweden 1988	Canada 1989
Infectious and Parasitic Diseases (01-07)	11.8	7.6	8.9	7.8	4.0	5.4	4.7
Malignant Neoplasms (08-14)	184.4	176.6	212.8	170.5	220.4	169.0	202.5
Malignant Neoplasm of Stomach (091)	27.9	35.1	21.2	27.8	12.7	10.3	8.6
Malignant Neoplasm of Trachea, Bronchus and Lung (101)	40.8	37.4	51.4	21.3	54.3	23.9	54.3
Malignant Neoplasm of Female Breast (113)	21.1	18.2	22.6	25.7	40.3	26.8	34.1
Diseases of the Circulatory System (25-30)	589.0	544.7	589.2	405.9	363.6	368.1	291.4
Ischemic Heart Disease (27)	317.1	336.0	121.0	85.6	215.3	209.3	172.2
Cerebrovascular Disease (29)	191.2	148.3	73.1	216.6	51.3	69.0	52.9
Diseases of the Respiratory System (31-32)	66.5	73.4	44.9	67.8	84.3	55.8	59.5
Bronchitis, Chronic and Unspecified; Emphysema and Asthma (323)	47.8	46.2	25.0	13.9	12.5	13.1	8.4
Diseases of the Digestive System (33-34)	29.7	22.7	34.5	44.7	26.9	24.2	27.7
Injury and Poisoning (E47-E56)	107.4	103.4	82.5	66.3	33.3	52.9	51.5
Motor Vehicle Accidents (E471)	23.0	23.2	22.4	26.9	9.0	8.8	15.4
Suicide and Self Inflicted Injury (E54)	20.5	21.3	13.8	8.5	7.8	17.8	13.1
All Causes	1141.9	1080.2	1123.7	954.2	820.4	753.1	726.7

Source: 1991 World Health Statistics Annual, WHO Geneva 1992
Note: 1. Standardized to the European population.

Table A.43

Age Specific Death Rates for Tuberculosis
Ukraine and Selected Countries

Causes of Death (ICD-9 Tabulation List) and Ages	Ukraine 1990 M	Ukraine 1990 F	Belarus 1990 M	Belarus 1990 F	Poland 1990 M	Poland 1990 F	Portugal 1990 M	Portugal 1990 F	United Kingdom 1990 M	United Kingdom 1990 F	Sweden 1988 M	Sweden 1988 F	Canada 1989 M	Canada 1989 F
020-021 Tuberculosis of Respiratory System														
<1 Year	0.9	1.3	-.-	-.-	-.-	-.-	-.-	-.-	0.2	-.-	-.-	-.-	-.-	-.-
1-4	0.3	0.1	-.-	0.3	-.-	-.-	-.-	-.-	-.-	-.-	-.-	-.-	-.-	-.-
5-14	-.-	0.1	0.1	-.-	-.-	-.-	-.-	0.5	0.0	0.0	-.-	-.-	-.-	-.-
15-24	0.6	0.3	0.3	0.1	0.1	0.0	0.1	0.5	-.-	0.0	-.-	0.2	-.-	-.-
25-34	8.3	0.9	2.8	0.2	0.9	0.4	2.0	0.5	0.1	0.0	-.-	-.-	-.-	-.-
35-44	22.1	2.2	8.5	0.6	3.2	0.7	2.3	1.1	0.1	0.0	0.2	-.-	-.-	0.0
45-54	34.0	2.4	17.2	2.0	9.9	1.4	5.9	0.9	0.5	0.2	0.2	0.4	0.4	0.3
55-64	32.4	2.9	18.7	2.3	16.0	2.3	10.7	1.6	1.4	0.5	0.5	0.9	1.2	1.5
65-74	27.7	4.9	15.6	5.5	26.1	5.8	10.7	...	3.5	1.0	1.5	2.9	2.4	2.4
75+	24.0	5.6	18.6	9.4	34.4	12.5	19.8	5.4	7.6	2.1	5.9	2.9	7.9	2.4
022-025 Tuberculosis, Other Forms														
<1 Year	0.3	0.3	-.-	-.-	-.-	-.-	-.-	1.8	-.-	-.-	-.-	-.-	-.-	-.-
1-4	-.-	0.1	-.-	-.-	-.-	-.-	-.-	-.-	-.-	-.-	-.-	-.-	-.-	-.-
5-14	0.0	0.1	-.-	-.-	-.-	0.0	-.-	-.-	-.-	-.-	-.-	-.-	-.-	-.-
15-24	0.1	0.1	-.-	-.-	-.-	0.0	0.1	-.-	-.-	0.0	-.-	-.-	0.1	-.-
25-34	0.3	0.1	0.1	0.3	0.3	0.0	-.-	0.3	0.0	0.1	-.-	-.-	0.1	-.-
35-44	0.5	0.3	0.9	0.4	0.2	0.0	0.3	0.2	0.1	0.0	-.-	-.-	0.1	0.1
45-54	2.7	0.7	1.2	1.2	0.3	0.1	0.8	-.-	0.2	0.1	-.-	-.-	0.1	0.1
55-64	4.6	1.5	0.5	1.5	0.2	0.0	1.7	0.9	0.3	0.2	-.-	-.-	-.-	0.1
65-74	7.0	1.2	1.6	-.-	0.2	0.4	1.8	0.9	0.5	0.3	0.5	-.-	0.3	0.3
75+	5.5	1.4	-.-	-.-	0.4	0.2	2.1	1.2	1.5	0.6	0.8	2.0	1.1	0.5

-.- Magnitude zero
0.0 Magnitude not zero, but less than 0.05

Source: 1991 World Health Statistics Annual, WHO Geneva 1992

169

Table A.44

Total Fertility[1], Infant Mortality[2], and Maternal Mortality[3] Rates
Ukraine and Selected Countries

	Ukraine	Belarus	Poland	Portugal	United Kingdom	Sweden	Canada
Total Fertility Rate Per Woman	1.9[4]		2.2	1.8	1.8	1.8	1.7
Infant Mortality Rate Per 1000 Live Births	13[4]	12[5]	19[6]	12	8	6	7
Maternal Mortality Rate Per 100,000 Live Births	32[4]	32[5]	11	10	8	5	4[7]

Sources:
1. Unless otherwise noted, 1991 World Health Statistics Annual, WHO Geneva, 1992 (1986-87 data).
2. Unless otherwise noted, World Development Report 1992, The World Bank, (1990 data)
3. Unless otherwise noted, WHO HFA Statistical Indicator Database (1989 data)
4. Khodorovsky, G., Family Planning and Health of Women in Ukraine, Kiev, July 1992 (1990 MOH data).
5. Ministry of Health, obtained during World Bank CEM Mission, May 1992 (1991 data)
6. Institute of Medical Statistics, Poland, 1991 (applying WHO methodology)
7. Statistics Canada, Health Reports, Mortality. Catalogue 82-003 (1989 data)

Table A.45

Infant Mortality Rate
Ukraine
1980-1992

	'80	'81	'82	'83	'84	'85	'86	'87	'88	'89	'90	'91	'92
Infant Mortality Per 100,000 Live Births	16.6	16.2	16.1	n/a	n/a	15.9	14.7	14.6	15.4	13.1	13.0	13.6	15.0

Source: HFA Statistical Indicator Database, WHO (1981-90) and MOH Ukraine (1991, 1992= 1st Q)

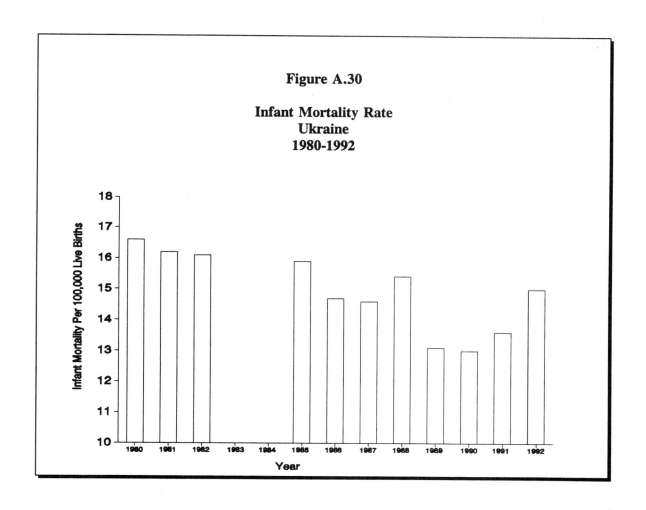

Figure A.30

Infant Mortality Rate
Ukraine
1980-1992

Table A.46

Age Specific Maternal and Infant Death Rates by Selected Causes and Ages
Ukraine and Selected Countries

Cause of Death (ICD-9 Basic Tabulation List) and Ages	Ukraine 1990		Belarus 1990		Poland 1990		Portugal 1990		United Kingdom 1990		Sweden 1988		Canada 1989	
	M	F	M	F	M	F	M	F	M	F	M	F	M	F
38 Abortion 15-24		0.4		--		0.1		0.1		0.1		--		--
25-34		0.4		0.5		0.3		0.1		0.1		--		0.0
35-44		0.4		0.4		0.2		0.2		0.1		--		0.0
390 Hemorrhage of Pregnancy and Childbirth 15-24		0.3		0.1		0.0		--		0.0		--		0.1
25-34		0.3		0.4		0.2		0.4		--		--		0.1
35-44		0.3		--		0.2		0.2		--		--		0.0
391 Toxaemia of Pregnancy 15-24		0.3		--		0.0		--		0.1		--		--
25-34		0.2		0.1		0.2		0.3		0.2		--		0.0
35-44		0.1		--		0.1		--		--		0.2		--
392-394, 399, 40, 41 Conditions of the Puerperium and Other Obstetrical Causes 15-24		1.2		0.3		0.3		--		0.1		0.5		0.2
25-34		1.2		1.3		0.5		0.1		0.2		0.9		0.2
35-44		0.7		0.7		0.3		0.3		0.1		0.2		0.0
440 Spina Bifida and Hydrocephalus <1 Year	37.2	34.8	38.2	47.9	80.9	97.3	16.7	21.3	9.3	6.9	10.4	3.7	14.4	15.7
442 Congenital Anomalies of Heart and Circulatory System <1 Year	181.2	148.6	169.2	129.2	214.6	160.2	105.1	93.9	81.7	64.9	72.6	71.9	93.0	85.6
441, 443-447, 449 Other Congenital Anomalies <1 Year	196.0	152.1	196.5	159.7	168.6	161.7	163.5	164.8	82.9	68.0	114.1	116.1	116.8	117.5
453 Birth Trauma <1 Year	76.9	48.0	110.5	45.0	103.7	59.6	16.7	3.5	15.4	9.7	25.9	18.4	10.4	6.3
450-452 454, 455, 459 Other Conditions Originating in the Perinatal Period <1 Year	504.9	351.8	462.5	294.7	816.2	611.9	580.5	382.8	362.2	293.0	273.3	154.8	334.1	242.3

-- Magnitude zero
0.0 Magnitude not zero, but less than 0.05

Source: 1991 World Health Statistics Annual, WHO Geneva 1992

Table A.47

Abortion Indicators
Ukraine
1986-1990

Indicator	1986	1987	1988	1989	1990	% Change Over 5 Years
Women in Fertile Age (15-49)	12,756,074	12,637,884	12,509,592	12,401,599	12,339,334	-3.0
Live Births	792,574	768,851	740,000[1]	690,981	657,202	-21.0
Abortions	1,166,039	1,113,229	1,080,029	1,058,414	1,019,038	-14.0
• In Women Under Age	3,950	-.-	4,306	5,717	6,137	
• Criminal Abortions	106,790	n/a	88,740	n/a	72,820	
• Miscarriages	29,800	n/a	28,970	n/a	25,130	
Live Births Per 1000 Women in Fertile Age	62.1	60.8	59.2	55.7	53.3	-17.0
Abortions Per 1000 Women in Fertile Age	91.4	88.1	86.3	85.3	82.6	-11.0
Abortions Per 100 Live Births	147.1	144.8	145.9	153.2	155.1	5.0

Sources: HFA Statistical Indicator Database WHO/EURO, Khodorovsky
Note: 1.   Estimate

Table A.48

Ministry of Health
Estimated Demand for Contraceptives for 1991
Ukraine

Denomination	Number	Value in Million Rubles	$US
Condoms	468 million items	702	14.04
Hormonal Contraceptives	9.9 million packs	114	18.05
Intrauterus Contraceptives	2.4 million items	39.6	40.32

Source: Ministry of Health

Table A.49

Prevalence and Incidence Rates Per 100,000 Total Population by Disease and Percent of Total Cases Registered at Health Care Institutions 1991

Main Categories of Diseases (ICD-9)	Prevalence Rate	% Cases	Incidence Rate	% Cases
All Categories	120,377.2	100.00	62,029.4	100.00
Infectious & Parasitic Diseases	4,110.2	3.4	2,697.8	4.0
Neoplasms	2,550.5	2.1	610.4	0.9
Endocrine & Metabolic	3,401.3	2.8	652.8	1.0
Blood & Blood-Forming Organs	620.9	0.5	243.5	0.4
Mental disorders	4,426.8	3.8	448.4	0.7
Nervous system & Sense Organs	11,180.7	9.3	5,426.8	8.1
Circulatory System	19,607.5	16.3	2,512.2	3.7
Respiratory System	40,912.6	33.9	36,024.6	53.5
Digestive System	9,826.1	8.2	2,541.7	3.8
Genitourinary System	4,948.0	4.1	2,559.9	3.8
Complications of Pregnancy	4,000.9	0.8	3,484.3	1.2
Skin & Subcutaneous Tissue	4,615.5	3.8	3,724.4	5.5
Musculoskeletal System	6,364.9	5.3	2,841.2	4.2
Congenital Anomalies	356.1	0.3	85.7	0.2
Injury & Poisoning	6,020.3	5.0	-.-	-.-
Symptoms & Ill-Defined Conditions	282.5	0.2	182.2	0.3

Source: Indicators of Health of the Population and Activity of Health Care Institutions of Ukraine for the Years 1990-1991. Statistical Material. Part I. MOH of Ukraine, Centre for Medical Statistics. Kiev 1992.

Note: Staff of the Centre noted that the reliability of data in Part I may be uneven because of inconsistencies in documentation at the institutional level.

Table A.50

Forecast Sources of Funds for Health Care in 1992

Source	Total (Rb.MM)	% of Total	% of Govt Revenues (1)
State and Local General Revenues	191,987	91.0	12.0 to 12.6
Payroll Taxes	12,079	5.8	0.8
Social Insurance Fund	7,211	3.4	0.5
Chernobyl Fund	4,868	2.3	0.3
Individuals	6,967	3.3	NA
TOTAL	211,032	100.0	12.8 to 13.4

(1) Includes state and local general revenues and resources of the Pension, Social Insurance, Employment and Chernobyl Funds. Ranges reflect disagreement between the Pension Fund and the Ministry of Finance about 1992 Pension Fund revenues.

Sources: June 1992 Drafts of the 1992 Budgets for the Ministry of Health, Social Insurance Fund, Chernobyl Fund, Pension Fund and Employment Fund.

Table A.51

Forecast 1992 Uses of Health Care Funds

	Total (Rb.MM)	% of Total	% GDP
Facilities	183,611	87.0	6.7
Hospitals	140,613	66.6	
Sanitoriums	21,980	10.4	
Ambulatory Clinics	11,280	5.6	
Other Health Centers	5,171	2.5	
Ambulance Services	2,368	1.1	
Blood Transfusion Services	1,459	0.7	
Capital Construction	200	0.1	
Public Health (1)	5,778	2.7	0.2
Education	5,342	2.5	0.2
Subsidies for Pharmaceutical	4,835	2.3	0.2
Research	1,608	0.8	0.1
Other (2)	9,860	4.7	0.4
TOTAL (3)	211,032	100.0	7.7

(1) Additional public health expenditures are included in the budgets for specific facilities.
(2) Additional treatment for Chernobyl victims and private payments for health services not included elsewhere.
(3) Does not sum exactly due to rounding

Sources: June 1992 Drafts of the 1992 Budgets for the Ministry of Health, Social Insurance Fund, Chernobyl Fund, Pension Fund and Employment Fund.

Table A.52

Ministry of Health and Local Health Inputs

Inputs	Percent of Total		
	1989 Actual	1991 Actual	1992 Forecast
Wages	53.3	47.4	27.0
Maintenance and Supplies	13.4	25.4	NA
Pharmaceutical	10.6	6.3	8.0
Food	8.2	6.9	NA
Construct	5.2	2.1	0.1
Capital Repair	4.0	3.6	NA
Equipment	3.9	5.9	11.0
Other	1.4	2.4	NA
TOTAL	100.0	100.0	100.0

Source: Ministry of Health

Table A.53

Human Health Service Resources of the Ministry of Health System 1991

Category	In MOH Health Care Facilities[1]		In MOH Network	
	Number	%	Number	%
MOH Network of Health Care Facilities				
• Physicians	201,923	16.8		
• Mid-Level Health Service Personnel	539,940	44.9		
• Non-Technical Support Personnel	333,791	27.8		
• Engineering-Technical Personnel (1990)	6,800	0.6		
• Administrative Personnel[2] (1990)	47,660	4.0		
• Other	61,219	5.7		
Total	1,201,333	100.00	1,201,333	88.9
Total Scientific-Research Institutes				
• Total Staff in 48 Institutes			9,704	0.7
• of which 4,433 are scientific personnel				
Institutes of Higher Health Education				
• Total Staff in 18 Institutions			22,387	1.7
• of which 7,770 are teaching personnel				
• teaching 51,928 students				
Staff of the Scientific-Manufacturing Union Ukraine Pharmaceuticals			82,558	6.1
Staff of the Trade and Manufacturing Union Poly Med Technology			11,487	0.8
Staff of Other Health Organizations[3]			24,013	1.8
Total 1991			1,351,482	100.0
1990			1,324,517	

Source: MOH, General Administration Finance, July 1992
Notes: 1.   There are 24,464 facilities in the MOH network of which 3,766 are hospital facilities with inpatient beds and 6,423 ambulatory care facilities. Of the total, 150 are under direct control of the Ministry. The vast majority of facilities are at the oblast and regional level. The Scientific-Research and Higher Health Eduction Institutes are under MOH control but retain considerable autonomous administration.
            2.   This includes staff of the MOH (203 persons) and staff at each oblast level health administration (15-30 persons each).
            3.   Bureau of Forensic Medicine, Bureau of Medical Statistics, Regional accounting centres, groups for Technical Supervision of Construction

Table A.54

Network of Hospital Facilities and Beds
of the Ministry of Health
1991

Type of Facility	Number	Beds	% Bed Total
Oblast	30	28,545	4.3
City	683	173,571	25.9
Specialist	125	21,165	3.2
City Children	124	23,170	3.2
Central Regional	481	171,732	25.6
District	1,481	53,001	7.9
Psychiatry and Substance Abuse	92	65,960	9.8
Childbirth Centres	83	17,055	2.5
Dyspanser (i.e., medical rehab preventive care centres)	411	63,211	9.4
Total	3,766	671,096	100.0

Source: Indicators of Resources for Health Care for the Population and Their Utilization in Ukraine. Networks and Personnel. Statistical Material for the Years 1990-1991. Part II. MOH of Ukraine, Centre for Medical Statistics. Kiev 1992

Notes: 1.   There are 24,464 health facilities in the MOH network. These are often grouped as follows: hospital facility types listed in this table, ambulatory facilities and polyclinics, ambulance stations, blood transfusion centres, sanatoria, sanitary-epidemiological stations, and 'other' facilities (bureau of forensic medical expertise, bureau of medical statistics, regionalized accounting centres, and centres for technical supervision of construction).

Table A.55

Network of Health Facilities and Health Care Personnel
of the Ministry of Health
Ukraine and OECD

	Total 1990	Ministry of Health Network 1991	OECD 1987	
			Low	High
Hospitals	3,882	3,766		
Ambulatory Care Facilities and Polyclinics	6,869	6,423		
Beds	700,331	671,096		
per 10,000	135.5	129.6	21.0	161.0
Physicians	221,408	201,923		
per 10,000	42.9	39.0	7.3	33.8
Mid-level Health Service Personnel	607,235	539,940		
per 10,000	117.5	104.2		
Admission per 100	-.-	24.3	5.5	22.6
Average Length of Stay	-.-	16.5	6.1	52.9
Patient Days Per Capita	-.-	4.0	0.7	4.9

Sources: 1.   Indicators of Resources for Health Care for the Population and Their Utilization in Ukraine. Networks and Personnel. Statistical Material for the Years 1990-1991. Part II. MOH of Ukraine, Centre for Medical Statistics. Kiev 1992

2.   OECD data as cited in World Bank Report 9182-POL.

Table A.56

Health Expenditures of Selected Countries as a Percent of GDP

	Ukraine[1] 1991	Belarus[2] 1992	Poland[2] 1992	Portugal[4] 1990	United Kingdom 1990	Sweden 1990	Canada 1990
Health Expenditures as Percent of GDP	6.2	2.8	5.7	5.5	6.1	9.0	8.6

Source:
1. MOH
2. GOSPLAN and Notes from Fourth Economic Mission, The World Bank, Feb 1992, Appendix, Table 2.
3. Poland Health System Reform, Meeting the Challenge, The World Bank, Jan 9, 1992, No. 9182-POL.
4. Portugal, UK, Canada, Sweden from **Health Care Systems in Transition**, OECD, 1990.

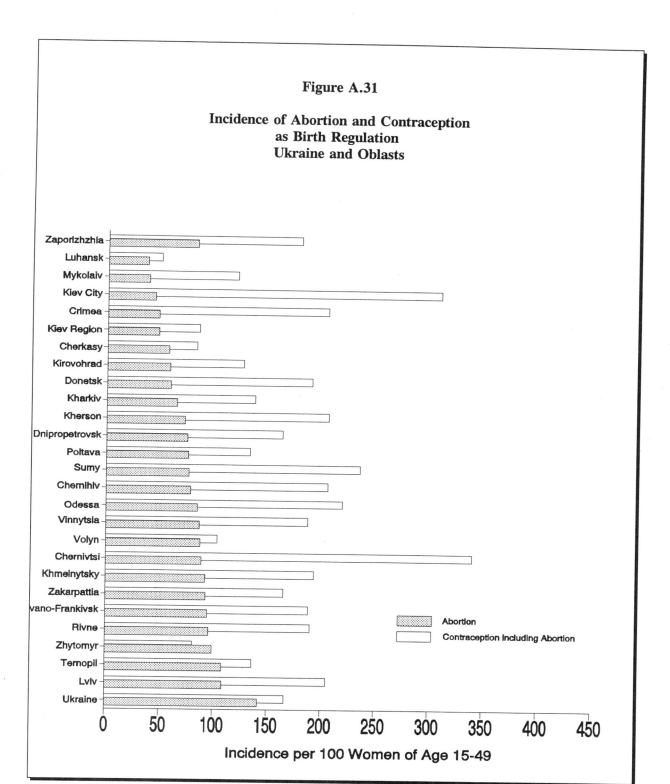

Figure A.31

**Incidence of Abortion and Contraception
as Birth Regulation
Ukraine and Oblasts**

Legend:
- Abortion
- Contraception Including Abortion

Incidence per 100 Women of Age 15-49

Source: Pirozhkov, S. and Lakiza-Sachuk, N. Demo-Social Consequences of Modern Family Planning in Ukraine and Their Influence on Development of the Republic, Kiev, July 1992

Figure A.32

Complications of Abortion

Complications After Abortion

Complication	Prevalence Per 100 Women After Abortion
Inflammation of Uterus and Uterine Organs	30
Secondary Sterility	50-60
Complications of Pregnancies	50
Miscarriages	22
Uterine Bleeding During Deliveries	13-15

Abortion Associated Chronic Morbidity 1990

	Women Under Physician Care in Dyspanser Medical Institutions (thousands)	Rate per 1000 Women Fertile Age
Salpingitis and Oophoritis	67.4	307
Endometriosis	5.0	23
Erosion and Ectropion of Cervix Uteri	136.2	620
Complications of Pregnancy, Delivery and Postnatal Period	70.4	570
Sterility	33.3	269

Source: Khodorovsky, G., Family Planning and Health of Women in Ukraine, Kiev, July 1992

Figure A.33

**Indicators of Hospital Resources Allocated to
Abortion Related Care 1991**

1. Supply of gynecological beds (including abortion cases)
   - rate per 10,000 total population
   - estimated rate per 10,000 females

   37,055
   7.2
   13.4

2. Excess average days occupancy of gynecological beds over average occupancy of total beds

   6 days

3. Number of women undergoing abortion

   957,000

4. Cost of an abortion in Kiev

   650 rubles

5. Percent of women undergoing abortion who are subsequently treated for complications of inflammation on an in- or out-patient basis

   30%

6. Proportion and number of treated women that can expect to be cured with one course of treatment

   half

7. Proportion and number requiring treatment for resulting chronic condition

   half
   143,550

8. Average number of courses of treatment for chronic condition

   5-6

9. Length of average course of treatment

   21 days

10. Average 1991 cost of course of treatment

    3,505 rubles

11. Number of women undergoing treatment for infertility (largely associated with complications of abortion)

    52,161

Source: Khodorovsky, G., 1992

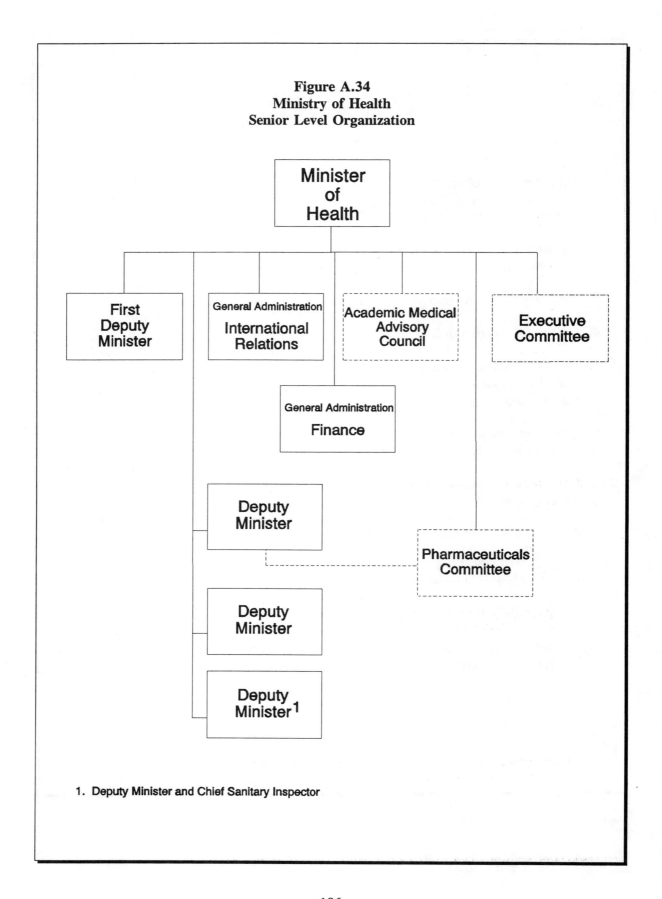

Figure A.34
Ministry of Health
Senior Level Organization

Minister of Health

First Deputy Minister

General Administration
International Relations

Academic Medical Advisory Council

Executive Committee

General Administration
Finance

Deputy Minister

Pharmaceuticals Committee

Deputy Minister

Deputy Minister[1]

1. Deputy Minister and Chief Sanitary Inspector

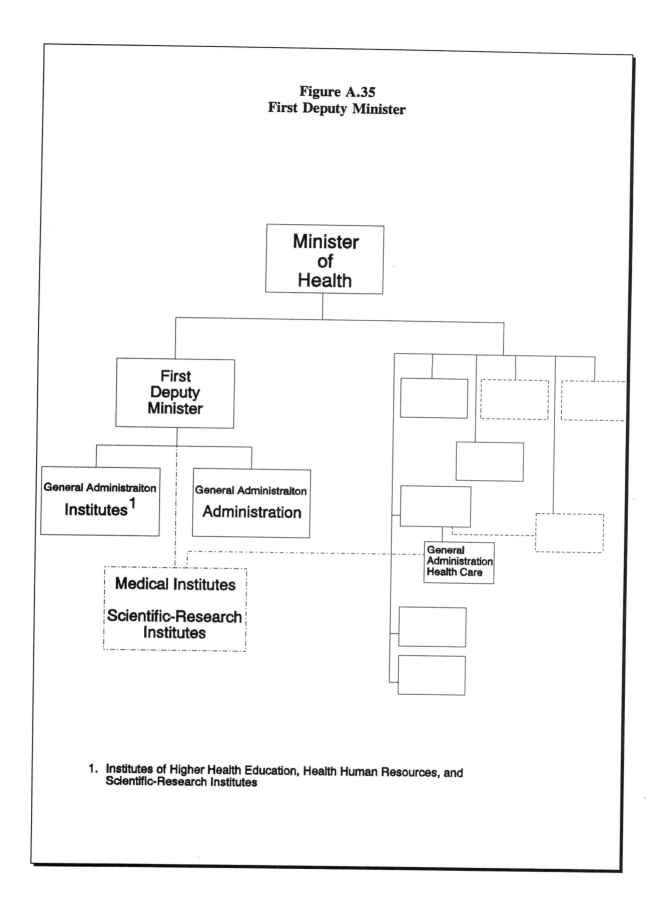

Figure A.35
First Deputy Minister

Minister of Health

First Deputy Minister

General Administraiton Institutes[1]

General Administraiton Administration

Medical Institutes
Scientific-Research Institutes

General Administration Health Care

1. Institutes of Higher Health Education, Health Human Resources, and Scientific-Research Institutes

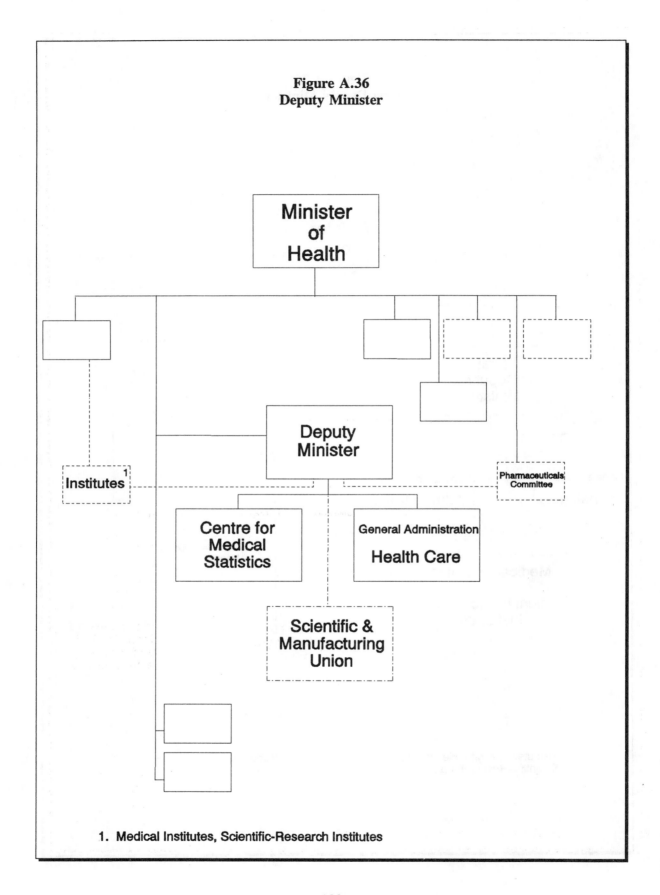

Figure A.36
Deputy Minister

Minister of Health

Deputy Minister

Institutes [1]

Pharmaceuticals Committee

Centre for Medical Statistics

General Administration

Health Care

Scientific & Manufacturing Union

1. Medical Institutes, Scientific-Research Institutes

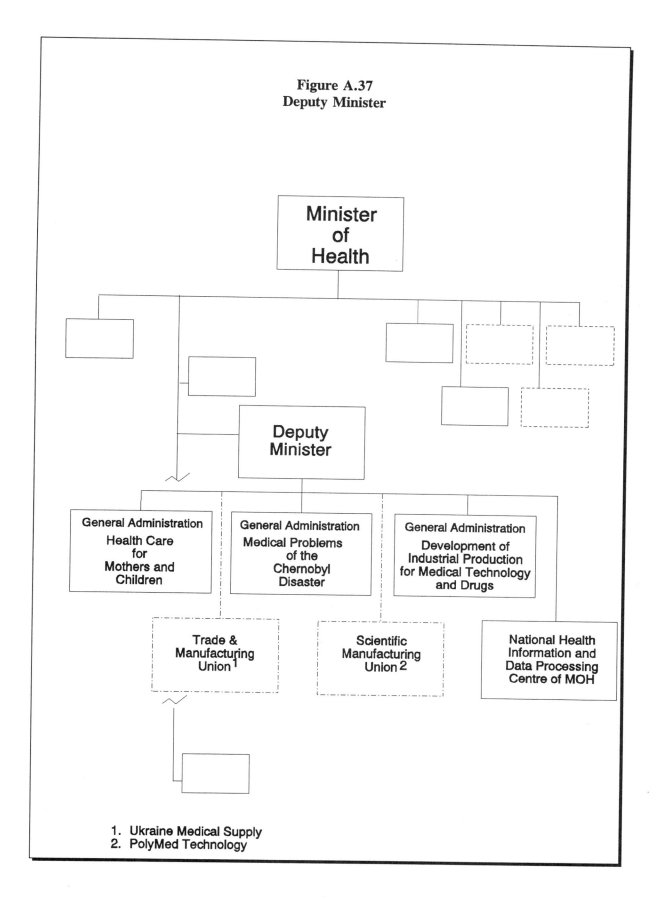

Figure A.37
Deputy Minister

Minister of Health

Deputy Minister

General Administration
Health Care
for
Mothers and
Children

General Administration
Medical Problems
of the
Chernobyl
Disaster

General Administration
Development of
Industrial Production
for Medical Technology
and Drugs

Trade &
Manufacturing
Union [1]

Scientific
Manufacturing
Union 2

National Health
Information and
Data Processing
Centre of MOH

1. Ukraine Medical Supply
2. PolyMed Technology

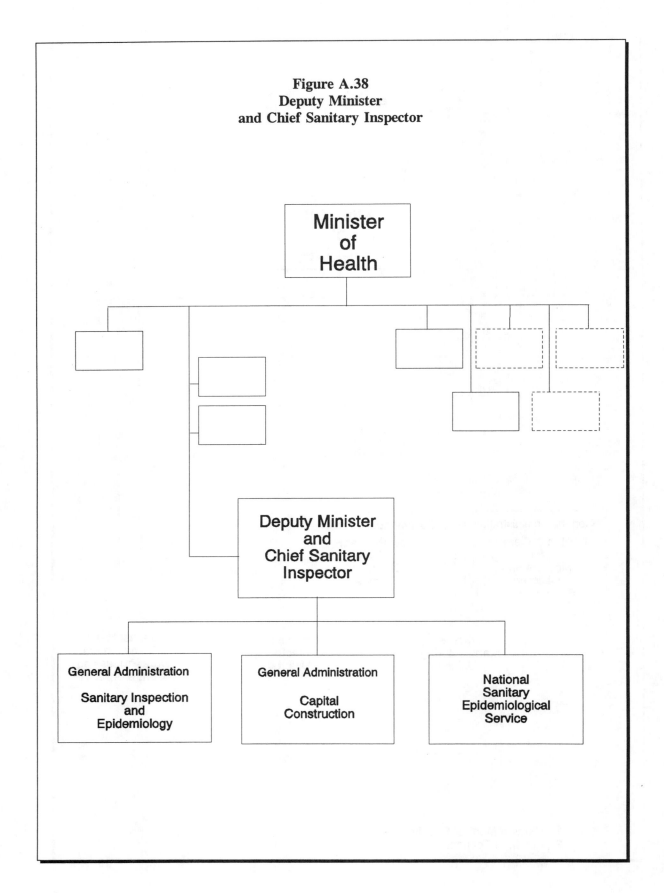

Figure A.38
Deputy Minister
and Chief Sanitary Inspector

Minister
of
Health

Deputy Minister
and
Chief Sanitary
Inspector

General Administration

Sanitary Inspection
and
Epidemiology

General Administration

Capital
Construction

National
Sanitary
Epidemiological
Service

Table A.57 UKRAINE: Monthly Wages; Annual Average
(In Rubles)

	1980	1985	1986	1987	1988	1989	1990	1991	QI'92
Ukraine	155.1	173.9	179.0	185.0	199.8	217.7	247.3	471.5	2,853.0
Crimea R.	154.2	169.1	174.6	181.1	196.0	214.7	250.0	464.4	2,318.8
Vinnytsia	136.7	155.3	160.2	166.4	179.1	194.7	222.0	406.5	1,966.0
Volyn	139.1	157.8	162.8	168.9	180.7	194.7	221.0	424.4	2,547.4
Dnipropetrovsk	163.1	181.1	185.7	190.2	207.4	227.4	225.0	508.2	3,666.9
Donetsk	174.3	195.4	199.5	203.6	217.5	236.8	268.0	547.7	4,684.4
Zhytomyr	137.1	155.8	160.3	169.3	179.0	194.4	227.0	470.0	2,139.9
Zakarpattia	141.5	159.7	165.5	172.8	185.8	200.1	223.0	387.5	1,479.1
Zaporizhzhia	159.5	178.1	182.6	187.1	203.8	223.0	257.0	500.3	3,221.8
Ivano-Frankivsk	141.1	163.3	167.4	175.6	188.9	204.2	227.0	429.4	2,211.2
Kiev Region	146.8	165.4	177.2	187.9	202.2	217.0	280.0	493.5	2,876.3
Kirovohrad	149.8	173.0	177.4	181.3	194.5	212.0	240.0	448.0	2,084.4
Luhansk	170.8	193.3	196.9	200.3	213.5	231.0	262.0	516.3	4,230.9
Lviv	147.9	165.7	170.3	177.6	193.1	208.5	234.0	443.5	2,352.4
Mykolaiv	151.3	171.7	178.5	183.7	198.0	215.9	250.0	439.9	1,941.2
Odessa	154.9	169.7	175.6	180.8	195.6	214.8	242.0	445.2	1,987.5
Poltava	151.2	171.7	177.3	184.9	198.7	215.2	243.0	470.8	2,613.7
Rivne	139.2	157.0	162.1	169.0	181.5	192.4	221.0	444.2	1,992.5
Sumy	143.7	167.6	173.6	197.7	194.0	207.8	237.0	471.1	2,093.2
Ternopil	135.4	152.3	157.6	165.6	178.4	191.0	218.0	417.1	2,204.2
Kharkiv	158.7	180.1	184.4	190.4	205.9	225.6	225.0	463.7	1,956.7
Kherson	150.2	166.4	172.5	177.2	190.3	209.3	241.0	443.0	1,890.5
Khmelnytsky	138.6	157.4	163.1	168.6	182.9	197.7	227.0	435.8	2,153.0
Cherkasy	142.9	163.0	168.2	176.0	191.4	208.6	238.0	461.7	1,978.4
Chernivtsi	134.7	152.1	157.3	163.2	175.6	191.5	218.0	392.9	1,958.2
Chernihiv	139.5	154.2	159.2	166.3	180.7	194.2	221.0	419.8	1,958.7
Kiev (City)	165.4	181.8	186.8	195.8	216.9	243.8	248.0	498.8	2,235.6

Source: Ministry of Labor

Table A.58 UKRAINE: Single-Headed Families a/
(From 1989 Census)

	Thousand Families
Ukraine	1898
Crimea R.	107
Vinnytsia	61
Volyn	29
Dnipropetrovsk	158
Donetsk	222
Zhytomyr	51
Zakarpattia	32
Zaporizhzhia	81
Ivano-Frankivsk	45
Kiev Region	65
Kirovohrad	40
Luhansk	111
Lviv	94
Mykolaiv	47
Odessa	105
Poltava	60
Rivne	31
Sumy	47
Ternopil	31
Kharkiv	134
Kherson	43
Khmelnytsky	47
Cherkasy	49
Chernivtsi	30
Chernihiv	48
Kiev (City)	130

Source: Ministry of Statistics.

a/ Incomplete families are those headed
by either mother or father, and/or one of
their parents, with children.

	Course a/ Places Offered	Course Places Needed	Number Placed In Re-/Train	Profess. Trained Total	First Trained	Re- Trained	Skill Upgrade
Trained Total	64,543	6,699	1,508	738	227	506	5
Laid-Off People	--	--	474	255	19	232	4
Women	27,488	3,231	930	517	144	371	2
Young People Up to 30 Yrs	--	--	767	383	197	185	1
Unemployed	--	--	486	136	10	126	--
Of Total:							
In Enterprises and Organizations	13,684	1,348	293	248	138	109	1
In Professional-Techn. Schools	27,051	2,841	224	75	27	48	--
o/w in State Techn.College	27,051	2,841	224	75	27	48	--
In Specialized College	2,369	85	21	15	--	15	
In University	3,258	290	196	109	11	97	1
o/w in State Univ. Contd. Educ.	2,807	290	196	109	11	97	1
in Branch Univ. Contd. Educ.	5,871	1,141	330	119	10	107	2
In Other Educational Institutions	12,310	994	444	172	41	130	1

Source: Ministry of Labor

a/ Based on a contract, employment centers have at their disposal course vacancies offered
by educational institutions, enterprises and organizations.

Note: Number of people continuing training: 1,712
                          o/w women   1,042
      Laid-off labor: 570 people

193

Table A.60 UKRAINE: Average Annual Wages in Industry
(In Percent and Ruble)

	1991		QI 1992	
	Rubles	% Total	Rubles	% Total
Industry Total	549	100	2,853	100
o/w				
Highly-Paid Branches				
Coal Mining	870	159	6,565	230
Oil Rafinery/Processing	522	101	2,729	96
Chemical	522	95	2,729	96
Low-Paid Branches				
Construction Materials	528	96	2,365	83
Light Industry	462	84	2,374	83

Source: Ministry of Labor

Table A.61   UKRAINE: Workforce Fluctuation; Construction
(In Thousand Employees)

| | ------- 1985 ---------- | | | ------- 1990 ---------- | | | ------- 1991 ---------- | | |
	Avg.No. Employed	Total Left	Left on Own Wish	Avg.No. Employed	Total Left	Left on Own Wish	Avg.No. Employed	Total Left	Left on Own Wish
Ukraine	932.8	359.5	112.4	1,159.7	372.5	151.2	1,149.4	345.9	150.7
Crimea R.	47.6	24.8	7.0	59.8	23.5	10.4	58.4	20.7	10.7
Vinnytsia	19.9	11.3	2.4	30.0	10.5	3.6	32.0	10.1	3.7
Volyn	12.3	5.9	1.6	18.8	5.9	2.1	18.9	4.9	1.9
Dnipropetrovsk	90.0	23.9	8.7	116.0	33.1	14.9	114.9	33.5	15.6
Donetsk	119.4	39.4	15.8	128.6	40.6	18.0	130.3	40.4	18.3
Zhytomyr	19.1	10.5	2.2	25.3	8.4	2.9	26.4	7.1	2.9
Zakarpattia	12.8	8.7	2.7	15.3	5.8	2.8	14.6	5.0	2.4
Zaporizhzhia	43.7	17.1	5.8	52.3	18.3	7.6	52.3	16.4	7.8
Ivano-Frankivsk	20.5	8.8	2.5	23.3	6.9	2.6	24.2	6.4	2.7
Kiev Region	47.4	20.4	6.1	58.5	19.4	7.9	53.2	14.9	7.0
Kirovohrad	73.1	16.9	5.4	82.9	21.1	8.7	78.8	20.0	7.9
Luhansk	16.5	9.3	2.3	20.6	7.8	2.9	20.9	7.9	2.9
Lviv	66.7	21.7	8.6	76.0	23.7	9.9	76.5	22.9	10.9
Mykolaiv	40.5	14.9	3.7	56.5	12.8	5.1	56.0	16.0	5.7
Odessa	25.9	12.4	3.8	32.0	12.4	5.1	31.2	10.6	5.0
Poltava	42.0	22.3	6.0	5.0	22.1	8.9	45.7	16.7	7.9
Rivne	28.3	11.0	3.4	40.4	10.7	4.6	40.9	11.0	4.8
Sumy	20.8	7.7	2.6	28.2	8.7	3.4	27.9	7.6	3.2
Ternopil	22.1	7.6	2.2	29.6	10.0	2.9	30.9	9.7	3.1
Kharkiv	12.2	4.4	1.3	18.5	5.8	2.2	18.0	5.0	2.2
Kherson	61.9	20.4	6.7	68.9	23.8	9.4	68.1	22.0	9.2
Khmelnytsky	24.3	10.5	3.4	34.2	12.0	4.3	32.6	10.8	4.7
Cherkasy	18.4	9.5	2.5	27.8	8.5	3.1	28.5	7.9	2.9
Chernivtsi	22.1	10.9	2.0	30.9	10.7	3.7	31.1	10.0	3.6
Chernihiv	9.3	3.9	1.5	14.0	3.7	1.9	14.0	3.5	1.7
Kiev (City)	16.2	5.3	2.2	21.2	6.1	2.4	22.9	5.0	2.2

Source: Ministry of Labor

195

Table A.62 UKRAINE: Mandatory Leaves Without Pay (December 1991 - February 1992)
(People)

	Number of Enterpris. Researched	Average Monthly Employm.	Mandatory Leaves w/o Pay	Of which, for Duration of:		
				up to 2 wks	2 Wks tp 1 Month	Over 1 Month
Crimea R.	7	7,145	1,199	--	500	699
Vinnytsia	8	13,018	3,285	--	1,138	2,147
Volyn	10	26,492	2,678	626	2,052	--
Dnipropetrovsk	7	37,151	3,054	757	2,297	--
Donetsk	6	9,433	492	200	232	60
Zhytomyr	8	6,835	2,111	262	1,610	239
Zakarpattia	11	14,104	6,216	99	5,279	838
Zaporizhzhia	12	18,028	13,461	6,342	7,089	30
Ivano-Frankivsk	10	12,003	2,005	450	821	734
Kiev Region	8	21,862	2,577	73	109	2,395
Kirovohrad	8	18,810	12,637	--	--	12,637
Luhansk	17	12,250	3,315	1,649	948	718
Lviv	59	44,952	7,243	--	--	7,243
Mykolaiv	4	7,799	3,289	37	--	3,252
Odessa	41	28,000	5,600	--	--	5,600
Poltava	7	15,648	2,148	1,588	560	--
Rivne	9	23,285	9,074	1,359	--	7,715
Sumy	9	17,646	4,561	437	184	3,940
Ternopil	10	8,517	1,268	1,173	72	23
Kharkiv	12	43,697	5,853	5,251	469	133
Kherson	11	31,736	4,563	330	--	4,233
Khmelnytsky	11	16,877	4,648	2,162	2,486	--
Cherkasy	6	15,578	8,396	7,700	14	682
Chernivtsi	11	15,097	3,633	3,126	400	107
Chernihiv	12	24,860	14,308	8,462	5,846	--
Kiev (City)	11	41,081	13,754	--	7,434	6,320
Sevastopol (City)	8	12,000	1,454	--	--	1,454
Ukraine Total	333	543,904	142,822	42,083	39,540	61,199

Source: Ministry of Labor

Table A.63 Forecast Sources of Funds for Health Care in 1992

Source	Total (Rb.MM)	% of Total	% of Govt Revenues (1)
State and Local General Revenues	191,987	91.0	12.0 to 12.6
Payroll Taxes	12,079	5.8	0.8
Social Insurance Fund	7,211	3.4	0.5
Chernobyl Fund	4,868	2.3	0.3
Individuals	6,967	3.3	NA
TOTAL	211,032	100.0	12.8 to 13.4

(1) Includes state and local general revenues and resources of the Pension, Social Insurance, Employment and Chernobyl Funds. Ranges reflect disagreement between the Pension Fund and the Ministry of Finance about 1992 Pension Fund revenues.

Sources: June 1992 Drafts of the 1992 Budgets for the Ministry of Health, Social Insurance Fund, Chernobyl Fund, Pension Fund and Employment Fund.

Table A.64 Forecast 1992 Uses of Health Care Funds

	Total (Rb.MM)	% of Total	% GDP
Facilities	183,611	87.0	6.7
Hospitals	140,613	66.6	
Sanitoriums	21,980	10.4	
Ambulatory Clinics	11,820	5.6	
Other Health Centers	5,171	2.5	
Ambulance Services	2,368	1.1	
Blood Transfusion Services	1,459	0.7	
Capital Construction	200	0.1	
Public Health (1)	5,778	2.7	0.2
Education	5,342	2.5	0.2
Subsidies for Pharmaceutical	4,835	2.3	0.2
Research	1,608	0.8	0.1
Other (2)	9,860	4.7	0.4
TOTAL (3)	211,032	100.0	7.7

(1) Additional public health expenditures are included in the budgets for specific facilities.
(2) Additional treatment for Chernobyl victims and private payments for health services not included elsewhere.
(3) Does not sum exactly due to rounding

Sources: June 1992 Drafts of the 1992 Budgets for the Ministry of Health, Social Insurance Fund, Chernobyl Fund, Pension Fund and Employment Fund.

Table A.65 Forecast 1992 Education Spending

Expenditure	1992 Budget (Rb. MM)	% Total Govt. Ed Budget	% Total Ed Expenditures	% of GDP
TOTAL STATE/LOCAL BUDGET	181,756	100.0	85.5	6.7
Total Personnel Costs	99,286	54.6	46.7	
Wages and Bonuses	72,648	40.0	34.2	
Payroll Tax (37%)	26,638	14.7	12.5	
Stipends	10,323	5.7	4.9	
Capital Repair	5,443	3.0	2.6	
Equipment Purchase	5,037	2.8	2.4	
Capital Investment	1,739	1.0	0.8	
Textbooks	980	0.5	0.5	
Computers	537	0.3	0.3	
Other (Inc. utilities and maintenance)	58,411	32.1	27.5	
Enterprises (16,031 Preschools) (1)	30,812	NA	14.5	1.1
TOTAL	212,567		100.0	7.8

(1) Mission estimate based on spending per preschool by the state government.

Sources: June 1992 draft of the Ministry of Education's 1992 budget, the Ministry of Finance's June 1992 draft consolidated local education budget, mission estimates.

Table A.66 Ministry of Health and Local Health Inputs

Inputs	Percent of Total		
	1989 Actual	1991 Actual	1992 Forecast
Wages	53.3	47.4	27.0
Maintenance and Supplies	13.4	25.4	NA
Pharmaceutical	10.6	6.3	8.0
Food	8.2	6.9	NA
Construct	5.2	2.1	0.1
Capital Repair	4.0	3.6	NA
Equipment	3.9	5.9	11.0
Other	1.4	2.4	NA
TOTAL	100.0	100.0	100.0

Source: Ministry of Health

200

Table A.67 UKRAINE: Student/Teacher Ratios; Comparative

	Ukraine	Developed Countries	Developing Countries
Total Enrollment (Millions)	9.3	231.2	720.3
Number of Teachers (Millions)	1.13	15.1	29.7
Student/Teacher Ratio	8.2	15.3	24.3

Source: Ministry of Education and UNESCO Annual Statistical Yearbook 1991.
Data for Developed Countries are for 1989.

Table A.68 UKRAINE: Enrollment and Teachers in Primary and Secondary Schools
(School Years 1991-92)

Total Enrollment (Thousand)   6,918

Number of Teachers (Thousand)   538

Student/Teacher Ratio   12.8

Source: Ministry of Statistics

Table A.69 UKRAINE: Universities (Academic Year 1991 - 92)

State University	Departm.	Full Time Students	Faculty	o/w Holding Masters Equival.	o/w Holding Doctor. Equival.
Dnepropetrovsk State University	12	8,835	1,277	559	83
Donetsk State University	11	5,593	1,062	524	64
Kiev State University	19	12,200	3,612	1,079	293
Lviv State University	13	7,230	1,911	529	96
Odessa State University	9	5,306	807	473	83
Simferopol State University	8	3,962	538	267	38
Ujgorof State University	10	4,340	916	329	75
Kharkiv State University	12	6,845	1,857	875	129
ZapojieState University	10	3,893	553	193	25
Chernivtsi State University	12	5,487	885	375	47
Kharkiv Law Institute	4	3,188	371	184	40
Total:	120	66,879	13,789	5,387	973

Source: Ministry of Education. All data are for 1992.

Table A.70 UKRAINE: Enrollments and Faculty in Universities a/

Country	Student Enrollment (Thousand)	Number of Faculty (Thousand)	Student/ Faculty Ratio
France	1,124	46	24.4
Federal Republic of German	1,465	151	13.3
Italy	1,349	54	25.0
Korea	1,143	34	33.6
Spain	978	51	19.2
United States	7,716	494	15.6
Ukraine	67	14	4.8

Source: For Ukraine: Ministry of Education; for other countries: UNESCO Statistical Yearbook 1991.

a/ Includes Equivalent Institutions.

Note: Data for Ukraine are not strictly comparable with those for other countries because they cover only the eleven universities in Ukraine and not "equivalent institutions." But this does not alter the fact that the student/faculty ratio is much lower than in the other countries. Data for the latter are for 1989 and 1992 for Ukraine.

Table A.71 UKRAINE: 1992 Education Spending: Forecast
(In Million Ruble and Percent)

Expenditure	1992 Budget (Rbl. Mln.)	Percent Total Govt. Ed. Budget	Percent Total Ed. Expenditure	Percent of GDP
Total State/Local Budget	181,756	100.0	85.5	6.7
Total Personal Costs	99,286	54.6	46.7	
Wages and Bonuses	72,648	40.0	34.2	
Payroll Tax (37%)	26,638	14.7	12.5	
Stipends	10,323	5.7	4.9	
Capital Repair	5,443	3.0	2.6	
Equipment Purchase	5,037	2.8	2.4	
Capital Investment	1,739	1.0	1.0	
Textbooks	980	0.5	0.5	
Computers	434	0.2	0.2	
Other (Incl. Utilities and Maintenance)	58,411	32.1	27.5	
Enterprises	30,812	n.a.	14.5	1.1
Total	212,567	100.0	7.8	

Sources: June 1992 draft of the Ministry of Education's 1992
budget, the Ministry of Finance's June 1992 drft consolidated
local education budget, mission estimates.

a/ Mission estimate based on daycare spending by the state government.

Table A.72 UKRAINE: Percentage of GNP Spent on Public Education

```
-------------------------------------------------------------------
Ukraine                                          7.8

Europe, including the former USSR                5.5

Developed Countries                              5.8

Developing Countries                             3.8

The World                                        5.5
-------------------------------------------------------------------
```

Source: UNESCO Statistical Yearbook, 1991, and Ukraine Ministry
of Finance.

ALLOWANCES
AND
SOCIAL ASSISTANCE

Table A.73 Family Allowances Available Without Regard to Financial Need

Name	Description	Benefit Size	Administration (1)	Funding (1)
Birth Allowance	One time allowance given to all families at birth of child	300% of min wage		
	If either parent employed:		Employer of either parent	SIF
	If parents unemployed:		SW	State GR
Child Allowance Under 3	Monthly allowance for children under age 3 given to all families with mothers who worked prior to childbirth or who were under age 18			
	If mother worked > 1 year	100% of min wage	Mother's Employer or School or SW (3)	PF and State GR passed thru PF (4)
	If mother worked < 1 year	50% of min wage	Mother's Employer or School or SW (3)	PF and State GR passed thru PF (4)
Child Allowance Under 2	Monthly allowance given to all families with mothers who did not work or attend higher education prior to childbirth for each child under age 2	50% of min wage	SW	PF and State GR passed thru PF (4)
Child Allowance for Military	Additional monthly allowance for each child of men called up for active military service	100% of min wage	SW	State GR passed thru PF
Funeral Allowance	One-time allowance given to family of deceased person			
	Working person	200% of min wage	Employer or School	SIF
	Unemployed person	200% of min wage	SW	State GR
	Retired person	2 months pension	SW	Pension Fund

Disabled Child Allowance	Additional monthly allowance to families with non-working mother caring for disabled child under 16	22.5% of min wage	SW	PF (service pension budget)
Diabetic Child Allowance	Additional monthly allowance for each child with diabetes ages 0 to 14	6.7-17.2% of min wage	SW	Local GR
Institutionalized Child Allowance	Monthly allowance for each child under 18 in institutions for physical or mental disability or disease	100% of min wage	Institutions	Local GR passed thru ed budget

(1) Cher= Chernobyl Fund; GR=General Revenues; PF=Pension Fund; SIF = Social Insurance Fund; SW =District Offices of Ministry of Social Welfare

(2) Included in this category are mothers who in the military or laid off from their job due to restructuring of their employer

(3) The mother's previous place of employment or school. If mother was laid off from work then district offices of the Ministry of Social Welfare.

(4) The Pension Fund finances allowances for children up to age 1.5, the state funds allowances from general revenues for children between 1.5 and 3 for mothers who previously worked and between 1.5 and 2 for mothers who did not work.

Sources: Interviews and reports from the Chernobyl Fund, Ministry of Finance, Ministry of Social Welfare, Pension Fund, and Social Insurance Fund.

Table A.74 Work-Related Benefits Available Without Regard to Financial Need

Name	Description	Benefit Size	Administration (1)	Funding (1)
Sick/Short-term Disabled	Sick leave and short term disability available for up to 4 months	100% of salary	employer	SIF
Maternity	Maternity leave for four months	100% of salary	employer	SIF
Vacation	Free vacations in holiday camps for workers and their families	Cost of camp	employer	SIF

(1) Cher= Chernobyl Fund; GR=General Revenues; PF=Pension Fund; SIF = Social Insurance Fund; SW=District Offices of Ministry of Social Welfare

Sources: Interviews and reports from the Social Insurance Fund.

Table A.75 Benefits for Specific Groups Available Without Regard to Financial Need

Name	Description	Benefit Size	Administration (1)	Funding (1)
Telephones For War Veterans	Telephone installation free of charge of veterans of WWII	Current cost	SW	State GR
Exonerated Citizens	Allowance to citizens exonerated of political crimes	NA	SW	Local GR

(1) Cher= Chernobyl Fund; GR=General Revenues; PF=Pension Fund; SIF = Social Insurance Fund; SW=District Offices of Ministry of Social Welfare

Sources: Interviews and reports from the Chernobyl Fund, Ministry of Finance, Ministry of Social Welfare, Pension Fund, and Social Insurance Fund.

Table A.76 Benefits for Disabled without Regard to Financial Need

Name	Description	Benefit Size	Administration (1)	Funding (1)
Cars	Certain disabled people are entitled to a free car or the equivalent sum in cash	Current car price	SW	State GR
Motorized Wheelchairs	Certain disabled people are entitled to a free motorized wheelchair	Current wheelchair price	SW	State GR
Prosthetics	Certain disabled people are entitled to free prosthetic devices	Current price	SW	State GR
Working Disabled Allowance	Additional allowance for the Working Disabled in Disabled Groups I and II (i.e. those seriously disabled)	49% of min wage	SW	State GR
Sanitarium Treatment	Additional allowance to some disabled people for sanitarium treatment	As necessary	SW	State GR
Telephones	Telephone installation for disabled people in disabled categories I and II	Current price	SW	State GR

(1) Cher = Chernobyl Fund; GR =General Revenues; PF=Pension Fund; SIF = Social Insurance Fund; SW =District Offices of Ministry of Social Welfare

Sources: Interviews and reports from the Chernobyl Fund, Ministry of Finance, Ministry of Social Welfare, Pension Fund, and Social Insurance Fund.

211

Table A.77 Benefits for Low-Income and Vulnerable Groups (1)

Name	Description	Benefit Size	Administration (2)	Funding (2)
Child Allowance 3 to 6	Monthly child allowance when mothers worked prior to childbirth for each child 3-6 in low-income families	50% of min wage	Employer or School of mother or SW (3)	State GR passed thru PF
Child Allowance 2 to 6	Monthly child allowance when mothers did not work prior to childbirth for each child 2-6 in low-income families	50% of min wage	Employer or School of Father or SW	State GR passed thru PF
Child Allowance 6-18 for Single Mothers	Monthly child allowance for single mothers for each child 6 to 18 (16 if child receives a student stipend)	50% of min wage	SW	State GR
Child Allowance 0-18 for Orphaned Parents	Monthly child allowance when parent is single parent brought up in an orphanage. For each child until 18 (16 if child receives a student stipend)	100% of min wage	SW	State GR
Child Allowance 6 to 16	Monthly child allowance for each child < 16 in low income families if child receives no other allowance, pension or stipend	22.5% of min wage	Employer or School of parent or child or SW	Local GR
Child Allowance Under 12	Additional monthly allowance for each child under 12 in very low income families (4)	30% of min wage	Employer or School of parent or SW	State GR through PF
Alimony Allowance	Additional monthly allowance for each child if estranged parent owes alimony for child under 18 but does not pay it	50% of min wage	SW	Local GR
Large Family Allowance	Additional monthly allowance to families with 3 or more children < 16 if mother does not work	22.5% of min wage	SW	State GR
Child Products Allowance	Annual compensation to low-income families for price increases in children's products (for each child 0-18)	100-140% of monthly min wage per year (5)	Employer or School of parent or child or SW	Local GR
Child Clothes Allowance	Annual compensation to low-income families for price increases in children's clothes (for each child 0 through middle school (or technical school if student must buy uniform)	100-125% of monthly min wage per year (5)	Employer or School of parent or child or SW	Local GR
Child and Pensioner Food Allowance	Additional monthly allowance for each child less than 18 or pension age adult if either are in low income families	30-40% of min wage	Employer or School of parent or child or SW	Local GR

212

Name	Description	Benefit Size	Administration (2)	Funding (2)
Extremely Low Income Allowance	Additional monthly allowance for <u>extremely</u> low income families (6)			
	For each adult in the family	200% of min wage	SW	Local GR
	For each child under 18	100% of min wage	SW	Local GR
Nursing Homes and Daycare (7)	The elderly infirmed who lack family support have free access to nursing homes or daytime care facilities that combine health care and leisure activities	As necessary	SW	Local GR
Housekeeping Aid (7)	Help cooking, cleaning and shopping for elderly infirmed	As necessary	SW	Local GR

(1) Available to families with incomes below 2 minimum wages per person (approximately 43 percent of Ukrainians) or to specific groups who are likely to have low incomes.
(2) Cher= Chernobyl Fund; GR=General Revenues; PF=Pension Fund; SIF = Social Insurance Fund; SW =District Offices of Ministry of Social Welfare
(3) The mother's previous place of employment or school. If mother was laid off from work then district offices of the Ministry of Social Welfare.
(4) Very low income families are those with incomes below 2/3 the minimum wage per family member. Families can receive this allowance in addition to any of the other allowances they qualify for.
(5) Payment increases as child ages up to 18 years old.
(6) Extremely low income families are those with incomes below 1/2 of the minimum wage per family member.
(7) New programs available only in some districts. Currently serve about 350,000 people.

Sources: Interviews and reports from the Chernobyl Fund, Ministry of Finance, Ministry of Social Welfare, Pension Fund, and Social Insurance Fund.

213

Table A.78 Benefits For People Affected By Chernobyl (1)

Name	Description	Benefit Size	Adminis-tration (2)	Funding (2)
Employment	**Benefits Relating to Employment**			
Job Loss or Change	Monetary compensation for people who lose their jobs due to sickness, required relocation or plant closing related to the disaster.	Average salary for 3 months		Cher
	Monetary compensation for people in categories I-IV to cover salary differential between their former job and their current, lower-paid position when change had to be made for health or required relocation reasons.	Salary differential for 12 months		Cher
Temporary Inability to Work	Monetary compensation for people in categories I - IV who are temporarily unable to work due to Chernobyl-related illness.	100% of salary		Cher
Salary Supplement	Wage bonus for people who work in contaminated areas. Size of wage bonus depends on contamination level.	20% to 100% of salary		Cher
Business Loan	Interest free loan for the purposes of starting one's own business or purchasing one's own farm for people in categories I-IV	As necessary		Cher
Vacation	Additional paid vacation (annual leave) for people in categories I and II. Paid vacation is 14 calendar days minimum up to 42 calendar days depending on whether employee is still working in the area and level of contamination at work site	100% of salary		Cher
Family Allowances	**Allowances For Children and Students**			
Pregnancy and Maternity	Additional 90 days of childbirth leave for "women who have suffered"	100% of salary for 90 days		Cher
	Doubled payment for childcare leave for "women who have suffered"	66 - 100% of min wage per month		Cher
Sick Child Allowance	Yearly allowance for each child who became sick due to the disaster until children reaches primary school age	NA		Cher
Evacuated Child Allowance	Monthly allowance for each child of school age who was evacuated from the area or who was born after April 1986 to parents in categories I and II	50% of min wage		Cher

214

Name	Description	Benefit Size	Adminis-tration (2)	Funding (2)
Disabled Child Allowance	Monthly allowance for each child who became disabled or is undergoing medical treatment as a result of the disaster and to each child whose parent has become disabled. (Replaces "Evacuated Child Allowance" above for relevant children)	100% of min wage		Cher
Previously Disabled Child Allowance	Annual allowance to families raising child disabled prior to the disaster whose health was harmed by the disaster	300% of monthly min wage per year		Cher
Low-Income Child Allowance	Doubled monthly low-income child allowance for low-income children who became sick due to the disaster	30-40% of min wage		Cher
Student Stipend	50% increase in the level of student stipends for people in categories I-IV eligible for stipends	50% of current stipend per month		Cher
Disability and Death	**Benefits for Disability and Death**			
Disability	One-time compensation for disability resulting from the disaster. Compensation varies depending on level of disability.	5,000 to 10,000 Rb.		Cher
	Annual allowance for recuperation from disaster-related disability. Compensation varies depending on level of disability.	100% to 300% of monthly min wage		Cher
Death	One-time compensation for loss of breadwinner or for loss of child	5,000 to 10,000 Rb.		Cher
Housing and Relocation	**Benefits Relating to Housing and Relocation**			
Apartment Rental	Monthly apartment rental subsidy for people in categories I and II	Rb. 58 per family		Cher
Fuel Subsidy	Annual fuel subsidy for people in categories I and II	Rb. 3,500 per family		Cher
	Compensation for 50% of the cost of fuel for people in categories III and IV who are waiting for relocation and who live in buildings without central heating	NA		Cher
Housing Purchase	Interest free loans with government repayment of 25% to 50% of principle for purchase of residence or dacha for people in categories I-IV	NA		Cher

Name	Description	Benefit Size	Administration (2)	Funding (2)
	Construction loans for relocating families	Rb. 10,000 per family member to max of Rb. 60,000		Cher
Relocation Allowance	One time allowance for each relocated family member	300% of min wage		Cher
Moving Expenses	Payment of moving expenses for relocating families	As necessary		Cher
Wages while moving	Payment of wages during moving period for relocating families	100% of average wage for 15 days		Cher
Household Furnishings	Receipt of 15 year interest free loan for furnishing new house for relocating families	8,500 per family member		Cher
Household Goods	State repayment of loan families received to purchase household goods when family was evacuated for people in categories I and II	NA		Cher
Contaminated Property	Compensation for contaminated structures, household property, furnishings, crops, and livestock that had to be destroyed.	NA		Cher
Contaminated Living Conditions	Allowances for families living in areas of high radiation	30-50% of min wage (3)		Cher
Food	**Benefits Relating to Food**			
	The right to purchase food at 50 to 75% of its actual cost for people in categories I and II and sick children	As necessary		Cher
	Free meals served in schools for students in primary, secondary and vocational schools who are in categories III and IV	As necessary		Cher
	Food items or cash equivalent compensation for families of children in categories III and IV who are too ill or too young to attend school	As necessary		Cher
Other	**Miscellaneous Benefits**			
Leisure	Medical treatment, camps and vacations outside the region for workers and their families	As necessary	Employer	SIF
	Cost-free round-trip travel once per year anywhere in the country by any means of transport for people in categories I-III	As necessary		Cher
Tax Exemptions	Exemptions from payment of all taxes and customs duties for people in categories I-IV and relocated families (relocated families for 3 years)	As necessary		Cher

Name	Description	Benefit Size	Adminis-tration (2)	Funding (2)
Public Transportation	Cost free use of public transportation for people in categories I and II, for children made ill by the disaster and adults accompanying them to medical treatment facilities	As necessary		Cher
Automobiles	Cost free provision of cars to people in Categories I and II	As necessary		Cher

(1) People affected by Chernobyl are divided into four categories. Category I individuals are those who participated in the Chernobyl cleanup and who have become very ill as a result. Category II individuals participated in the cleanup and are suffering medical problems as a result (but are not as sick as those in Category I). Category III individuals are those who worked on the cleanup from 1988 to 1990 and those who have lived or worked in the territory with heavy radiation (15 curies/sq. km. or more). Category IV individuals live or work (or lived or worked) in areas with moderate radiation (from 5 to 15 curies/sq. km).

(2) Cher = Chernobyl Fund; GR=General Revenues; PF=Pension Fund; SIF = Social Insurance Fund; SW=District Offices of Ministry of Social Welfare

(3) Size of allowance depends on level of radiation

Sources: Interviews and reports from the Chernobyl Fund, Ministry of Finance, Ministry of Social Welfare, Pension Fund, and Social Insurance Fund.

Table A.79 Projected Uses of Pension Funds for 1992
(Ranges Reflect Pension Fund and MOF Estimates)

USE	1992F Rb. MM	Share of 1992F Vol.	% of GDP
Total Pension Fund	320,354 to 369,302	90 to 91	11.7 to 13.5
Cash Benefits (1)	306,597 to 332,554	82 to 86	
Retired	241,341 to 263,858	65 to 68	
Disabled	28,639 to 31,129	8	
Dependent	16,198 to 16,589	4 to 5	
Other (2)	11,409 to 11,693	3	
Military	6,126 to 6,968	2	
Additional Benefits	2,600	1	
Delivery Costs	5,957 to 8,893	2	
Repayment of 1991 Loan	4,200 to 4,292	1	
Addl Benefits Owed (3)	1,600 to 21,563	1 to 5	
Partial Administration Costs (4)	2,000	1	
Chernobyl Victims Addl. Benefits	10,918	3	0.4
Min of Defense	23,647	6 to 7	0.9
TOTAL PENSIONS	354,919 to 403,867	100	13.0 to 14.8
SURPLUS (DEFICIT)	(83,120) to 37,738	-21 to 11	

(1) Estimates for the breakdown of cash benefits between types of beneficiary were made based on the number of beneficiaries in each group and the average pension received.
(2) People who never worked including those disabled in childhood and hobos.
(3) Benefits accrued but not paid in 1991
(4) Includes only Pension Fund administration costs.
Sources: Pension Fund Draft Budget for 1992 (Ministry of Finance and Pension Fund June 1992 versions), 1992 Draft Consolidate State Budget for Ukraine (June 1992 version) and mission estimates.

218

Table A.80 UKRAINE: Retirement Age Population and Dependency Ratio Projections
(Mid-Year Population, Both Sexes) a/

Retirement Age	1989	2000	2010
Retirement Age Population			
Current b/	14,144,886	13,073,841	13,518,377
62 years	9,203,606	10,727,242	10,331,134
65 years	10,959,470	9,103,750	8,458,111
Dependency Ratio			
Current b/	47.6	42.5	44.5
62 years	26.6	32.4	30.8
65 years	33.3	26.2	23.9

Source: IBRD EC3HR population projections.

a/ Projections are based on different definitions of the retirement age.

b/ Envisages 54 years for women and 59 years for men.

c/ Calculated as the ratio of the retirement age population per 100 people
of working ages, i.e. 15 years of age till retirement age.

219

Table A.81 Types of Pensioners and Level of Benefits to Each
As of January 1, 1992

Pensioners	Number (000)	% of Total	Avg. Amount as % of Minimum Pension (1)
Pension Fund Supported	12,997	97	122
Retirees	10,318	77	125
Disabled	1,224	9	123
Dependents	693	5	96
Other (2)	500	4	75
Military	262	2	144
Military Paid from Ministry of Defence	362	3	522
Total	13,359	100	133

(1) Figures do not reflect July and October 1992 increases.
(2) People who never worked included people disabled from childhood and hobos.

Source: Ministry of Social Welfare

220

Table A.82 1992 Projected Sources of Funds for Pensions
(Ranges Reflect Pension Fund and MOF Estimates)

SOURCE	1992F (Rb. MM)	% of Total	% Govt Revenue (1)
Total Pension Fund	286,182 to 358,092	89.2 to 91.2	25.0 to 29.4
Employer Payroll Tax	287,320 to 356,268	89.6 to 90.7	
Employee Payroll Tax	8,493 to 11,082	2.6 to 2.8	
Other (2)	150 to 200	0.1	
Non-Pension Commitments	(9,458) to (9,781)	(2.4) to (3.1)	
State General Revenues (3)	23,647	6.0 to 7.4	1.9 to 2.1
State Chernobyl Fund (4)	10,918	2.8 to 3.4	0.9 to 1.0
Total	320,747 to 392,657	100	28.1 to 32.3

(1) Includes state and local general revenues and revenues from the Pension, Social Insurance, Employment and Chernobyl Funds.

Table A.83 UKRAINE: Orphans and Single People by Age
(In Thousand People) a/

```
-------------------------------------------------------
Total:                          3134
   up to 19 years of age         101
   20-24                         166
   25-29                         128
   30-39                         211
   40-49                         265
   50-54                         233
   55-59                         263
   60-64                         428
   65-69                         377
   70 and older                  962
-------------------------------------------------------
```

Source: Ministry of Statistics

a/ Population Census of 1989.

Table A.84   UKRAINE: Families with Children Under 18

	Thousand Families
Total	7,931
of which:	
With 1 Child	4,130
With 2 Children	3,132
With 3 Children	511
With 4 Children	102
With 5 and More Children	56

Source: Ministry of Statistics

Note: Based on 1989 Population Census.

Distributors of World Bank Publications

ARGENTINA
Carlos Hirsch, SRL
Galeria Guemes
Florida 165, 4th Floor-Ofc. 453/465
1333 Buenos Aires

**AUSTRALIA, PAPUA NEW GUINEA,
FIJI, SOLOMON ISLANDS,
VANUATU, AND WESTERN SAMOA**
D.A. Information Services
648 Whitehorse Road
Mitcham 3132
Victoria

AUSTRIA
Gerold and Co.
Graben 31
A-1011 Wien

BANGLADESH
Micro Industries Development
Assistance Society (MIDAS)
House 5, Road 16
Dhanmondi R/Area
Dhaka 1209

Branch offices:
Pine View, 1st Floor
100 Agrabad Commercial Area
Chittagong 4100

76, K.D.A. Avenue
Kulna 9100

BELGIUM
Jean De Lannoy
Av. du Roi 202
1060 Brussels

CANADA
Le Diffuseur
C.P. 85, 1501B rue Ampère
Boucherville, Québec
J4B 5E6

CHILE
Invertec IGT S.A.
Av. Santa Maria 6400
Edificio INTEC, Of. 201
Santiago

CHINA
China Financial & Economic
Publishing House
8, Da Fo Si Dong Jie
Beijing

COLOMBIA
Infoenlace Ltda.
Apartado Aereo 34270
Bogota D.E.

COTE D'IVOIRE
Centre d'Edition et de Diffusion
Africaines (CEDA)
04 B.P. 541
Abidjan 04 Plateau

CYPRUS
Center of Applied Research
Cyprus College
6, Diogenes Street, Engomi
P.O. Box 2006
Nicosia

DENMARK
SamfundsLitteratur
Rosenoerns Allé 11
DK-1970 Frederiksberg C

DOMINICAN REPUBLIC
Editora Taller, C. por A.
Restauración e Isabel la Católica 309
Apartado de Correos 2190 Z-1
Santo Domingo

EGYPT, ARAB REPUBLIC OF
Al Ahram
Al Galaa Street
Cairo

The Middle East Observer
41, Sherif Street
Cairo

FINLAND
Akateeminen Kirjakauppa
P.O. Box 128
SF-00101 Helsinki 10

FRANCE
World Bank Publications
66, avenue d'Iéna
75116 Paris

GERMANY
UNO-Verlag
Poppelsdorfer Allee 55
D-5300 Bonn 1

HONG KONG, MACAO
Asia 2000 Ltd.
46-48 Wyndham Street
Winning Centre
2nd Floor
Central Hong Kong

INDIA
Allied Publishers Private Ltd.
751 Mount Road
Madras - 600 002

Branch offices:
15 J.N. Heredia Marg
Ballard Estate
Bombay - 400 038

13/14 Asaf Ali Road
New Delhi - 110 002

17 Chittaranjan Avenue
Calcutta - 700 072

Jayadeva Hostel Building
5th Main Road, Gandhinagar
Bangalore - 560 009

3-5-1129 Kachiguda
Cross Road
Hyderabad - 500 027

Prarthana Flats, 2nd Floor
Near Thakore Baug, Navrangpura
Ahmedabad - 380 009

Patiala House
16-A Ashok Marg
Lucknow - 226 001

Central Bazaar Road
60 Bajaj Nagar
Nagpur 440 010

INDONESIA
Pt. Indira Limited
Jalan Borobudur 20
P.O. Box 181
Jakarta 10320

IRELAND
Government Supplies Agency
4-5 Harcourt Road
Dublin 2

ISRAEL
Yozmot Literature Ltd.
P.O. Box 56055
Tel Aviv 61560

ITALY
Licosa Commissionaria Sansoni SPA
Via Duca Di Calabria, 1/1
Casella Postale 552
50125 Firenze

JAPAN
Eastern Book Service
Hongo 3-Chome, Bunkyo-ku 113
Tokyo

KENYA
Africa Book Service (E.A.) Ltd.
Quaran House, Mfangano Street
P.O. Box 45245
Nairobi

KOREA, REPUBLIC OF
Pan Korea Book Corporation
P.O. Box 101, Kwangwhamun
Seoul

MALAYSIA
University of Malaya Cooperative
Bookshop, Limited
P.O. Box 1127, Jalan Pantai Baru
59700 Kuala Lumpur

MEXICO
INFOTEC
Apartado Postal 22-860
14060 Tlalpan, Mexico D.F.

NETHERLANDS
De Lindeboom/InOr-Publikaties
P.O. Box 202
7480 AE Haaksbergen

NEW ZEALAND
EBSCO NZ Ltd.
Private Mail Bag 99914
New Market
Auckland

NIGERIA
University Press Limited
Three Crowns Building Jericho
Private Mail Bag 5095
Ibadan

NORWAY
Narvesen Information Center
Book Department
P.O. Box 6125 Etterstad
N-0602 Oslo 6

PAKISTAN
Mirza Book Agency
65, Shahrah-e-Quaid-e-Azam
P.O. Box No. 729
Lahore 54000

PERU
Editorial Desarrollo SA
Apartado 3824
Lima 1

PHILIPPINES
International Book Center
Suite 1703, Cityland 10
Condominium Tower 1
Ayala Avenue, H.V. dela
Costa Extension
Makati, Metro Manila

POLAND
International Publishing Service
Ul. Piekna 31/37
00-677 Warzawa

For subscription orders:
IPS Journals
Ul. Okrezna 3
02-916 Warszawa

PORTUGAL
Livraria Portugal
Rua Do Carmo 70-74
1200 Lisbon

SAUDI ARABIA, QATAR
Jarir Book Store
P.O. Box 3196
Riyadh 11471

**SINGAPORE, TAIWAN,
MYANMAR, BRUNEI**
Information Publications
Private, Ltd.
Golden Wheel Building
41, Kallang Pudding, #04-03
Singapore 1334

SOUTH AFRICA, BOTSWANA
For single titles:
Oxford University Press
Southern Africa
P.O. Box 1141
Cape Town 8000

For subscription orders:
International Subscription Service
P.O. Box 41095
Craighall
Johannesburg 2024

SPAIN
Mundi-Prensa Libros, S.A.
Castello 37
28001 Madrid

Librería Internacional AEDOS
Consell de Cent, 391
08009 Barcelona

SRI LANKA AND THE MALDIVES
Lake House Bookshop
P.O. Box 244
100, Sir Chittampalam A.
Gardiner Mawatha
Colombo 2

SWEDEN
For single titles:
Fritzes Fackboksforetaget
Regeringsgatan 12, Box 16356
S-103 27 Stockholm

For subscription orders:
Wennergren-Williams AB
P. O. Box 1305
S-171 25 Solna

SWITZERLAND
For single titles:
Librairie Payot
Case postale 3212
CH 1002 Lausanne

For subscription orders:
Librairie Payot
Service des Abonnements
Case postale 3312
CH 1002 Lausanne

THAILAND
Central Department Store
306 Silom Road
Bangkok

**TRINIDAD & TOBAGO, ANTIGUA
BARBUDA, BARBADOS,
DOMINICA, GRENADA, GUYANA,
JAMAICA, MONTSERRAT, ST.
KITTS & NEVIS, ST. LUCIA,
ST. VINCENT & GRENADINES**
Systematics Studies Unit
#9 Watts Street
Curepe
Trinidad, West Indies

TURKEY
Infotel
Narlabahçe Sok. No. 15
Cagaloglu
Istanbul

UNITED KINGDOM
Microinfo Ltd.
P.O. Box 3
Alton, Hampshire GU34 2PG
England

VENEZUELA
Libreria del Este
Aptdo. 60.337
Caracas 1060-A